Simple Program Design:
A Step-By-Step Approach

Third Edition

Lesley Anne Robertson

Contributing authors
Wendy Doube
Kim Styles

COURSE
TECHNOLOGY

Thomson Learning™

Simple Program Design – A Step-By-Step Approach, Third Edition
is published by Course Technology.

Associate Publisher	Kristen Duerr	Editor	Bruce Gillespie
Product Manager	Jennifer Muroff	Illustrations	Rick Noble
Production Editor	Melissa Panagos	Text Designer	Angela Donarelli
Marketing Manager	Susan Ogar		
Associate Product Manager	Tricia Coia		
Editorial Assistant	Jennifer Adams		
Cover Designer	Efrat Reis		

Disclaimer
Course Technology reserves the right to revise this publication and make changes from time to time in its content without notice.

The Web addresses in this book are subject to change from time to time as necessary without notice.

For more information, contact Course Technology, One Main Street, Cambridge, MA 02142;
or find us on the World Wide Web at www.course.com

For permission to use material from this text or product, contact us by

- Web: www.thomsonrights.com
- Phone: 1-800-730-2214
- Fax: 1-800-730-2215

ISBN 0-619-01590-X

Printed in China by L. Rex Printing Co,. Ltd.

Contents

4   Selection control structures

Expands the selection control structure by introducing multiple selection, nested selection, and the case construct in pseudocode. Several algorithms, using variations of the selection control structure, are developed.

5   Repetition control structures

Develops algorithms which use the repetition control structure in the form of DOWHILE, REPEAT...UNTIL, and counted repetition loops.

6   Pseudocode algorithms using sequence, selection and repetition

Develops algorithms to eight simple programming problems using combinations of sequence, selection and repetition constructs. Each problem is properly defined; the control structures required are established; a pseudocode algorithm is developed; and the solution is manually checked for logic errors.

7   Array processing

Introduces arrays, operations on arrays, and algorithms which manipulate arrays. Algorithms for single and two-dimensional arrays, which initialise the elements of an array, search an array and write out the contents of an array, are presented.

8 First steps in modularisation

Introduces modularisation as a means of dividing a problem into subtasks. Hierarchy charts and parameter passing are introduced and several algorithms which use a modular structure are developed.

9 Further modularisation, cohesion and coupling

Develops modularisation further, using a more complex problem. Module cohesion and coupling are introduced, several levels of cohesion and coupling are described and pseudocode examples of each level are provided.

10 General algorithms for common business problems

Develops a general pseudocode algorithm for four common business applications. All problems are defined; a hierarchy chart is established; and a pseudocode algorithm is developed, using a mainline and several subordinate modules. The topics covered include report generation with page break, a single-level control break, a multiple-level control break, and a sequential file update program.

11 Object-oriented design

Introduces object-oriented design, objects, classes, attributes, methods and information hiding. The steps required to create an object-oriented solution to a problem are provided and solution algorithms developed.

12 More object-oriented design

Introduces the concept of multiple classes, polymorphism and method overriding in object-oriented design. Discusses the relationship between classes and lists the steps required to create an object-oriented design to a problem with multiple classes.

13 Conclusion

A revision of the steps involved in good top-down program design.

Appendix 1
Flowcharts

Introduces flowcharts for those students who prefer a more graphic approach to program design. Algorithms which use a combination of sequence, selection and repetition are developed in some detail.

Appendix 2
Nassi-Schneiderman diagrams

Introduces Nassi-Schneiderman diagrams for those students who prefer a more diagrammatic approach to program design. Algorithms which use a combination of sequence, selection and repetition constructs are developed in some detail.

Appendix 3
Special algorithms

Contains a number of algorithms which are not included in the body of the textbook and yet may be required at some time in a programmer's career.

Preface

With the increased popularity of programming courses in our universities, colleges and technical institutions, there is a need for an easy-to-read textbook on computer program design. There are already dozens of introductory programming texts using specific languages such as PASCAL, BASIC, COBOL or C, but they usually gloss over the important step of designing a solution to a given programming problem.

This textbook tackles the subject of program design by using structured programming techniques and pseudocode to develop a solution algorithm. The recommended pseudocode has been chosen because of its closeness to written English, its versatility and ease of manipulation, and its similarity to the syntax of most structured programming languages.

Simple Program Design is designed for programmers who want to develop good programming skills for solving common business problems. Too often, programmers who are faced with a problem launch straight into the code of their chosen programming language, instead of concentrating on the actual problem at hand. They become bogged down with the syntax and format of the language, and often spend many hours getting the program to work. Using this textbook, the programmer will learn how to define the problem, how to design a solution algorithm, and how to prove the algorithm's correctness, before coding a single statement from any programming language. By using pseudocode and structured programming techniques, the programmer can concentrate on developing a well-designed and correct solution, and thus eliminate many frustrating hours at the testing phase.

The book is divided into thirteen chapters, beginning with a basic explanation of structured programming techniques, top-down development and modular design. Then, concept by concept, the student is introduced to the syntax of pseudocode; methods of defining the problem; the application of basic control structures in the development of the solution algorithm; desk-checking techniques; arrays; hierarchy charts; module design; parameter passing; object-oriented design methodology; and many common algorithms.

Each chapter thoroughly covers the topic at hand, giving practical examples relating to business applications, and a consistently structured approach when representing algorithms and hierarchy charts.

This third edition of *Simple Program Design* contains additional material which complements the information provided in the first two editions. A new chapter on array processing has been included, covering single and multidimensional arrays, together with common operations on arrays and algorithms for their manipulation. Modularisation has been extended to cover two chapters, with communication between modules and parameter passing introduced at an earlier stage in the design process.

Two new chapters covering object-oriented design methodology have been included in this third edition. These chapters were written by Kim Styles and Wendy Doube, lecturers in computing at the Gippsland School of Computing and Information Technology, Monash University. They introduce the concepts of object-oriented design and the steps involved in creating an object-oriented solution to a problem. Step-by-step algorithms using OO design are provided, as well as material on multiple objects and interfaces.

Many courses now require students to be proficient in more than one algorithm design technique. As in the first two editions, pseudocode has been chosen as the main algorithm design technique throughout the book. However, this third edition now offers two alternate methods of representing algorithms: flowcharts, in Appendix 1, and Nassi-Schneiderman diagrams, in Appendix 2. All algorithms developed in pseudocode in Chapters 2, 3, 4 and 5 have been presented again in Appendix 1 — using flowcharts — and Appendix 2 — using Nassi-Schneiderman diagrams.

This third edition also provides ten programming problems, of increasing complexity, at the end of each chapter, so that teachers now have a choice of exercises that matches the widely varying abilities of their students.

I would like to thank Kim Styles and Wendy Doube, lecturers in Computing at Monash University, for their wonderful input on object-oriented design methodology, Paul Moriarty, of Saranac Lake, New York, for his enthusiastic suggestions, and my brother, Rick Noble, for his amusing cartoons at the beginning of each chapter.

Lesley Anne Robertson

The Author

Lesley Anne Robertson was introduced to structured programming techniques and top-down design when she joined IBM, Australia, in 1973 as a trainee programmer. Since then, she has consistently used these techniques as a programmer, a systems analyst, and finally a Lecturer in Computing at the University of Western Sydney, NSW, where she taught computer programming for eleven years.

Lesley now lives on a vineyard and winery in Mudgee, NSW, with her husband, David, and daughters, Lucy and Sally.

Program design

Objectives

- To describe the steps in the program development process
- To explain structured programming
- To introduce algorithms and pseudocode
- To describe program data

Outline

1.1 STEPS IN PROGRAM DEVELOPMENT

Computer programming is an art. Many people believe that a programmer must be good at mathematics, have a memory for figures and technical information, and be prepared to spend many hours sitting at a computer, typing programs. However, given the right tools, and steps to follow, anyone can write well-designed programs. It is a task worth doing, as it is both stimulating and fulfilling.

Programming can be defined as the development of a solution to an identified problem, and the setting up of a related series of instructions which, when directed through computer hardware, will produce the desired results. It is the first part of this definition that satisfies the programmer's creative needs: that is, to design a solution to an identified problem. Yet this step is so often overlooked. Leaping straight into the coding phase without first designing a proper solution usually results in programs that contain a lot of errors. Often the programmer needs to spend a significant amount of time finding these errors and correcting them. A more experienced programmer will design a solution to the program first, desk check this solution, and then code the program in a chosen programming language.

There are seven basic steps in the development of a program. An outline of these seven steps follows.

1 Define the problem

This step involves carefully reading and rereading the problem until you understand completely what is required. To help with this initial analysis, the problem should be divided into three separate components:

- The inputs,
- The outputs, and
- The processing steps to produce the required outputs.

A defining diagram as described in Chapter 3 is recommended in this analysis phase, as it helps to separate the define the three components.

2 Outline the solution

Once the problem has been defined, you may decide to break the problem up into smaller tasks or steps, and establish an outline solution. This initial outline is usually a rough draft of the solution which may include:

- The major processing steps involved,
- The major subtasks (if any),
- The major control structures (e.g. repetition loops),
- The major variables and record structures, and
- The mainline logic.

The solution outline may also include a hierarchy or structure chart. The steps involved in creating this outline solution are detailed in Chapters 2 to 6.

3 Develop the outline into an algorithm

The solution outline developed in Step 2 is then expanded into an algorithm: a set of precise steps that describe exactly the tasks to be performed and the order in which they are to be carried out. This book uses pseudocode (a form of structured English) to represent the solution algorithm, as well as structured programming techniques. Flowcharts and Nassi-Schneiderman diagrams are also provided in Appendix 1 and Appendix 2 for those who prefer a more pictorial method of algorithm representation. Algorithms using pseudocode and the Structure Theorem are developed thoroughly in Chapters 2 to 7.

4 Test the algorithm for correctness

This step is one of the most important in the development of a program, and yet it is the step most often forgotten. The main purpose of desk checking the algorithm is to identify major logic errors early, so that they may be easily corrected. Test data needs to be walked through each step in the algorithm to check that the instructions described in the algorithm will actually do what they are supposed to. The programmer walks through the logic of the algorithm, exactly as a computer would, keeping track of all major variables on a sheet of paper. Chapter 3 recommends the use of a desk check table to desk check the algorithm, and many examples of its use are provided.

5 Code the algorithm into a specific programming language

Only after all design considerations have been met in the previous four steps should you actually start to code the program into your chosen programming language.

6 Run the program on the computer

This step uses a program compiler and programmer-designed test data to machine test the code for syntax errors (those detected at compile time) and logic errors (those detected at run time). This is usually the most rewarding step in the program development process. If the program has been well designed, the usual time-wasting frustration and despair often associated with program testing are reduced to a minimum. This step may need to be performed several times until you are satisfied that the program is running as required.

7 Document and maintain the program

Program documentation should not be listed as the last step in the program development process, as it is really an ongoing task from the initial definition of the problem to the final test result.

Documentation involves both external documentation (such as hierarchy charts, the solution algorithm, and test data results) and internal documentation that may have been coded in the program. Program maintenance refers to changes which may need to be made to a program throughout its life. Often these changes are performed by a different programmer from the one who initially wrote the program. If the program has been well designed using structured programming techniques, the code will be seen as self documenting, resulting in easier maintenance.

1.2 STRUCTURED PROGRAMMING

Structured programming helps you to write effective, error-free programs. The original concept of structured programming was set out in a paper published in 1964 in Italy by Bohm and Jacopini. They established the idea of designing programs using a Structure Theorem based on three control structures. Since then a number of authors, such as Edsger Dijkstra, Niklaus Wirth, Ed Yourdon and Michael Jackson, have developed the concept further and have contributed to the establishment of the popular term 'structured programming'. This term now refers not only to the Structure Theorem itself, but also to top-down development and modular design.

Top-down development

Traditionally, programmers presented with a programming problem would start coding at the beginning of the problem and work systematically through each step until reaching the end. Often they would get bogged down in the intricacies of a particular part of the problem, rather than considering the solution as a whole. In the top-down development of a program design, a general solution to the problem is outlined first. This is then broken down gradually into more detailed steps until finally the most detailed levels have been completed. It is only after this process of 'functional decomposition' (or 'stepwise refinement') that the programmer starts to code. The result of this systematic, disciplined approach to program design is a higher precision of programming than was possible before.

Modular design

Structured programming also incorporates the concept of modular design, which involves grouping tasks together because they all perform the same function (e.g. calculating sales tax or printing report headings). Modular design is connected directly to top-down development, as the steps or subtasks into which the programmer breaks up the program solution will actually form the future modules of the program. Good modular design aids in the reading and understanding of the program.

The Structure Theorem

The Structure Theorem revolutionised program design by eliminating the GOTO statement and establishing a structured framework for representing the solution. The theorem states that it is possible to write any computer program by using only three basic control structures. These control structures are:

- Sequence;
- Selection, or IF-THEN-ELSE; and
- Repetition, or DOWHILE.

They are covered in detail in Chapter 2.

1.3 AN INTRODUCTION TO ALGORITHMS AND PSEUDOCODE

Structured programming techniques require a program to be properly designed before coding begins, and it is this design process that results in the construction of an algorithm.

What is an algorithm?

An algorithm is like a recipe: it lists the steps involved in accomplishing a task. It can be defined in programming terms as a set of detailed, unambiguous and ordered instructions developed to describe the processes necessary to produce the desired output from a given input. The algorithm is written in simple English and is not a formal document. However, to be useful, there are some principles which should be adhered to. An algorithm must:

- be lucid, precise and unambiguous;
- give the correct solution in all cases; and
- eventually end.

For example, if you want to instruct someone to add up a list of prices on a pocket calculator, you might write an algorithm such as the following:

```
Turn on calculator
Clear calculator

Repeat the following instructions
        Key in dollar amount
        Key in decimal point (.)
        Key in cents amount
        Press addition (+) key
Until all prices have been entered

Write down total price
Turn off calculator
```

Notice that in this algorithm the first two steps are performed once, before the repetitive process of entering the prices. After all the prices have been entered and summed, the total prices can be written down and the calculator can be turned off. These final two activities are also performed only once. This algorithm satisfies the desired list of properties: it lists all the steps in the correct order from top to bottom, in a definite and unambiguous fashion, until a correct solution is reached. Notice that the steps to be repeated (entering and summing the prices) are indented, both to separate them from those steps performed only once and to emphasise the repetitive nature of their action. It is important to use indentation when writing solution algorithms because it helps to differentiate between the three control structures.

What is pseudocode?

Pseudocode, flowcharts and Nassi-Schneiderman diagrams are all popular ways of representing algorithms. Flowcharts and Nassi-Schneiderman diagrams are covered in Appendix 1 and Appendix 2 of this text, while pseudocode has been chosen as the primary method of representing an algorithm because it is easy to read and write. Pseudocode is really structured English. It is English that has been formalised and abbreviated to look very like high-level computer languages.

There is no standard pseudocode at present. Authors seem to adopt their own special techniques and sets of rules, which often resemble a particular programming language. This book attempts to establish a standard pseudocode for use by all programmers, regardless of the programming language they choose. Like many versions of pseudocode, this version has certain conventions, as follows:

1   Statements are written in simple English.
2   Each instruction is written on a separate line.
3   Keywords and indentation are used to signify particular control structures.
4   Each set of instructions is written from top to bottom, with only one entry and one exit.
5   Groups of statements may be formed into modules, and that group given a name.

Pseudocode has been chosen to represent the solution algorithms in this book because its use allows the programmer to concentrate on the logic of the problem.

1.4 PROGRAM DATA

Because programs are written to process data, you must also have a good understanding of the nature and structure of the data being processed. Data within a program may be a single variable, such as an integer or a character; or a group item (sometimes called an aggregate), such as an array, or a file.

Variables, constants and literals

A variable is the name given to a collection of memory cells, designed to store a particular data item. It is called a variable because the value stored in that variable may change or vary as the program executes. For example, the variable total_amount may contain several values during the execution of the program.

A constant is a data item with a name and a value that remain the same during the execution of the program. For example, the name fifty may be given to a data item that contains the value 50.

A literal is a constant whose name is the written representation of its value. For example, the program may contain the literal '50'.

Elementary data items

An elementary data item is one containing a single variable that is always treated as a unit. These data items are usually classified into data types. A data type consists of a set of data values and a set of operations that can be performed on those values. The most common elementary data types are:

integer:
  representing a set of whole numbers, positive or negative

real:
  representing a set of numbers, positive or negative, which may include values before or after a decimal point

character:
  representing the set of characters of the alphabet, plus some special characters

Boolean :
  representing a control flag or switch, which may contain one of two possible values; true or false.

Data structures

A data structure is an aggregate of other data items. The data items that it contains are its components, which may be elementary data items or another data structure. In a data structure, data is grouped together in a particular way, which reflects the situation with which the program is concerned. The most common data structures are:

record:
  a collection of data items or fields that all bear some relationship to one another. For example, a student record may contain the student's number, name, address and enrolled subjects.

file:
  a collection of records. For example, a student file may contain a collection of the above student records.

array:
  a data structure, which is made up of a number of variables or data items that all have the same data type and are accessed by the same name. For example, an array called scores may contain a collection of students' exam scores. Access to the individual items in the array is made by the use of an index or subscript beside the name of the array, for example, scores (3).

string:
  a collection of characters. For example, the string 'Jenny Parker' may represent a student's name.

1.5 Chapter summary

In this chapter, the steps in program development were introduced and briefly described. These seven steps are:

1 Define the problem.
2 Outline the solution.
3 Develop the outline into an algorithm.
4 Test the algorithm for correctness.

5　Code the algorithm into a specific programming language.
6　Run the program on the computer.
7　Document and maintain the program.

Structured programming was presented as a combination of three separate concepts: top-down development, modular design, and the use of the Structure Theorem when designing a solution to a problem.

An algorithm was defined as a set of detailed, unambiguous and ordered instructions developed to describe the processes necessary to produce the desired output from the given input. Pseudocode is an English-like way of representing the algorithm; its advantages and some conventions for its use were listed.

Programmers need to have a good understanding of the data to be processed, therefore data variables, constants and literals were defined, as well as elementary data items and data structures.

Pseudocode

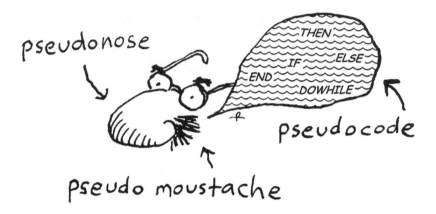

Objectives

- To introduce common words and keywords used when writing pseudocode
- To define the three basic control structures as set out in the Structure Theorem
- To illustrate the three basic control structures using pseudocode

Outline

2.1 HOW TO WRITE PSEUDOCODE

When designing a solution algorithm, you need to keep in mind that the set of instructions written will eventually be performed by a computer. That is, if you use words and phrases in the pseudocode which are in line with basic computer operations, the translation from the pseudocode algorithm to a specific programming language becomes quite simple.

This chapter establishes six basic computer operations and introduces common words and keywords used to represent these operations in pseudocode. Each operation can be represented as a straightforward English instruction, with keywords and indentation to signify a particular control structure.

Six basic computer operations

1 A computer can receive information

When a computer is required to receive information or input from a particular source, whether it be a terminal, a disk or any other device, the verbs Read and Get are used in pseudocode. Read is usually used when the algorithm is to receive input from a record on a file, while Get is used when the algorithm is to receive input from the keyboard. For example, typical pseudocode instructions to receive information are:

```
Read student name
Get system date
Read number_1, number_2
Get tax_code
```

Each example uses a single verb, Read or Get, followed by one or more nouns to indicate what data is to be obtained. At no stage is it necessary to specify the source of the data, as this information is not required until run time.

2 A computer can put out information

When a computer is required to supply information or output to a device, the verbs Print, Write, Put, Output or Display are used in pseudocode. Print is usually used when the output is to be sent to the printer, while Write is used when the output is to be written to a file. If the output is to be written to the screen, the words Put, Output or Display are used in pseudocode. Typical pseudocode examples are:

```
Print 'Program Completed'
Write customer record to master file
Put out name, address and postcode
Output total_tax
Display 'End of data'
```

In each example, the data to be put out is described concisely using mostly lower-case letters.

3 A computer can perform arithmetic

Most programs require the computer to perform some sort of mathematical calculation, or formula, and for these, a programmer may use either actual mathematical symbols or the words for those symbols. For instance, the same pseudocode instruction can be expressed as either of the following:

```
Add number to total
total = total + number
```

Both expressions clearly instruct the computer to add one value to another, so either is acceptable in pseudocode. The equal symbol '=' has been used to indicate assignment of a value as a result of some processing.

To be consistent with high-level programming languages, the following symbols can be written in pseudocode:

+ for Add
− for Subtract
* for Multiply
/ for Divide
( ) for Parentheses

The verbs Compute and Calculate are also available. Some pseudocode examples to perform a calculation are:

```
Divide total_marks by student_count
sales_tax = cost_price * 0.10
Compute C = (F − 32) * 5/9
```

When writing mathematical calculations for the computer, the 'order of operations', common to all programming languages, should be considered. The first operation carried out will be any calculation contained within parentheses. Next, any multiplication or division, as it occurs from left to right, will be performed. Then, any addition or subtraction, as it occurs from left to right, will be performed.

4 A computer can assign a value to a variable or memory location

There are three cases where you may write pseudocode to assign a value to a variable or memory location:

1 To give data an initial value in pseudocode, the verbs Initialise or Set are used.
2 To assign a value as a result of some processing, the symbol '=' is written.
3 To keep a piece of information for later use, the verbs Save or Store are used.

Some typical pseudocode examples are:

```
Initialise total accumulators to zero
Set student_count to 0
Total_price = cost_price + sales_tax
Store customer_num in last_customer_num
```

5 A computer can compare two variables and select one of two alternative actions

An important computer operation available to the programmer is the ability to compare two variables and then, as a result of the comparison, select one of two alternative actions. To represent this operation in pseudocode, special keywords are used: IF, THEN, and ELSE. The comparison of data is established in the IF clause, and the choice of alternatives is determined by the THEN or ELSE options. Only one of these alternatives will be performed. A typical pseudocode example to illustrate this operation is:

```
IF student is part_time THEN          True or false
    add 1 to part_time_count
ELSE
    add 1 to full_time_count
ENDIF
```

In this example the attendance status of the student is investigated, with the result that either the part_time_count or the full_time_count accumulator is incremented. Note the use of indentation to emphasise the THEN and ELSE options, and the use of the delimiter ENDIF to close the operation.

6 A computer can repeat a group of actions

When there is a sequence of processing steps which need to be repeated, two special keywords, DOWHILE and ENDDO, are used in pseudocode. The condition for the repetition of a group of actions is established in the DOWHILE clause, and the actions to be repeated are listed beneath it. For example:

```
DOWHILE student_total < 50
    Read student record
    Print student name, address to report
    Add 1 to student_total
ENDDO
```

In this example it is easy to see the statements which are to be repeated, as they immediately follow the DOWHILE statement and are indented for added emphasis. The condition which controls and eventually terminates the repetition is established in the DOWHILE clause, and the keyword ENDDO acts as a delimiter. As soon as the condition for repetition is found to be false, control passes to the next statement after the ENDDO.

Some teachers of PASCAL as a first programming language prefer to use the keywords WHILE...DO and ENDWHILE to start and end this operation, as follows:

```
WHILE student_total < 50 DO
    Read student record
    Print student name, address to report
    Add 1 to student_total
ENDWHILE
```

Note that the format, indentation and operation of DOWHILE and WHILE...DO are exactly the same. The only difference is the actual keywords which are used.

2.2 THE STRUCTURE THEOREM

The Structure Theorem forms the basic framework for structured programming. It states that it is possible to write any computer program by using only three basic control structures that are easily represented in pseudocode: sequence, selection, and repetition.

The three basic control structures

1 Sequence

The sequence control structure is the straightforward execution of one processing step after another. In pseudocode we represent this construct as a sequence of pseudocode statements.

```
statement a
statement b
statement c
```

The sequence control structure can be used to represent the first four basic computer operations listed previously: to receive information, put out information, perform arithmetic, and assign values. For example, a typical sequence of statements in an algorithm might read:

```
Add 1 to page_count
Print heading line
Set linecount to zero
Read customer record
```

These instructions illustrate the sequence control structure as a straightforward list of steps written one after the other, in a top-to-bottom fashion. Each instruction will be executed in the order in which it appears.

2 Selection

The selection control structure is the presentation of a condition and the choice between two actions, The choice depending on whether the condition is true or false. This construct represents the decision-making abilities of the computer and is used to illustrate the fifth basic computer operation, namely to compare two variables and select one of two alternate actions.

In pseudocode, selection is represented by the keywords IF, THEN, ELSE and ENDIF:

```
IF condition p is true THEN
      statement(s) in true case
ELSE
      statement(s) in false case
ENDIF
```

If condition p is true then the statement or statements in the true case will be executed, and the statements in the false case will be skipped. Otherwise (the ELSE statement) the statements in the true case will be skipped and statements in the false case will be executed. In either case, control then passes to the next processing step after the delimiter ENDIF. A typical pseudocode example might read:

```
IF student is part_time THEN
      add 1 to part_time_count
ELSE
      add 1 to full_time_count
ENDIF
```

A variation of the selection control structure is the null ELSE structure, which is used when a task is performed only if a particular condition is true. The null ELSE construct is written in pseudocode as:

```
IF condition p is true THEN
      statement(s) in true case
ENDIF
```

Note that the keyword ELSE is omitted. This construct tests the condition in the IF clause and, if that is found to be true, performs the statement or statements listed in the THEN clause. However, if the initial condition is found to be false, no action will be taken and processing will proceed to the next statement after the ENDIF.

3 Repetition

The repetition control structure can be defined as the presentation of a set of instructions to be performed repeatedly, as long as a condition is true. The basic idea of repetitive code is that a block of statements is executed again and again, until a terminating condition occurs. This construct represents the sixth basic computer operation, namely to repeat a group of actions. It is written in pseudocode as:

```
DOWHILE condition p is true
      statement block
ENDDO
```

The DOWHILE loop is a leading decision loop; that is, the condition is tested before any statements are executed. If the condition in the DOWHILE statement is found to be true, the block of statements following that statement is executed once. The delimiter ENDDO then triggers a return of control to the retesting of the condition. If the condition is still true the statements are repeated, and so the repetition process continues until the condition is found to be false. Control then passes to the statement which follows the ENDDO statement. It is imperative that at least one statement within the statement block can alter the condition and eventually render it false, because otherwise the logic may result in an endless loop.

The DOWHILE statement could also have been written as a WHILE...DO statement using exactly the same format, indentation and operation, as follows:

```
WHILE condition p is true DO
      statement block
ENDWHILE
```

Here is a pseudocode example which represents the repetition control structure:

```
Set student_total to zero
DOWHILE student_total < 50
    Read student record
    Print student name, address to report
    Add 1 to student_total
ENDDO
```

This example illustrates a number of points:

1. The variable student_total is initialised before the DOWHILE condition is executed.
2. As long as student_total is less than 50 (i.e. the DOWHILE condition is true), the statement block will be repeated.
3. Each time the statement block is executed, one instruction within that block will cause the variable student_total to be incremented.
4. After 50 iterations, student_total will equal 50, which causes the DOWHILE condition to become false and the repetition to cease.

It is important to realise that the initialising and subsequent incrementing of the variable tested in the condition is an essential feature of the DOWHILE construct.

2.3 CHAPTER SUMMARY

In this chapter, six basic computer operations were listed, along with pseudocode words and keywords to represent them. These operations were: to receive information, put out information, perform arithmetic, assign a value to a variable, decide between two alternate actions, and repeat a group of actions. Typical pseudocode examples were given as illustrations.

The Structure Theorem was introduced. It states that it is possible to write any computer program by using only three basic control structures: sequence, selection, and repetition. Each control structure was defined, and its association with each of the six basic computer operations was indicated. Pseudocode examples for each control structure were provided.

CHAPTER

Developing an algorithm

Objectives

- To introduce methods of analysing a problem and developing a solution
- To develop simple algorithms using the sequence control structure
- To introduce methods of manually checking the developed solution

Outline

3.1 DEFINING THE PROBLEM

Chapter 1 described seven steps in the development of a computer program. The very first step, and one of the most important, is defining the problem. This involves carefully reading and rereading the problem until you understand completely what is required. Quite often, additional information will need to be sought to help resolve any ambiguities or deficiencies in the problem specifications. To help with this initial analysis, the problem should be divided into three separate components:

1 Input: a list of the source data provided to the problem.
2 Output: a list of the outputs required.
3 Processing: a list of actions needed to produce the required outputs.

When reading the problem statement, the input and output components are easily identified, because they use descriptive words such as nouns and adjectives. The processing component is also identified easily. The problem statement usually describes the processing steps as actions, using verbs and adverbs.

When dividing a problem into its three different components, you should simply analyse the actual words used in the specification, and divide them into those which are descriptive and those which imply actions. It may help to underline the nouns, adjectives and verbs used in the specification.

In some programming problems, the inputs, processes and outputs may not be clearly defined. In such cases it is best to concentrate on the outputs required. Doing this will then decide most inputs, and the way will then be set for determining the processing steps required to produce the desired output.

At this stage the processing section should be a list of what actions need to be performed, not how they will be accomplished. Do not attempt to find a solution until the problem has been completely defined. Let's look at a simple example.

Example 3.1 *Add three numbers*

A program is required to read three numbers, add them together, and print their total.

Tackle this problem in two stages. Firstly, underline the nouns and adjectives used in the specification. This will establish the input and output components as well as any objects which are required. With the nouns and adjectives underlined, our example would look like this:

A program is required to read three numbers, add them together, and print their total.

By looking at the underlined nouns and adjectives you can see that the input for this problem is three numbers and the output is the total. It is helpful to write down these first two components in a simple diagram, called a defining diagram.

Input	Processing	Output
number_1 number_2 number_3		total

Second, underline (in a different colour) the verbs and adverbs used in the specification. This will establish the actions required. Example 3.1 should now look like this:

A program is required to <u>read</u> three numbers, <u>add</u> them <u>together</u>, and <u>print</u> their total.

By looking at the underlined words, you can see that the processing verbs are read, add together and print. These steps can now be added to our defining diagram to make it complete. Note that when writing down each processing verb, also include the objects or nouns associated with each verb. The defining diagram now becomes:

Input	Processing	Output
number_1	Read three numbers	total
number_2	Add numbers together	
number_3	Print total number	

Now that all the nouns and verbs in the specification have been considered and the defining diagram is complete, the problem has been properly defined. That is, we now understand the input to the problem, the output to be produced, and the processing steps required to convert the input to the output.

Meaningful names

At this stage in defining the problem it is a good idea to introduce some unique names, which will be used to represent the variables or objects in the problem and describe the processing steps. All names should be meaningful. A name given to a variable is simply a method of identifying a particular storage location in the computer.

The uniqueness of the name will differentiate it from other locations. Often a name describes the type of data stored in a particular variable. For instance, a variable may be one of the three simple data types, namely an integer, a real number or a character. The name itself should be transparent enough to adequately describe the variable: number_1, number_2 and number_3 are more meaningful names for three numbers than A, B and C.

Underscores are useful when choosing variable names, as the underscore is used as a word separator; for example, number_1 and word_count. Most programming languages do no tolerate a space in a variable name.

When it comes to writing down the processing component of the defining diagram, you should use words that describe the work to be done in terms of single, specific tasks or functions. In Example 3.1 the processing steps would be written down as verbs accompanied by their associated objects:

Read three numbers
Add numbers together
Print total number

There is a pattern in the words chosen to describe these steps. Each action is described as a single verb followed by a two-word object. Studies have shown that if you follow this convention to describe a processing step, two benefits result. First, you are using a disciplined approach to defining the problem; second, the processing is being dissected into separate tasks or functions. This simple operation of dividing a problem into separate functions and choosing a proper name for each function is extremely important later, when considering modules.

Example 3.2 *Find average temperature*

A program is required to prompt the terminal operator for the maximum and minimum temperature readings on a particular day, accept those readings as integers, and calculate and display to the screen the simple average temperature, calculated by (maximum temperature + minimum temperature)/2.

First establish the input and output components by underlining the nouns and adjectives in the problem statement.

A program is required to prompt the terminal operator for the <u>maximum</u> <u>and minimum</u> <u>temperature</u> <u>readings</u> on a particular day, accept those readings as integers, and calculate and display to the screen the <u>simple</u> <u>average</u> <u>temperature</u>, calculated by (maximum temperature + minimum temperature)/2.

The input component is the maximum and minimum temperature readings and the output is the average temperature. Using meaningful names, these components can be set up in a defining diagram as follows:

Input	Processing	Output
max_temp min_temp		avg_temp

Now establish the processing steps by underlining the verbs in the problem statement.

A program is required to <u>prompt</u> the terminal operator for the maximum and minimum temperature readings on a particular day, <u>accept</u> those readings as integers, and <u>calculate</u> and <u>display</u> to the screen the simple average temperature, calculated by (maximum temperature + minimum temperature)/2.

The processing verbs are prompt, accept, calculate and display. By finding the associated objects of these verbs, the defining diagram can now be completed, as follows:

Input	Processing	Output
max_temp min_temp	Prompt for temperatures Get max, min temperatures Calculate average temperature Display average temperature	avg_temp

Remember that at this stage you are only concerned with the fact that the simple average temperature must be calculated, not how the calculation will be performed. That will come later, when the solution algorithm is established.

Example 3.3 *Compute mowing time*

A program is required to read in the <u>length</u> and <u>width</u> of a rectangular house block, and the <u>length</u> and <u>width</u> of the rectangular house which has been built on the block. The algorithm should then compute and display the <u>time</u> required to cut the grass around the house, at the rate of two square metres per minute.

To establish the input and output components in this problem, the nouns or objects have been underlined. By reading these words, you can see that the input is the length and width of the block, and the length and width of the house. The output is the time to cut the grass.

The input and output components can be set up in a defining diagram, as follows:

Input	Processing	Output
block_length block_width house_length house_width		mowing_time

Now the verbs and adverbs in the problem statement can be underlined.

A program is required to <u>read</u> in the length and width of a rectangular house block, and the length and width of the rectangular house which has been built on the block. The algorithm should then <u>compute</u> and <u>display</u> the time required to cut the grass around the house, at the rate of two square metres per minute.

The processing steps can now be added to the defining diagram:

Input	Processing	Output
block_length block_width house_length house_width	Prompt for block measurements Get block measurements Prompt for house measurements Get house measurements Calculate mowing area Calculate mowing time	mowing_time

These steps are sufficient to establish the requirements of the problem. You must be absolutely confident of what is to be done in the program before you attempt to establish how it is done.

3.2 DESIGNING A SOLUTION ALGORITHM

Designing a solution algorithm is the most challenging task in the life cycle of a program. Once the program has been properly defined, you usually begin with a rough sketch of the steps required to solve the problem. Look at what is required and, using these requirements and the three basic control structures defined in the Structure Theorem, attempt to establish how the processing will take place.

The first attempt at designing a particular algorithm usually does not result in a finished product. Steps may be left out, or some that are included may later be altered or deleted. Pseudocode is useful in this trial and error process, since it is relatively easy to add, delete or alter an instruction. Do not hesitate to alter algorithms, or even discard one and start again, if you are not completely satisfied with it. If the algorithm is not correct, the program will never be.

There is some argument that the work of a programmer ends with the algorithm design. After that, a coder or trainee programmer could take over and code the solution algorithm into a specific programming language. In practice, this usually doesn't happen. However, it is important that you not be too anxious to start coding until the necessary steps of defining the problem and designing the solution algorithm have been completed.

Here are solution algorithms for the preceding three examples. All involve sequence control structures only; there are no decisions or loops so the solution algorithms are relatively simple.

Example 3.4 *Solution algorithm for Example 3.1*

A program is required to read three numbers, add them together and print their total.

A Defining diagram

Input	Processing	Output
number_1	Read three numbers	total
number_2	Add numbers together	
number_3	Print total number	

This diagram shows what is required, and a simple calculation will establish how. Using pseudocode, and the sequence control structure, establish the solution algorithm as follows.

B Solution algorithm

```
Add_three_numbers
      Read number_1, number_2, number_3
      total = number_1 + number_2 + number_3
      Print total
END
```

There are a number of points to consider in this solution algorithm:

1   A name has been given to the algorithm, namely Add_three_numbers. Names should briefly describe the function of the algorithm, and are usually expressed as a single verb followed by a two-word object. Other names which are equally suitable include Process_three_numbers and Total_three_numbers.
2   An END statement at the end of the algorithm indicates that the algorithm is complete.
3   All processing steps between the algorithm name and the END statement have been indented for readability.
4   Each processing step in the defining diagram relates directly to one or more statements in the algorithm. For instance, 'Read three numbers' in the defining diagram becomes 'Read number_1, number_2, number_3' in the algorithm; and 'Add number together' becomes 'total = number_1 + number_2 + number_3'.

   Now that the algorithm is complete, you should desk check the solution and then translate it into a programming language. (Desk checking is covered in Section 3.3.)

Example 3.5 *Solution algorithm for Example 3.2*

A program is required to prompt the terminal operator for the maximum and minimum temperature readings on a particular day, accept those readings as integers, and calculate and display to the screen the simple average temperature, calculated by (maximum temperature + minimum temperature)/2.

A *Defining diagram*

Input	Processing	Output
max_temp min_temp	Prompt for temperatures Get max, min temperatures Calculate average temperature Display average temperature	avg_temp

Using pseudocode, a simple calculation and the sequence control structure, the algorithm can be expressed as follows:

B *Solution algorithm*

```
Find_average_temperature
      Prompt operator for max_temp, min_temp
      Get max_temp, min_temp
      avg_temp = (max_temp + min_temp)/2
      Output avg_temp to the screen
END
```

In this example the step 'Calculate average temperature' in the defining diagram has been expressed in the algorithm as actual calculations to compute and display the average temperature.

Example 3.6 *Solution algorithm for Example 3.3*

A program is required to read in the length and width of a rectangular house block, and the length and width of the rectangular house which has been built on the block. The algorithm should then compute and display the time required to cut the grass around the house, at the rate of two square metres per minute.

A Defining diagram

Input	Processing	Output
block_length	Prompt for block measurements	mowing_time
block_width	Get block measurements	
house_length	Prompt for house measurements	
house_width	Get house measurements	
	Calculate mowing area	
	Calculate mowing time	

The actions to be carried out in this algorithm are listed sequentially in the processing component of the defining diagram. At this stage the processing steps still only describe the steps to be performed, in their correct order. Meaningful names such as block_length and mowing_time have been given to the variables within the algorithm for readability.

B The solution algorithm

```
Calculate_mowing_time
      Prompt operator for block_length, block_width
      Get block_length, block_width
      block_area = block_length * block_width
      Prompt operator for house_length, house_width
      Get house_length, house_width
      house_area = house_length * house_width
      mowing_area = block_area — house_area
      mowing _time = mowing_area/2
      Output mowing_time to screen
END
```

3.3 CHECKING THE SOLUTION ALGORITHM

After a solution algorithm has been constructed it must be tested for correctness. This step is necessary, because most major logic errors occur during the development of the algorithm, and if not detected, these errors would be passed on to the program. It is much easier to detect errors in pseudocode than in the corresponding program code. This is because once programming begins you usually assume that the logic of the algorithm is correct. Then, when you detect errors your attention is focused on the individual lines of code to identify the problems rather than the initial logic expressed in the algorithm. It is often too difficult to step back and analyse the program as a whole. As a result, many frustrating hours can be wasted during testing, which could have been avoided by just five minutes spent desk checking the solution algorithm.

Desk checking involves tracing through the logic of the algorithm with some chosen test data. That is, you walk through the logic of the algorithm exactly as a computer would, keeping track of all major variable values on a sheet of paper. This playing computer not only helps to detect errors early, but also helps you become familiar with the way the program runs. The closer you are to the execution of the program, the easier it is to detect errors.

Selecting test data

When selecting test data to desk check an algorithm, you must look at the program specification and choose simple test cases only, based on the requirements of the specification, not the algorithm. By doing this you will still be able to concentrate on what the program is supposed to do, not how.

To desk check the algorithm, you need only a few simple test cases which will follow the major paths of the algorithm logic. A much more comprehensive test will be performed once the algorithm has been coded into a programming language.

Steps in desk checking an algorithm

There are six simple steps to follow when desk checking an algorithm:

1 Choose simple input test cases that are valid. Two or three test cases are usually sufficient.
2 Establish what the expected result should be for each test case. This is one of the reasons for choosing simple test data in the first place: it is much easier to determine the total of 10, 20 and 30 than 3.75, 2.89 and 5.31!
3 Make a table of the relevant variable names within the algorithm on a piece of paper.
4 Walk the first test case through the algorithm, keeping a step-by-step record of the contents of each variable in the table as the data passes through the logic.
5 Repeat the walk-through process using the other test data cases, until the algorithm has reached its logical end.
6 Check that the expected result established in Step 2 matches the actual result developed in Step 5.

By desk checking an algorithm you are attempting to detect early errors. Desk checking will eliminate most errors, but it still cannot prove that the algorithm is 100% correct!

Now let us desk check each of the algorithms developed in this chapter:

Example 3.7 *Desk check of Example 3.1*

A *Solution algorithm*

```
Add_three_numbers
      Read number_1, number_2, number_3
      total = number_1 + number_2 + number_3
      Print total
END
```

B *Desk checking*

(i)   Choose two sets of input test data. The three numbers selected will be 10, 20 and 30 for the first test case and 40, 41 and 42 for the second.

Input data:

	First data set	**Second data set**
number_1	10	40
number_2	20	41
number_3	30	42

(ii) Establish the expected result for each test case.
Expected results:

	First data set	**Second data set**
total	60	123

(iii) Set up a table of relevant variable names, and pass each test data set through the solution algorithm, statement by statement.

Statement		**number_1**	**number_2**	**number_3**	**total**	**Print**
First Pass	Read	10	20	30		
	total				60	
	Print					yes
Second Pass	Read	40	41	42		
	total				123	
	Print					yes

(iv) Check that the expected results (60 and 123) match the actual results (the total column in the table).

This desk check, which should take no more than five minutes, indicates that the algorithm is correct. You can now proceed to code the algorithm into a programming language. Note that if, at the end of a desk check, the actual results do not match the expected results, the solution algorithm probably contains a logic error. In this case, the programmer needs to go back to the solution algorithm, fix the error, then desk check the algorithm again. See Example 3.10.

Example 3.8 *Desk check of Example 3.2*

A *Solution algorithm*

```
Find_average_temperature
        Prompt operator for max_temp, min_temp
        Get max_temp, min_temp
        avg_temp = (max_temp + min_temp)/2
        Output avg_temp to the screen
END
```

B *Desk checking*

(i)   Choose two sets of input test data. The max_temp and min_temp values will be 30 and 10 for the first case, and 40 and 20 for the second.

Input data:

	First data set	Second data set
max_temp	30	40
min_temp	10	20

(ii) Establish the expected result for each test case.
Expected results:

	First data set	Second data set
avg_temp	20	30

(iii) Set up a table of variable names, and pass each test data set through the solution algorithm, statement by statement.

Statement		Prompt	max_temp	min_temp	avg_temp	Output
First Pass	Prompt	yes				
	Get		30	10		
	Calculate				20	
	Output					yes
Second Pass	Prompt	yes				
	Get		40	20		
	Calculate				30	
	Output					yes

(iv) Check that the expected results in step (ii) match the actual results in step (iii).

Example 3.9 *Desk check of Example 3.3*

A *Solution algorithm*

Calculate_mowing_time
      Prompt operator for block_length, block_width
      Get block_length, block_width
      block_area = block_length * block_width
      Prompt operator for house_length, house_width
      Get house_length, house_width
      house_area = house_length * house_width
      mowing_area = block_area − house_area
      mowing _time = mowing_area/2
      Output mowing_time to screen
END

B *Desk checking*

(i) Choose two sets of valid input data. The data chosen will be as illustrated in the diagram.

Input data:

	First data set	Second data set
block_length	30	40
block_width	30	20
house_length	20	20
house_width	20	10

(ii) Expected results

	First data set	Second data set
mowing_time	250 minutes	300 minutes

(iii) Set up a table of variable names and pass each test data set through the solution algorithm, statement by statement.

Statement	block length	block width	house length	house width	block area	house area	mowing area	mowing time
First Pass								
Get	30	30						
block_area					900			
Get			20	20				
house_area						400		
mowing_area							500	
mowing_time								250
Output								yes
Second Pass								
Get	40	20						
block_area					800			
Get			20	10				
house_area						200		
mowing_area							600	
mowing_time								300
Output								yes

(iv) Check that the expected results match the actual results. Yes, the expected result for each set of data matches the calculated result.

EXAMPLE 3.10 *Desk check of Example 3.3, which now contains a logic error*

A Solution Algorithm

```
Calculate_mowing_time
      Prompt operator for block_length, block_width
      Get block_length, block_width
      block_area = block_length * block_width
      Prompt operator for house_length, house_width
      Get house_length, house_width
      house_area = block_length * block_width
      mowing_area = block_area − house_area
      mowing_time = mowing_area / 2
      Output mowing_time to screen
END
```

B Desk Checking

(i) Choose two sets of valid input data.

Input data:

	First data set	Second data set
block_length	30	40
block_width	30	20
house_length	20	20
house_width	20	10

(ii) Expected results

	First data set	Second data set
mowing_time	250 minutes	300 minutes

(iii) Set up a table of variable names and pass each test data set through the solution algorithm, statement by statement.

Statement	block length	block width	house length	house width	block area	house area	mowing area	mowing time
First Pass								
Get	30	30						
block_area					900			
Get			20	20				
house_area						900		
mowing_area							0	
mowing_time								0
Output								yes
Second Pass								
Get	40	20						
block_area					800			
Get			20	10				
house_area						800		
mowing_area							0	
mowing_time								0
Output								yes

(iv) Check that the expected results match the actual results. Here, you can see that the calculation for house_area is incorrect, because when house_area is subtracted from block_area, the result is zero, which cannot be right. The algorithm needs to be adjusted, so that the statement

house_area = block_length * block_width

is changed to

house_area = house_length * house_width

Another desk check would establish that the algorithm is now correct.

3.4 CHAPTER SUMMARY

The first section of this chapter was devoted to methods of analysing and defining a programming problem. You must fully understand a problem before you can attempt to find a solution. The method suggested was to analyse the actual words used in the specification with the aim of dividing the problem into three separate components: input, output and processing. Several examples were explored and the use of a defining diagram was established. It was emphasised that the processing steps should list what tasks need to be performed, rather than how they are to be accomplished.

The second section was devoted to the establishment of a solution algorithm. After the initial analysis of the problem you must attempt to find a solution and express this solution as an algorithm. To do this you must use correct pseudocode statements, the three basic control structures, and the defining diagram which had previously been established. Only algorithms using the sequence control structure were used as examples.

The third section was concerned with checking the algorithm for correctness. A method of playing computer by tracing through the algorithm step by step was introduced, with examples to previous problems given.

3.5 PROGRAMMING PROBLEMS

In the following problems you will need to:

- define the problem by constructing a defining diagram,
- create a solution algorithm using pseudocode, and
- desk check the solution algorithm using two valid test cases.

1   Construct an algorithm that will prompt an operator to input three characters, receive those three characters, and display a welcoming message to the screen such as 'Hello xxx! We hope you have a nice day'.

2   You require an algorithm that will receive two integer items from a terminal operator, and display to the screen their sum, difference, product and quotient.

3   You require an algorithm that will receive an integer from the screen, add 5 to it, double it, subtract 7 from it, and display the final number to the screen.

4 You require an algorithm that will read in a tax rate (as a percentage) and the prices of five items. The program is to calculate the total price, before tax, of the items, then the tax payable on those items. The tax payable is calculated by applying the tax rate percentage to the total price. Print the total price and the tax payable as output.

5 You require an algorithm to read in one customer's account balance at the beginning of the month, a total of all withdrawals for the month, and a total of all deposits made during the month. A federal tax charge of 1% is applied to all transactions made during the month. The program is to calculate the account balance at the end of the month by (1) subtracting the total withdrawals from the account balance at the beginning of the month, (2) adding the total deposits to this new balance, (3) calculating the federal tax (1% of total transactions, i.e. total withdrawals + total deposits), and (4) subtracting this federal tax from the new balance. After these calculations, print the final end-of-month balance.

6 You require a program to read in the values from an employee's time sheet, and calculate and print the weekly pay owing to that employee. The values read in are the total number of regular hours worked, the total overtime hours, and the hourly wage rate. Weekly pay is calculated as payment for regular hours worked, plus payment for overtime hours worked. Payment for regular hours worked is calculated as (wage rate times regular hours worked); payment for overtime hours worked is calculated as (wage rate times overtime hours worked times 1.5).

Selection control structures

Objectives

- To elaborate on the uses of simple selection, multiple selection and nested selection in algorithms
- To introduce the case construct in pseudocode
- To develop algorithms using variations of the selection control structure

Outline

4.1 THE SELECTION CONTROL STRUCTURE

The selection control structure was introduced in Chapter 2, as the second construct in the Structure Theorem. This structure represents the decision-making capabilities of the computer. That is, you can use the selection control structure in pseudocode to illustrate a choice between two or more actions, depending on whether a condition is true or false. This 'condition' is based on a comparison of two items, and is usually expressed with one of the following relational operators:

<	less than
>	greater than
=	equal to
<=	less than or equal to
>=	greater than or equal to
<>	not equal to

Thus, in the IF statement, a choice is made between two alternate paths, based on a decision about whether the 'condition' is true or false.

There are a number of variations of the selection structure, as follows.

1 Simple selection (simple IF statement)

Simple selection occurs when a choice is made between two alternative paths, depending on the result of a condition being true or false. The structure is represented in pseudocode using the keywords IF, THEN, ELSE and ENDIF. For example:

```
IF account_balance < $300 THEN
    service_charge = $5.00
ELSE
    service_charge = $2.00
ENDIF
```

Only one of the THEN or ELSE paths will be followed, depending on the result of the condition in the IF clause.

2 Simple selection with null false branch (null ELSE statement)

The null ELSE structure is a variation of the simple IF structure. It is used when a task is performed only when a particular condition is true. If the condition is false, then no processing will take place and the IF statement will be bypassed. For example:

```
IF student_attendance = part_time THEN
    add 1 to part_time_count
ENDIF
```

In this case, the part_time_count field will be altered only if the student's attendance pattern is part time.

3 Combined selection (combined IF statement)

A combined IF statement is one that contains multiple conditions, each connected with the logical operators AND or OR. If the conditions are combined using the connector AND, both conditions must be true for the combined condition to be true. For example:

```
IF student_attendance = part_time
AND student_gender = female THEN
      add 1 to fem_part_time_count
ENDIF
```

In this case, each student record will undergo two tests. Only those students who are female and who attend part time will be selected, and the variable fem_part_time_count will be incremented. If either condition is found to be false, the counter will remain unchanged.

If the connector OR is used to combine any two conditions, only one of the conditions needs to be true for the combined condition to be considered true. If neither condition is true, the combined condition is considered false. Changing the AND in the above example to OR dramatically changes the outcome from the processing of the IF statement.

```
IF student_attendance = part_time
OR student_gender = female THEN
      add 1 to fem_part_time_count
ENDIF
```

In this example, if either or both conditions is found to be true, the combined condition will be considered true. That is, the counter will be incremented:

1   if the student is part time, regardless of gender; or
2   if the student is female, regardless of attendance pattern.

Only students who are not female and not part time will be ignored. So fem_part_time_count will contain the total count of female part-time students, male part-time students, and female full-time students. As a result, fem_part_time_count is no longer a meaningful name for this variable. You must fully understand the processing that takes place when combining conditions with the AND or OR logical operators.

More than two conditions can be linked together with the AND or OR operators. However, if both operators are used in the one IF statement, parentheses must be used to avoid ambiguity. Look at the following example:

```
IF record_code = '23'
OR update_code = delete
AND account_balance = zero THEN
      delete customer record
ENDIF
```

The logic of this statement is confusing. It is uncertain whether the first two conditions should be grouped together and operated on first, or the second two conditions should be grouped together and operated on first. Pseudocode algorithms should never be ambiguous. There are no precedence rules for logical operators in pseudocode, but there are precedence rules in most programming languages. Therefore parentheses must be used in pseudocode to avoid ambiguity as to the meaning intended, as follows:

```
IF (record_code = '23'
OR update_code = delete)
AND account_balance = zero THEN
    delete customer record
ENDIF
```

The IF statement is now no longer ambiguous, and it is clear as to what conditions are necessary for the customer record to be deleted: the record will only be deleted if the account balance equals zero and either the record code = 23 or the update code = delete.

The NOT operator

The NOT operator can also be used for the logical negation of a condition, as follows:

```
IF NOT (record_code = '23') THEN
    update customer record
ENDIF
```

Here, the IF statement will be executed for all record codes other than code '23', i.e. for record codes *not* equal to '23'.

Note that the AND and OR operators can also be used with the NOT operator, but great care must be taken and parentheses must be used to avoid ambiguity, as follows:

```
IF NOT (record_code = '23'
    AND update_code = delete) THEN
    update customer record
ENDIF
```

Here, the customer record will only be updated if the record code is not equal to '23' *and* the update code is not equal to delete.

4   Nested selection (nested IF statement)

Nested selection occurs when the word IF appears more than once within an IF statement. Nested IF statements can be classified as linear or non-linear.

Linear nested IF statements

The linear nested IF statement is used when a field is being tested for various values and a different action is to be taken for each value.

This form of nested IF is called linear because each ELSE immediately follows the IF condition to which it corresponds. Comparisons are made until a true condition is encountered, and the specified action is executed until the next ELSE statement is reached. Linear nested IF statements should be indented for readability, with each IF, ELSE and corresponding ENDIF aligned. For example:

```
IF record_code = 'A' THEN
      increment counter_A
ELSE
      IF record_code = 'B' THEN
            increment counter_B
      ELSE
            IF record_code = 'C' THEN
                  increment counter_C
            ELSE
                  increment error_counter
            ENDIF
      ENDIF
ENDIF
```

Note that there are an equal number of IF, ELSE and ENDIF statements, and that the correct indentation makes it easy to read and understand.

Non-linear nested IF statements

A non-linear nested IF occurs when a number of different conditions need to be satisfied before a particular action can occur. It is termed non-linear because the ELSE statement may be separated from the IF statement with which it is paired. Indentation is once again important when expressing this form of selection in pseudocode. Each ELSE statement should be aligned with the IF condition to which it corresponds.

For instance:

```
IF student_attendance = part_time THEN
      IF student_gender = female THEN
            IF student_age > 21 THEN
                  add 1 to mature_fem_pt_students
            ELSE
                  add 1 to young_fem_pt_students
            ENDIF
      ELSE
            add 1 to male_pt_students
      ENDIF
ELSE
      add 1 to full_time_students
ENDIF
```

Note that there are an equal number of IF conditions as ELSE and ENDIF statements. Using correct indentation helps to see which pair of IF and ELSE statements match. However, non-linear nested IF statements may contain logic errors that could be difficult to correct, so they should be used sparingly in pseudocode. If possible, replace a series of non-linear nested IF statements with a combined IF statement. This replacement is possible in pseudocode because two consecutive IF statements act like a combined IF statement which uses the AND operator. Take as an example the following non-linear nested IF statement:

```
IF student_attendance = part_time THEN
    IF student_age > 21 THEN
        increment mature_pt_student
    ENDIF
ENDIF
```

This can be written as a combined IF statement:

```
IF student_attendance = part_time
AND student_age > 21 THEN
    increment mature_pt_student
ENDIF
```

The same outcome will occur for both pseudocode expressions, but the format of the latter is preferred, if the logic allows it, simply because it is easier to understand.

4.2 ALGORITHMS USING SELECTION

Let us look at some programming examples that use the selection control structure. In each example, the problem will be defined, a solution algorithm will be developed and the algorithm will be manually tested. To help define the problem, the processing verbs in each example have been underlined.

Example 4.1 *Read three characters*

Design an algorithm that will:
prompt a terminal operator for three characters, accept those characters as input, sort them into ascending sequence and output them to the screen.

A *Defining diagram*

Input	Processing	Output
char_1	Prompt for characters	char_1
char_2	Accept three characters	char_2
char_3	Sort three characters	char_3
	Output three characters	

B *Solution algorithm*

The solution algorithm requires a series of IF statements to sort the three characters into ascending sequence.

```
Read_three_characters
    Prompt the operator for char_1, char_2, char_3
    Get char_1, char_2, char_3
    IF char_1 > char_2 THEN
        temp = char_1
        char_1 = char_2
        char_2 = temp
    ENDIF
    IF char_2 > char_3 THEN
        temp = char_2
        char_2 = char_3
        char_3 = temp
    ENDIF
    IF char_1 > char_2 THEN
        temp = char_1
        char_1 = char_2
        char_2 = temp
    ENDIF
    Output to the screen char_1, char_2, char_3
END
```

If this solution, most of the logic of the algorithm is concerned with the sorting of the three characters into alphabetic sequence. This sorting is carried out with the use of pseudocode that 'swaps' two items, as follows:

```
temp = char_1
char_1 = char_2
char_2 = temp
```

Here, the values in the variables char_1 and char_2 are 'swapped', with the use of the temporary variable, temp. Pseudocode such as this must be written carefully to ensure that items are not lost in the shuffle.

To make the algorithm easier to read, this sorting logic could have been performed in a single module, as will be demonstrated in Chapter 7.

C Desk checking

Two sets of valid characters will be used to check the algorithm; the characters k, b and g as the first set, and z, s and a as the second.

(i) Input data:

	First data set	Second data set
char_1	k	z
char_2	b	s
char_3	g	a

(ii) Expected results:

	First data set	Second data set
char_1	b	a
char_2	g	s
char_3	k	z

(iii) Desk check table:

Note that when desk checking the logic, each IF statement is treated as a single statement.

Statement		char_1	char_2	char_3	temp	IF statement executed?
First Pass	Get	k	b	g		
	IF	b	k		k	yes
	IF		g	k	k	yes
	IF					no
	output	yes	yes	yes		
Second Pass	Get	z	s	a		
	IF	s	z		z	yes
	IF		a	z	z	yes
	IF	a	s		s	yes
	output	yes	yes	yes		

Example 4.2 *Process customer record*

A program is required to <u>read</u> a customer's name, a purchase amount and a tax code. The tax code has been validated and will be one of the following:

0   tax exempt (0%)
1   state sales tax only (3%)
2   federal and state sales tax (5%)
3   special sales tax (7%)

The program must then <u>compute</u> the sales tax and the total amount due and <u>print</u> the customer's name, purchase amount, sales tax and total amount due.

A *Defining diagram*

Input	Processing	Output
cust_name	Read customer details	cust_name
purch_amt	Compute sales tax	purch_amt
tax_code	Compute total amount	sales_tax
	Print customer details	total_amt

B Solution algorithm

The solution algorithm requires a linear nested IF statement to calculate the sales tax.

```
Process_customer_record
        Read cust_name, purch_amt, tax_code
        IF tax_code = 0 THEN
            sales_tax = 0
        ELSE
            IF tax_code = 1 THEN
                sales_tax = purch_amt * 0.03
            ELSE
                IF tax_code = 2 THEN
                    sales_tax = purch_amt * 0.05
                ELSE
                    sales_tax = purch_amt * 0.07
                ENDIF
            ENDIF
        ENDIF
        total_amt = purch_amt + sales_tax
        Print cust_name, purch_amt, sales_tax, total_amt
    END
```

C Desk checking

Two sets of valid input data for purchase amount and tax code will be used to check the algorithm.

(i) Input data:

	First data set	Second data set
purch_amt	10.00	20.00
tax_code	0	2

(ii) Expected results:

	First data set	Second data set
sales_tax	0	1.00
total_amt	10.00	21.00

Note that when desk checking the logic, the whole linear nested IF statement (13 lines of pseudocode) is counted as a single pseudocode statement.

(iii) Desk check table:

Statement	purch_amt	tax_code	sales_tax	total_ amt	IF statement executed?
First Pass					
Read	10.00	0			
IF			0		IF tax_code = 0
total_amt				10.00	
Print	yes		yes	yes	
Second Pass					
Read	20.00	2			
IF			1.00		IF tax_code = 2
total_amt				21.00	
Print	yes		yes	yes	

As the expected result for the two test cases matches the calculated result, the algorithm is correct.

Example 4.3 *Calculate employee's pay*

A program is required by a company to <u>read</u> an employee's number, pay rate and the number of hours worked in a week. The program is then to <u>compute</u> the employee's weekly pay and <u>print</u> it along with the input data.

According to the company's rules, no employee may be paid for more than 60 hours per week, and the maximum hourly rate is $25.00 per hour. If more than 35 hours are worked, payment for the overtime hours worked is calculated at time-and-a-half. If the hours worked field or the hourly rate field is out of range, the input data and an appropriate message is to be <u>printed</u> and the employee's weekly pay is not to be calculated.

A *Defining diagram*

Input	Processing	Output
emp_no	Read employee details	emp_no
pay_rate	Validate input fields	pay_rate
hrs_worked	Calculate employee pay	hrs_worked
	Print employee details	emp_weekly_pay
		error_message

B Solution algorithm

The solution to this problem will require a series of simple IF and nested IF statements. First, the variables 'pay_rate' and 'hrs_worked' must be validated, and if either is found to be out of range, an appropriate message is to be placed into a variable called 'error_message'.

The employee's weekly pay is only to be calculated if the input variables 'pay_rate' and 'hrs_worked' are valid, so another variable, 'valid_input_fields', will be used to indicate to the program whether or not these input fields are valid.

Boolean variables

The variable valid_input_fields is a Boolean variable; that is, it may contain only one of two possible values (true or false). When using the IF statement with a Boolean variable, the IF statement can be simplified in pseudocode, as follows:

```
IF valid_input_fields = true THEN
    statement
ENDIF
```

can be simplified to imply '= true', and so can be written as:

```
IF valid_input_fields THEN
    statement
ENDIF
```

Similarly, if we want to test if valid_input_fields is false, we can say in pseudocode:

```
IF NOT valid_input_fields THEN
    statement
ENDIF
```

The variable valid_input_fields acts as an internal switch or flag to the program. It will initially be set to true, and will be assigned the value false if one of the input fields is found to be invalid. The employee's weekly pay will be calculated only if valid_input_fields is true.

```
Compute_employee_pay
    Set valid_input_fields to true
    Set error_message to blank
    Read emp_no, pay_rate, hrs_worked
    IF pay_rate > $25 THEN
        error_message = 'Pay rate exceeds $25.00'
        valid_input_fields = false
        Print emp_no, pay_rate, hrs_worked, error_message
    ENDIF
    IF hrs_worked > 60 THEN
        error_message = 'Hours worked exceeds limit of 60'
        valid_input_fields = false
        Print emp_no, pay_rate, hrs_worked, error_message
    ENDIF
    IF valid_input_fields THEN
        IF hrs_worked <= 35 THEN
            emp_weekly_pay = pay_rate * hrs_worked
        ELSE
            overtime_hrs = hrs_worked − 35
            overtime_pay = overtime_hrs * pay_rate * 1.5
            emp_weekly_pay = (pay_rate * 35) + overtime_pay
        ENDIF
        Print emp_no, pay_rate, hrs_worked, emp_weekly_pay
    ENDIF
END
```

In this solution there are two separate functions to be performed in the algorithm: the validation of the input data, and the calculation and printing of the employee's weekly pay. These two tasks could have been separated into modules before the algorithm was developed in pseudocode (see Chapter 7).

C Desk checking

Two sets of valid input data for pay rate and hours worked will be used to check this algorithm.

(i) Input data:

	First data set	Second data set
pay_rate	10.00	40.00
hrs_worked	40	35

(ii) Expected results:

	First data set	Second data set
pay_rate	10.00	40.00
hrs_worked	40	35
emp_weekly_pay	425.00	—
error_message	blank	Pay rate exceeds $25.00

(iii) Desk check table:

Statement	pay_rate	hrs_worked	over-time_hrs	over-time_pay	emp_weekly_pay	valid_input_fields	error_message	IF statement executed?
First Pass								
Initialise						true		
Initialise							blank	
Read	10.00	40						
IF								no
IF								no
IF			5	75.00	425.00			valid input fields
Print	yes	yes				yes		
Second Pass								
Initialise						true		
Initialise							blank	
Read	40.00	35						
IF						false	Pay rate exceeds $25.00	Pay rate >25.00
Print	yes	yes					yes	
IF								no
IF								no

4.3 THE CASE STRUCTURE

The case control structure in pseudocode is another way of expressing a linear nested IF statement. It is used in pseudocode for two reasons: it can be directly translated into many high-level languages, and it makes the pseudocode easier to write and understand. Nested IFs often look cumbersome in pseudocode and depend on correct structure and indentation for readability. Let us look at the example used earlier in this chapter:

```
IF record_code = 'A' THEN
      increment counter_A
ELSE
      IF record_code = 'B' THEN
            increment counter_B
      ELSE
            IF record_code = 'C' THEN
                  increment counter_C
            ELSE
                  increment error_counter
            ENDIF
      ENDIF
ENDIF
```

This linear nested IF structure can be replaced with a case control structure. Case is not really an additional control structure. It simplifies the basic selection control structure and extends it from a choice between two values to a choice from multiple values. In one case structure, several alternative logical paths can be represented. In pseudocode, the keywords CASE OF and END-CASE serve to identify the structure, with the multiple values indented, as follows:

```
CASE OF single variable
      value_1 : statement block_1
      value_2 : statement block_2
                  .
                  .
                  .
      value_n : statement block_n
      value_other : statement block_other
ENDCASE
```

The path followed in the case structure depends on the value of the variable specified in the CASE OF clause. If the variable contains value_1, statement block_1 is executed; if it contains value_2, statement block_2 is executed, and so on. The value_other is included in the event that the variable contains none of the listed values. We can now rewrite the above linear nested IF statement with a case statement, as follows:

```
CASE OF record_code
      'A'   : increment counter_A
      'B'   : increment counter_B
      'C'   : increment counter_C
      other : increment error_counter
ENDCASE
```

In both forms of pseudocode the processing logic is exactly the same. However, the case solution is much more readable.

Let us now look again at Example 4.2. The solution algorithm for this example was earlier expressed as a linear nested IF statement, but it could equally have been expressed as a CASE statement.

Example 4.4 *Process customer record*

A program is required to <u>read</u> a customer's name, a purchase amount and a tax code. The tax code has been validated and will be one of the following:

0 tax exempt (0%)
1 state sales tax only (3%)
2 federal and state sales tax (5%)
3 special sales tax (7%)

The program must then <u>compute</u> the sales tax and the total amount due and <u>print</u> the customer's name, purchase amount, sales tax and total amount due.

A *Defining diagram*

Input	Processing	Output
cust_name	Read customer details	cust_name
purch_amt	Compute sales tax	purch_amt
tax_code	Compute total amount	sales_tax
	Print customer details	total_amt

B *Solution algorithm*

The solution algorithm will be expressed using a CASE statement.

```
Process_customer_record
      Read cust_name, purch_amt, tax_code
      CASE OF tax_code
            0 : sales_tax = 0
            1 : sales_tax = purch_amt * 0.03
            2 : sales_tax = purch_amt * 0.05
            3 : sales_tax = purch_amt * 0.07
      ENDCASE
      total_amt = purch_amt + sales_tax
      Print cust_name, purch_amt, sales_tax, total_amt
END
```

C *Desk checking*

Two sets of valid input data for purchase amount and tax code will be used to check the algorithm. Note that the case structure serves as a single pseudocode statement.

(i) Input data:

	First data set	Second data set
purch_amt	10.00	20.00
tax_code	0	2

(ii) Expected results:

	First data set	Second data set
sales_tax	0	1.00
total_amt	10.00	21.00

(iii) Desk check table:

Statement	purch_amt	tax_code	sales_tax	total_amt	CASE statement executed?
First Pass					
Read	10.00	0			
CASE			0		CASE 0
total_amt				10.00	
Print	yes		yes	yes	
Second Pass					
Read	20.00	2			
CASE			1.00		CASE 2
total_amt				21.00	
Print	yes		yes	yes	

As the expected result matches the actual result, the algorithm is shown to be correct.

4.4 CHAPTER SUMMARY

This chapter covered the selection control structure in detail. Descriptions and pseudocode examples were given for simple selection, null ELSE, combined IF and nested IF statements. Several solution algorithms which used the selection structure were developed.

The case structure was introduced as a means of expressing a linear nested IF statement in a simpler and more concise form. Case is available in many high-level languages, and so is a useful construct to write in pseudocode.

4.5 PROGRAMMING PROBLEMS

Construct a solution algorithm for the following programming problems. Your solution should contain: a defining diagram, a pseudocode algorithm, and a desk check of the algorithm.

1 Design an algorithm that will receive two integer items from a terminal operator, and display to the screen their sum, difference, product and quotient. Note that the quotient calculation (first integer divided by second integer) is only to be performed if the second integer does not equal zero.

2 Design an algorithm that will read two numbers and an integer code from the screen. The value of the integer code should be 1, 2, 3 or 4. If the value of the code is 1, compute the sum of the two numbers. If the code is 2, compute the difference (first minus second). If the code is 3, compute the product of the two numbers. If the code is 4, and the second number is not zero, compute the quotient (first divided by second). If the code is not equal to 1, 2, 3 or 4, display an error message. The program is then to display the two numbers, the integer code and the computed result to the screen.

3 Design an algorithm that will prompt an operator for a student's serial number and the student's exam score out of 100. Your program is then to match the exam score to a letter grade and print the grade to the screen. Calculate the letter grade as follows:

Exam score	Assigned grade
90 and above	A
80–89	B
70–79	C
60–69	D
below 60	F

4 Design an algorithm that will receive the weight of a parcel and determine the delivery charge for that parcel. Calculate the charges as follows:

Parcel weight (kg)	Cost per kg ($)
<2.5 kg	$3.50 per kg
2.5–5 kg	$2.85 per kg
>5 kg	$2.45 per kg

5 Design an algorithm that will prompt a terminal operator for the price of an article and a pricing code. Your program is then to calculate a discount rate according to the pricing code and print to the screen the original price of the article, the discount amount and the new discounted price. Calculate the pricing code and accompanying discount amount as follows:

Pricing code	Discount rate
H	50%
F	40%
T	33%
Q	25%
Z	0%

If the pricing code is Z, the words 'No discount' are to be printed on the screen. If the pricing code is not H, F, T, Q or Z, the words 'Invalid pricing code' are to be printed.

6 An architect's fee is calculated as a percentage of the cost of a building. The fee is made up as follows:

8% of the first $5000.00 of the cost of a building and
3% on the remainder if the remainder is less than or equal to $80 000.00 or
$2\frac{1}{2}$ % on the remainder if the remainder is more than $80 000.00.

Design an algorithm that will accept the cost of a building and calculate and display the architect's fee.

7 A home mortgage authority requires a deposit on a home loan according to the following schedule:

Loan $	Deposit
less than $25 000	5% of loan value
$25 000–$49 999	$1250 + 10% of loan over $25 000
$50 000–$100 000	$5000 + 25% of loan over $50 000

Loans in excess of $100 000 are not allowed. Design an algorithm that will read a loan amount and compute and print the required deposit.

8 Design an algorithm that will receive a date in the format dd/mm/yyyy (e.g. 21/07/1998) and validate it as follows:
(i) the month must be in the range 1–12, and
(ii) the day must be in the range of 1–31 and acceptable for the corresponding month. (Don't forget a leap year check for February.)

9 The tax payable on taxable incomes for employees in a certain country is set out in the following table:

Taxable income	Tax payable
From $1.00–$4461.99	Nil
From $4462.00–$17 893.99	Nil plus 30 cents for each $ in excess of $4462.00
From $17 894.00–$29 499.99	$4119.00 plus 35 cents for each $ in excess of $17 894.00
From $29 500.00–$45 787.99	$8656.00 plus 46 cents for each $ in excess of $29 500.00
$45788.00 and over	$11 179.00 plus 60 cents for each $ in excess of $45 788.00

Design an algorithm that will read as input the taxable income amount and calculate and print the tax payable on that amount.

10 A transaction record on a Sales Commission File contains the retail price of an item sold, a transaction code that indicates the sales commission category to which an item can belong, and the employee number of the person who sold the item. The transaction code can contain the values S, M or L, which indicate that the percentage commission will be 5%, 7% or 10% respectively. Construct an algorithm that will read a record on the file, calculate the commission owing for that record, and print the retail price, commission and employee number.

Repetition control structures

" DESK CHECKING "

DOWHILE
you've got
nothing better
to do ...

Objectives

- To develop algorithms which use the DOWHILE and REPEAT...UNTIL control structures
- To introduce a pseudocode structure for counted repetition loops
- To develop algorithms using variations of the repetition construct

Outline

5.1 REPETITION USING THE DOWHILE STRUCTURE

The solution algorithms developed so far have one characteristic in common: they show the program logic required to process just one set of input values. However, most programs require the same logic to be repeated for several sets of data. The most efficient way to deal with this situation is to establish a looping structure in the algorithm that will cause the processing logic to be repeated a number of times.

In Chapter 2, the DOWHILE construct was introduced as the pseudocode representation of a repetitive loop. Its format is:

```
DOWHILE condition p is true
     statement block
ENDDO
```

As the DOWHILE loop is a leading decision loop, the following processing takes place:

(a) The logical condition p is tested.
(b) If condition p is found to be true, the statements within the statement block are executed once. Control then returns to the retesting of condition p (step a).
(c) If condition p is found to be false, control passes to the next statement after ENDDO and no further processing takes place within the loop.

As a result, the DOWHILE structure will continue to repeat a group of statements while a condition remains true. As soon as the condition becomes false, the construct is exited.

There are two important considerations about which you must be aware before designing a DOWHILE loop.

First, the testing of the condition is at the beginning of the loop. This means that the programmer may need to perform some initial processing to adequately set up the condition before it can be tested.

Second, the only way to terminate the loop is to render the DOWHILE condition false. This means you must set up some process within the statement block that will eventually change the condition so that the condition becomes false. Failure to do this results in an endless loop.

Example 5.1 *Fahrenheit–Celsius conversion*

Every day, a weather station receives 15 temperatures expressed in degrees Fahrenheit. A program is to be written which will <u>accept</u> each Fahrenheit temperature, <u>convert</u> it to Celsius and <u>display</u> the converted temperature to the screen. After 15 temperatures have been processed, the words 'All temperatures processed' are to be <u>displayed</u> on the screen.

A Defining diagram

Input	Processing	Output
f_temp (15 temperatures)	Get Fahrenheit temperatures Convert temperatures Display Celsius temperatures Display screen message	c_temp (15 temperatures)

The defining diagram still only lists what needs to be done; the equation to convert the temperature will not need to be known until the algorithm is developed.

Having defined the input, output and processing, you are ready to outline a solution to the problem. This can be done by writing down the control structures needed and any extra variables which are to be used in the solution algorithm. In this example you need:

- a DOWHILE structure to repeat the necessary processing, and
- a counter, initialised at zero, which will control the fifteen repetitions. This counter, called temperature_count, will contain the number of temperatures read and processed.

You should now write down the solution algorithm.

B Solution algorithm

```
Fahrenheit_Celsius_conversion
    Set temperature_count to zero
    DOWHILE temperature_count < 15
        Prompt operator for f_temp
        Get f_temp
        Compute c_temp = (f_temp − 32) * 5/9
        Display c_temp
        Add 1 to temperature_count
    ENDDO
    Display 'All temperatures processed' to the screen
END
```

Note that the temperature_count variable is initialised before the loop, tested in the DOWHILE condition at the top of the loop, and incremented within the body of the loop. It is essential that the variable controlling the loop is acted upon in these three places. Notice also that the statement that alters the value of temperature_count in the loop is the last statement in the statement block. That is, immediately after incrementing temperature_count, its value will be tested when control returns to the DOWHILE condition at the top of the loop.

This solution algorithm could also have been expressed using the keywords WHILE...DO and ENDWHILE, as follows:

```
Fahrenheit_Celsius_conversion
    Set temperature_count to zero
    WHILE temperature_count < 15 DO
        Prompt operator for f_temp
        Get f_temp
        Compute c_temp = (f_temp − 32) * 5/9
        Display c_temp
        Add 1 to temperature_count
    ENDDO
    Display 'All temperatures processed' to the screen
END
```

This is identical to the first algorithm; only the repetition keywords used are different.

C Desk checking

Although the program will require 15 records to process properly, it is still only necessary to check the algorithm at this stage with two valid sets of data.

(i) Input data:

	First data set	Second data set
f_temp	32	50

(ii) Expected results:

	First data set	Second data set
c_temp	0	10

(iii) Desk check table:

Statement	temperature_count	DOWHILE condition	f_temp	c_temp
Initialise	0			
DOWHILE		true		
Get			32	
Compute				0
Display				yes
Add	1			
DOWHILE		true		
Get			50	
Compute				10
Display				yes
Add	2			

Desk checking this algorithm shows the exact processing of a DOWHILE loop. There is some initial processing (first statement), which will be executed only once. Then the DOWHILE condition is tested and found to be true. The body of the loop is then executed before returning to the testing of the DOWHILE condition. Processing will continue to repeat until the DOWHILE condition becomes false, i.e. until the temperature counter equals 15.

Although only two test cases were used to desk check the algorithm, you can see that, given more test cases, the temperature counter will eventually reach 15, so the looping will cease.

Let us now look at a problem where an unknown number of records are to be processed. In this situation, you cannot use a counter to control the loop, so another method is required. Often this takes the form of a trailer record, or sentinel. This sentinel is a special record or value placed at the end of valid data to signify the end of that data. It must contain a value that is clearly distinguishable from the other data to be processed. It is referred to as a sentinel because it indicates that no more data follows.

Example 5.2 *Print examination scores*

A program is required to <u>read</u> and <u>print</u> a series of names and exam scores for students enrolled in a mathematics course. The class average is to be <u>computed</u> and <u>printed</u> at the end of the report. Scores can range from 0 to 100. The last record contains a blank name and a score of 999 and is not to be included in the calculations.

A Defining diagram

Input	Processing	Output
name	Read student details	name
exam_score	Print student details	exam_score
	Compute average score	average_score
	Print average score	

You will need to consider the following requirements when establishing a solution algorithm:

- a DOWHILE structure to control the reading of exam scores, until it reaches a score of 999,
- an accumulator for total scores, namely total_score, and
- an accumulator for the total students, namely total_students.

B Solution algorithm

```
Print_examination_scores
        Set total_score to zero
        Set total_students to zero
        Read name, exam_score
        DOWHILE exam_score not = 999
                Add 1 to total_students
                Print name, exam_score
                Add exam_score to total_score
                Read name, exam_score
        ENDDO
        If total_students not = zero THEN
                average_score = total_score/total_students
                Print average_score
        ENDIF
END
```

This solution algorithm is a typical example of the basic algorithm design required for processing sequential files of data. There is an unknown number of records, so the condition controlling the exam score processing is the testing for the trailer record or sentinel (Record_999). It is this test that appears in the DOWHILE clauses (DOWHILE exam_score not = 999).

However, this test cannot be made until at least one exam score has been read. Hence, the initial processing, which sets up the condition, is a Read statement immediately before the DOWHILE clause (Read name, exam_score). This is known as a priming Read, and its use is extremely important when processing sequential files.

The algorithm will require another Read statement, this time within the body of the loop. Its position is also important. The trailer record or sentinel must not be included in the calculation of average score, so each time an exam score is read, it must be tested for a 999 value, before further processing can take place. For this reason, the Read statement is placed at the end of the loop, immediately before ENDDO, so that its value can be tested when control returns to the DOWHILE condition. As soon as the trailer record or sentinel has been read, control will exit from the loop to the next statement after ENDDO, which is the calculation of average_score.

The priming Read before the DOWHILE condition, together with the subsequent Read within the loop, immediately before the ENDDO statement, form the basic framework for DOWHILE repetitions in pseudocode. In general, all algorithms using a DOWHILE construct to process a sequential file should have the same basic pattern, as follows:

```
Process_sequential_file
        Initial processing
        Read first record
        DOWHILE more records exist
                Process this record
                Read next record
        ENDDO
        Final processing
END
```

C Desk checking

Two valid records and a trailer record should be sufficient to desk check this algorithm.

(i) Input data:

	First record	Second record	Third record
score	50	100	999

(ii) Expected results:

1st name, and score of 50
2nd name, and score of 100
Average score 75

(iii) Desk check table:

Statement	total_ score	total_ students	exam_ score	DOWHILE condition	average_ score
Initialise	0	0			
Read			50		
DOWHILE				true	
Add		1			
Print			yes		
Add	50				
Read			100		
DOWHILE				true	
Add		2			
Print			yes		
Add	150				
Read			999		
DOWHILE				false	
Compute					75
Print					yes

The expected results are confirmed, which proves that the algorithm is correct for this set of data.

Example 5.3 *Process student enrolments*

A program is required which will <u>read</u> a file of student records, and <u>select</u> and <u>print</u> only those students enrolled in a course unit named Programming I. Each student record contains student number, name, address, postcode, gender and course unit number. The course unit number for Programming I is 18500. Three totals are to be <u>printed</u> at the end of the report: total females enrolled in the course, total males enrolled in the course, and total students enrolled in the course.

A Defining diagram

Input	Processing	Output
student_record	Read student records	selected student
• student_no	Select student records	records
• name	Print selected records	totals
• address	Compute total females enrolled	
• postcode	Compute total males enrolled	
• gender	Compute total students enrolled	
• course_unit	Print totals	

You will need to consider the following requirements, when establishing a solution algorithm:

- a DOWHILE structure to perform the repetition,
- an IF statement to select the required students, and
- accumulators for the three total fields.

Note that there is no trailer record for this student file. In cases like this, the terms 'more data', 'more records', 'records exist' or 'not EOF' (end of file) can be used in the DOWHILE or WHILE...DO condition clause. For example, these are all equivalent conditions:

```
DOWHILE more data
DOWHILE more records
DOWHILE records exist
DOWHILE NOT EOF
WHILE success DO
```

By expressing the condition in this way, you leave it to the computer to indicate to the program when there are no more records in the file. This occurs when an attempt is made to read a record but no more records exist. A signal is sent to the program to indicate that there are no more records, so the 'DOWHILE more records' or 'DOWHILE NOT EOF' clause is rendered false.

B Solution algorithm

```
Process_student_enrolments
        Set total_females_enrolled to zero
        Set total_males_enrolled to zero
        Set total_students_enrolled to zero
        Read student record
        DOWHILE records exist
                IF course_unit = 18500 THEN
                        print student details
                        increment total_students_enrolled
                        IF student_gender = female THEN
                                increment total_females_enrolled
                        ELSE
                                increment total_males_enrolled
                        ENDIF
                ENDIF
                Read student record
        ENDDO
        Print total_females_enrolled
        Print total_males_enrolled
        Print total_students_enrolled
    END
```

This solution algorithm sues the same basic framework as the previous example. A non-linear nested IF statement was used to determine the required selection logic.

C Desk checking

Three valid student records should be sufficient to desk check this algorithm. Since student_no, name, address, and postcode are not operated upon in this algorithm, they do not need to be given in the input data sets.

(i) Input data:

	First record	Second record	Third record
course_unit	20000	18500	18500
gender	F	F	M

(ii) Expected results:

Student number, name, address, postcode, F (2nd student)
Student number, name, address, postcode, M (3rd student)

Total females enrolled	1
Total males enrolled	1
Total students enrolled	2

The non-linear nested IF statement in this example will be considered a single statement when desk checking the algorithm.

Statement	course_unit	gender	DOWHILE condition	IF condition	total_females_enrolled	total_males_enrolled	total_students_enrolled
Initialise					0	0	0
Read	20000	F					
DOWHILE			true				
IF				false			
Read	18500	F					
DOWHILE			true				
IF	Print	Print		true			1
IF				true	1		
Read	18500	M					
DOWHILE			true				
IF	Print	Print		true			2
IF				false		1	
Read	EOF						
DOWHILE			false				
Print					yes	yes	yes

5.2 REPETITION USING THE REPEAT...UNTIL STRUCTURE

The REPEAT...UNTIL structure is similar to the DOWHILE structure, in that a group of statements are repeated in accordance with a specified condition. However, where the DOWHILE structure tests the condition at the <u>beginning</u> of the loop, a REPEAT...UNTIL structure tests the condition at the <u>end</u> of the loop. This means that the statements within the loop will be executed once before the condition is tested. If the condition is false, the statements will then be repeated UNTIL the condition becomes true.

The format of the REPEAT...UNTIL structure is:

```
REPEAT
     statement
     statement
        :
        :
UNTIL condition is true
```

You can see that REPEAT…UNTIL is a trailing decision loop; the statements are executed once before the condition is tested.

There are two other considerations about which you need to be aware before using REPEAT…UNTIL.

First, REPEAT…UNTIL loops are executed when the condition is false; it is only when the condition becomes true that repetition ceases. Thus the logic of the condition clause of the REPEAT…UNTIL structure is the opposite of DOWHILE. For instance, 'DOWHILE more records' is equivalent to 'REPEAT…UNTIL no more records', and 'DOWHILE number NOT = 99' is equivalent to 'REPEAT…UNTIL number = 99'.

Second, the statements within a REPEAT…UNTIL structure will always be executed at least once. As a result, there is no need for a priming Read when using REPEAT…UNTIL. One Read statement at the beginning of the loop is sufficient.

Let us now compare an algorithm which uses a DOWHILE structure with the same problem using a REPEAT…UNTIL structure. Consider the following DOWHILE loop:

```
Process_student_records
       Set student_count to zero
       Read student record
       DOWHILE student number NOT = 999
            Write student record
            Increment student_count
            Read student record
       ENDDO
       Print student_count
   END
```

This can be rewritten (incorrectly) as a trailing decision loop, using the REPEAT…UNTIL structure as follows:

```
Process_student_records
       Set student_count to zero
       REPEAT
                Read student record              INCORRECT
                Write student record             REPEAT...UNTIL logic
                Increment student_count
            UNTIL student number = 999
       Print student_count
   END
```

This algorithm is incorrect, because the statements within the loop will be repeated just one time too many. Instead of immediately terminating the repetition once the trailer record has been read (Read student record), there are two more statements in the loop to be executed before the condition is tested. That is, the trailer record will be written to the file and added to student_count before establishing that is is the trailer record. To avoid this, logic must be included to prevent data being processed once the trailer record has been read. This logic takes the form of an IF statement immediately after the Read statement, as follows:

```
Process_student_records
      Set student_count to zero
      REPEAT
            Read student record
            IF student number NOT = 999 THEN          CORRECT
                  Write student record                REPEAT...UNTIL logic
                  Increment student_count
            ENDIF
            UNTIL student number = 999
            Print student_count
END
```

REPEAT...UNTIL loops are used less frequently in pseudocode than DOWHILE loops for sequential file processing because of this extra IF statement required within the loop.

The majority of examples given in this book will use the DOWHILE construct in preference to REPEAT...UNTIL because of its simple structure. However, the following programming example does use REPEAT...UNTIL.

Example 5.4 *Process inventory items*

A program is required to <u>read</u> a series of inventory records that contain item number, item description and stock figure. The last record in the file has an item number of zero. The program is to <u>produce</u> a 'Low Stock Items' report, by <u>printing</u> only those records which have a stock figure of less than 20 items. A heading is to be <u>printed</u> at the top of the report and a total low stock item count to be <u>printed</u> at the end.

A Defining diagram

Input	Processing	Output
inventory record	Read inventory records	heading
• item_number	Select low stock items	selected records
• item_description	Print low stock records	• item_number
• stock_figure	Print total low stock items	• item_description
		• stock_figure
		total_low_stock_items

You will need to consider the following requirements when establishing a solution algorithm:

- a REPEAT...UNTIL to perform the repetition (a DOWHILE could also have been used),
- an IF statement to select stock figures of less than 20,
- an accumulator for total_low_stock_items, and
- an extra IF, within the REPEAT loop, to ensure the trailer record is not processed.

B1 Solution algorithm using REPEAT…UNTIL

```
Process_inventory_records
      Set total_low_stock_items to zero
      Print 'Low Stock Items' heading
      REPEAT
            Read inventory record
            IF item_number > zero THEN
                  IF stock_figure < 20 THEN
                        print item_number, item_description, stock_figure
                        increment total_low_stock_items
                  ENDIF
            ENDIF
      UNTIL item_number = zero
      Print total_low_stock_items
END
```

The solution algorithm has a simple structure, with a single Read statement at the beginning of the REPEAT…UNTIL loop and an extra IF statement within the loop to ensure the trailer record is not incorrectly incremented into the total_low_stock_items accumulator.

B2 Solution algorithm using DOWHILE

```
Process_inventory_records
      Set total_low_stock_items to zero
      Print 'Low Stock Items' heading
      Read inventory record
      DOWHILE item_number > zero
            IF stock_figure < 20 THEN
                  print item_number, item_description, stock_figure
                  increment total_low_stock_items
            ENDIF
            Read inventory record
      ENDDO
      Print total_low_stock_items
END
```

This solution, using DOWHILE, also has simple structure, with a priming Read and a Read at the end of the loop just before ENDDO. When a record containing an item number of zero is read, the DOWHILE condition will become false and the looping will cease.

C Desk checking

The first solution algorithm, which uses a REPEAT…UNTIL structure, will be the algorithm that is desk checked. Two valid records and a trailer record (item number equal to zero) will be used to test the algorithm:

(i) Input data:

	First record	Second record	Third record
item_number	123	124	0
stock_figure	8	25	

(ii) Expected results:

Low Stock Items
123   8   (first record)

Total Low Stock Items = 1

(iii) Desk check table:

Statement	item_ number	stock_ figure	REPEAT UNTIL	first IF condition	second IF condition	total_low stock_items	heading
Initialise						0	
Print							yes
Read	123	8					
IF				true			
IF	Print	Print			true	1	
UNTIL			false				
Read	124	25					
IF				true			
IF					false		
UNTIL			false				
Read	0						
IF				false			
UNTIL			true				
Print						yes	

5.3 COUNTED REPETITION CONSTRUCTS

Counted repetition occurs when the exact number of loop iterations is known in advance. The execution of the loop is controlled by a loop index, and instead of using DOWHILE, or REPEAT...UNTIL, the simple keyword DO is used as follows:

```
DO loop_index — initial_value to final_value
    statement block
ENDDO
```

The DO loop does more than just repeat the statement block. It will:

1 initialise the loop_index to the required initial_value,
2 increment the loop_index by 1 for each pass through the loop,
3 test the value of loop_index at the beginning of each loop to ensure that it is within the stated range of values, and
4 terminate the loop when the loop_index has exceeded the specified final_value.

In other words, a counted repetition construct will perform the initialising, incrementing and testing of the loop counter automatically. It will also terminate the loop once the required number of repetitions have been executed.

Let us look again at Example 5.1, which processes 15 temperatures at a weather station each day. The solution algorithm can be redesigned to use a DO loop.

Example 5.5 *Fahrenheit–Celsius conversion*

Every day, a weather station receives 15 temperatures expressed in degrees Fahrenheit. A program is to be written which will <u>accept</u> each Fahrenheit temperature, <u>convert</u> it to Celsius and <u>display</u> the converted temperature to the screen. After 15 temperatures have been processed, the words 'All temperatures processed' are to be <u>displayed</u> on the screen.

A *Defining diagram*

Input	Processing	Output
f_temp (15 temperatures)	Get Fahrenheit temperatures Convert temperatures Display Celsius temperatures Display screen message	c_temp (15 temperatures)

B *Solution algorithm*

The solution will require a DO loop and a loop counter (temperature_count) to process the repetition.

```
Fahrenheit_Celsius_conversion
    DO temperature_count = 1 to 15
        Prompt operator for f_temp
        Get f_temp
        Compute c_temp = (f_temp − 32) * 5/9
        Display c_temp
    ENDDO
    Display 'All temperatures processed' to the screen
END
```

Note that the DO loop controls all the repetition:

- it initialises temperature_count to 1,
- it increments temperature_count by 1 for each pass through the loop,
- it tests temperature_count at the beginning of each pass to ensure that it is within the range 1 to 15, and
- it automatically terminates the loop once temperature_count has exceeded 15.

C Desk checking

Two valid records should be sufficient to test the algorithm for correctness. It is not necessary to check the DO loop construct for all 15 records.

(i) Input data:

	First data set	Second data set
f_temp	32	50

(ii) Expected results:

	First data set	Second data set
c_temp	0	10

(iii) Desk check table:

Statement	temperature_count	DO	f_temp	c_temp
DO	1	set to 1		
Get			32	
Compute				0
Display				yes
DO	2	increment		
Get			50	
Compute				10
Display				yes

Desk checking the algorithm with the two input test cases indicates that the expected results have been achieved.

A requirement of counted repetition loops is that the exact number of input data items or records needs to be known before the algorithm can be written. This is an artificial situation in real life, but counted repetition loops are used extensively with arrays or tables, as can be seen in Chapter 7.

5.4 CHAPTER SUMMARY

This chapter covered the repetition control structure in detail. Descriptions and pseudocode examples were given for DOWHILE, REPEAT...UNTIL, and counted repetition loops. Several solution algorithms which used each of the three control structures were defined, developed and desk checked.

We saw that most of the solution algorithms had the same general pattern. This pattern consisted of:

1 some initial processing before the loop;
2 some processing for each record within the loop; and
3 some final processing once the loop has been exited.

Expressed as a solution algorithm using the DOWHILE construct this basic pattern was developed as a general solution:

```
Process_sequential_file
        Initial processing
        Read first record
        DOWHILE more records exist
                Process this record
                Read next record
        ENDDO
        Final processing
END
```

5.5 PROGRAMMING PROBLEMS

Construct a solution algorithm for the following programming problems. Your solution should contain:

• a defining diagram
• a pseudocode algorithm, and
• a desk check of the algorithm.

1 Design an algorithm that will output the seven times table, as follows:

$$7 \times 1 = 7$$
$$7 \times 2 = 14$$
$$7 \times 3 = 21 \ldots$$

2 Design an algorithm that will display to the screen the first twenty numbers, with their squares and cubes, as follows:

1	1	1
2	4	8
3	9	27 ...

3 Design an algorithm that will prompt for, receive and total a collection of payroll amounts entered at the terminal until a sentinel amount of 999 is entered. After the sentinel has been entered, display the total payroll amount to the screen.

4 Design an algorithm that will read a series of integers at the terminal. The first integer is special, as it indicates how many more integers will follow. Your algorithm is to calculate and print the sum and average of the integers, excluding the first integer, and display these values to the screen.

5 Design an algorithm that will prompt for and receive the time expressed in 2400 format (e.g. 2305 hours), convert it to 12 hour format (eg 11.05 p.m.) and display the new time to the screen. Your program is to repeat the processing until a sentinel time of 9999 is entered.

6 Design a program that will read a file of product records, each containing the item number, item name, the quantity sold this year and the quantity sold last year. The program is to produce a product list showing the item number, item name and the increase or decrease in the quantity sold this year for each item.

7 The first record of a set of records contains a bank account number and an opening balance. Each of the remaining records in the set contains the amount of a cheque drawn on that bank account. The trailer record contains a zero amount. Design a program that will read and print the bank account number and opening balance on a Statement of Account Report. The following cheque amounts are to be read and printed on the report, each with a new running balance. Print a closing balance at the end of the report.

8 Design a program that will read a file of employee records containing employee number, employee name, hourly pay rate, regular hours worked and overtime hours worked. The company pays its employees weekly, according to the following rules:

> regular pay = regular hours worked × hourly rate of pay
> overtime pay = overtime hours worked × hourly rate of pay × 1.5
> total pay = regular pay + overtime pay

Your program is to read the input data on each employee's record and compute and print the employee's total pay on the Weekly Payroll Report. All input data and calculated amounts are to appear on the report. A total payroll amount is to appear at the end of the report.

9 Design an algorithm that will process the weekly employee time cards for all the employees of an organisation. Each employee time card will have three data items: an employee number, an hourly wage rate and the number of hours worked during a given week. Each employee is to be paid time and a half for all hours worked over 35. A tax amount of 15% of gross salary is to be deducted. The output to the screen should display the employee's number and net pay. At the end of the run, display the total payroll amount and the average amount paid.

10 As a form of quality control, the Pancake Kitchen has recorded, on a Pancake file, two measurements for each of its pancakes made in a certain month, the thickness in mm (millimetres) and the diameter in cm (centimetres). Each record on the file contains two measurements for a pancake, thickness followed by diameter. The last record in the file contains values of 99 for each measurement. Design a program that will read the Pancake file, calculate the minimum, maximum and average for both the dimensions, and print these values on a report.

Pseudocode algorithms using sequence, selection and repetition

Objectives

- To develop solution algorithms to eight typical programming problems using sequence, selection and repetition constructs

Outline

6.1 EIGHT SOLUTION ALGORITHMS

This chapter develops solution algorithms to eight programming problems of increasing complexity. All the algorithms will use a combination of sequence, selection and repetition constructs. The algorithms have been designed to be interactive or to process sequential files. Reading these algorithms should consolidate the groundwork developed in the previous chapters.

Each programming problem will be defined, the control structures required will be determined, and a solution algorithm will be devised.

(a) Defining the problem

It is extremely important that you divide the problem into its three components: input, output and processing. The processing component should list the tasks to be performed, i.e. what needs to be done, not how. The verbs in each problem have been underlined to help identify the actions to be performed.

(b) The control structures required

Once the problem has been defined, write down the control structures (sequence, selection and repetition) that may be needed, as well as any extra variables which the solution may require.

(c) The solution algorithm

Having defined the problem and determined the required control structures, devise a solution algorithm and represent it using pseudocode. Each solution algorithm presented in this chapter is only one solution to the particular problem: many different solutions could be equally correct.

(d) Desk checking

You will need to desk check each of the algorithms with two or more test cases.

Example 6.1 *Process number pairs*

Design an algorithm that will <u>prompt</u> for and <u>receive</u> pairs of numbers from an operator at a terminal and <u>display</u> their sum, product and average on the screen. If the calculated sum is over 200, an asterisk is to be <u>displayed</u> beside the sum. The program is to terminate when a pair of zero values is entered.

A Defining diagram

Input	Processing	Output
number_1 number_2	Prompt for numbers Get two numbers Calculate sum Calculate product Calculate average Display sum, product, average Display '*'	sum product average '*'

B Control structures required

1 A DOWHILE loop to control the repetition, and
2 An IF statement to determine if an asterisk is to be displayed.
3 Note the use of the NOT operand with the AND logical operator.

C Solution algorithm

```
Process_number_pairs
      Set sum to zero
      Prompt for number_1, number_2
      Get number_1, number_2
      DOWHILE NOT (number_1 = 0 AND number_2 = 0)
            sum = number_1 + number_2
            product = number_1 * number_2
            average = sum/2
            IF sum > 200 THEN
                  Display sum, '*', product, average
            ELSE
                  Display sum, product, average
            ENDIF
            Prompt for number_1, number_2
            Get number_1, number_2
      ENDDO
END
```

Example 6.2 *Print student records*

A file of student records consists of 'S' records and 'U' records. An 'S' record contains the student's number, name, age, gender, address and attendance pattern; full time (F/T) or part time (P/T). A 'U' record contains the number and name of the unit or units in which the student has enrolled. There may be more than one 'U' record for each 'S' record. Design a solution algorithm that will <u>read</u> the file of student records and <u>print</u> only the student's number, name and address on a 'STUDENT LIST'.

A *Defining diagram*

Input	Processing	Output
's' records	Print heading	heading line
• number	Read student records	selected student records
• name	Select 's' records	• number
• address	Print selected records	• name
• age		• address
• gender		
• attendance_pattern		
'u' records		

B *Control structures required*

1 A DOWHILE loop to control the repetition, and
2 An IF statement to select 'S' records.

C *Solution algorithm*

```
Print_student records
       Print 'STUDENT LIST' heading
       Read student record
       DOWHILE more records exist
           IF student record = 'S' record THEN
                  print student_number, name, address
           ENDIF
           Read student record
       ENDDO
END
```

Example 6.3 *Print selected students*

Design a solution algorithm that will <u>read</u> the same student file as in Example 6.2, and <u>produce</u> a report of all female students who are enrolled part time. The report is to be headed 'PART TIME FEMALE STUDENTS' and is to <u>show</u> the student's number, name, address and age.

A Defining diagram

Input	Processing	Output
's' records	Print heading	heading line
• number	Read student records	selected student records
• name	Select P/T female students	• number
• address	Print selected records	• name
• age		• address
• gender		• age
• attendance_pattern		
'u' records		

B Control structures required

1 A DOWHILE loop to control the repetition, and
2 An IF statement or statements to select 'S', female and part-time (P/T) students.

C Solution algorithm

Several algorithms for this problem will be presented, and all are equally correct. The only place the algorithms differ is in the expression of the IF statement. It is interesting to compare the three different solutions.

Solution 1 uses a non-linear nested IF:

```
Produce_part_time_female_list
        Print 'PART TIME FEMALE STUDENTS' heading
        Read student record
        DOWHILE more records
            IF student record = 'S' record THEN
                IF attendance_pattern = P/T THEN
                    IF gender = female THEN
                        print student_number, name, address, age
                    ENDIF
                ENDIF
            ENDIF
            Read student record
        ENDDO
    END
```

Solution 2 uses a nested and compound IF statement:

```
Produce_part_time_female_list
      Print 'PART TIME FEMALE STUDENTS' heading
      Read student record
      DOWHILE more records
            IF student record = 'S' record THEN
                  IF (attendance_pattern = P/T
                  AND gender = female) THEN
                        print student_number, name, address, age
                  ENDIF
            ENDIF
            Read student record
      ENDDO
END
```

Solution 3 also uses a compound IF statement:

```
Produce_part_time_female_list
      Print 'PART TIME FEMALE STUDENTS' heading
      Read student record
      DOWHILE more records
            IF student record = 'S' record
            AND attendance_pattern = P/T
            AND gender = female THEN
                  print student_number, name, address, age
            ENDIF
            Read student record
      ENDDO
END
```

Example 6.4 *Print and total selected students*

Design a solution algorithm that will <u>read</u> the same student file as in Example 6.3 and <u>produce</u> the same 'PART TIME FEMALE STUDENTS' report. In addition, you are to <u>print</u> at the end of the report the number of students who have been selected and listed, and the total number of students on the file.

A Defining diagram

Input	Processing	Output
's' records	Print heading	heading line
• number	Read student records	selected student records
• name	Select P/T female students	• number
• address	Print selected records	• name
• age	Compute total students	• address
• gender	Compute total selected students	• age
• attendance_pattern	Print totals	total_students
'u' records		total_selected_students

B Control structures required

1 A DOWHILE loop to control the repetition,
2 IF statements to select 'S', female and P/T students, and
3 Accumulators for total_selected_students and total_students.

C Solution algorithm

```
Produce_part_time_female_list
      Print 'PART TIME FEMALE STUDENTS' heading
      Set total_students to zero
      Set total_selected_students to zero
      Read student record
      DOWHILE records exist
            IF student record = 'S' record THEN
                  increment total_students
                  IF (attendance_pattern = P/T
                  AND gender = female) THEN
                        increment total_selected_students
                        print student_number, name, address, age
                  ENDIF
            ENDIF
            Read student record
      ENDDO
      Print total_students
      Print total_selected_students
END
```

Note the positions where the total accumulators are incremented. If these statements are not placed accurately within their respective IF statements, the algorithm could produce erroneous results.

Example 6.5 *Print Student Report*

Design an algorithm that will <u>read</u> the same student file as in Example 6.4 and, for each student, <u>print</u> the name, number and attendance pattern from the 'S' records (student records) and the unit number and unit name from the 'U' records (enrolled units records) as follows.

STUDENT REPORT

Student name	. . . .	
Student number	. . . .	
Attendance	. . . .	
Enrolled units	. . . .	. . . .
	. . . .	. . . .
	. . . .	. . . .

At the end of the report, print the total number of students enrolled.

A Defining diagram

Input	Processing	Output
's' records	Print heading	heading line
number	Read student records	detail lines
name	Print 's' record details	• student name
attendance_pattern	Print 'u' record details	• student number
'u' records	Compute total students	• attendance
unit_number	Print total students	• enrolled units
unit_name		total_students

B Control structures required

1   A DOWHILE loop to control the repetition,
2   An IF statement to select 'S' or 'U' records, and
3   An accumulator for total_students.

C Solution algorithm

```
Print_student_report
       Print 'STUDENT REPORT' heading
       Set total_students to zero
       Read student record
       DOWHILE records exist
              IF student record = 'S' THEN
                      add 1 to total_students
                      Print 'Student name', name
                      Print 'Student number', number
                      Print 'Attendance', attendance_pattern
                      Print 'Enrolled units'
              ELSE
                      IF student record = 'U' THEN
                             Print unit_number, unit_name
                      ELSE
                             Print 'student record error'
                      ENDIF
              ENDIF
              Read student record
       ENDDO
       Print 'Total students', total_students
    END
```

Example 6.6 *Produce sales report*

Design a program that will <u>read</u> a file of sales records and <u>produce</u> a sales report. Each record in the file contains a customer's number, name, a sales amount and a tax code. The tax code is to be applied to the sales amount to determine the sales tax due for that sale, as follows:

tax code	sales tax
0	tax exempt
1	3%
2	5%

The report is to print a heading 'SALES REPORT', and detail lines listing the customer number, name, sales amount, sales tax and the total amount due from the customer.

A Defining diagram

Input	Processing	Output
sales records • customer_number • name • sales_amt • tax_code	Print heading Read sales records Calculate sales tax Calculate total amount Print customer details	heading line detail lines • customer_number • name • sales_amt • sales_tax • total_amt

B Control structures required

1 A WHILE...DO loop, to control the repetition, and
2 A case statement to calculate the sales_tax.

Assume that the tax_code field has been validated and will contain only a value of 0, 1 or 2.

C Solution algorithm

```
Produce_sales_report
        Print 'SALES REPORT' heading
        Read sales record
        WHILE success DO
            CASE of tax_code
                0 : sales_tax = 0
                1 : sales_tax = sales_amt * 0.03
                2 : sales_tax = sales_amt * 0.05
            ENDCASE
            total_amt = sales_amt + sales_tax
            Print customer_number, name, sales_amt, sales_tax, total_amt
            Read sales record
        ENDWHILE
    END
```

A linear nested IF statement could have been used in place of the case statement in this example. The case statement, however, expresses the logic so simply that it should be used wherever appropriate.

Example 6.7 *Student test results*

Design a solution algorithm that will <u>read</u> a file of student test results and <u>produce</u> a Student Test Grades report. Each test record contains the student number, name and test score (out of 50). The program is to <u>calculate</u> for each student the test score as a percentage and to <u>print</u> the student's number, name, test score (out of 50) and letter grade on the report. The letter grade is determined as follows:

A = 90–100%
B = 80–89%
C = 70–79%
D = 60–69%
F = 0–59%

A *Defining diagram*

Input	Processing	Output
student test records • student_number • name • test_score	Print heading Read student records Calculate test percentage Calculate letter grade Print student details	heading line student details • student_number • name • test_score • grade

B *Control structures required*

1 A DOWHILE loop to control the repetition,
2 A linear nested IF statement to calculate the grade, and
3 A formula to calculate the percentage.
   (The case construct cannot be used here, as it is not designed to cater for a range of values, e.g. 0–59%).

C Solution algorithm

```
Print_student_results
        Print 'STUDENT TEST GRADES' heading
        Read student record
        DOWHILE not EOF
                percentage = test_score * 2
                IF percentage > 89 THEN
                        grade = A
                ELSE
                        IF percentage > 79 THEN
                                grade = B
                        ELSE
                                IF percentage > 69 THEN
                                        grade = C
                                ELSE
                                        IF percentage > 59 THEN
                                                grade = D
                                        ELSE
                                                grade = F
                                        ENDIF
                                ENDIF
                        ENDIF
                ENDIF
                Print student_number, name, test_score, grade
                Read student record
        ENDDO
END
```

Note that the linear nested IF has been worded so that all alternatives have been considered.

Example 6.8 *Gas supply billing*

The Domestic Gas Supply Company records its customers' gas usage figures on a Customer Usage File. Each record on the file contains the customer number, customer name, customer address and gas usage expressed in cubic metres.

The company bills its customers according to the following rate: if the customer's usage is 60 cubic metres or less, a rate of $2.00 per cubic metre is applied; if the customer's usage is more than 60 cubic metres, then a rate of $1.75 per cubic metre is applied for the first 60 cubic metres and $1.50 per cubic metre for the remaining usage.

Design a solution algorithm that will read the Customer Usage File and produce a report listing each customer's number, name, address, gas usage and the amount owing.

At the end of the report, print the total number of customers and the total amount owing to the company.

A Defining diagram

Input	Processing	Output
customer usage records • customer_number • name • address • gas_usage	Print heading Read usage records Calculate amount owing Print customer details Compute total customers Compute total amount owing Print totals	heading line customer details • customer_number • name • address • gas_usage • amount_owing total_customers total_amount_owing

B Control structures required

1 A DOWHILE loop to control the repetition,
2 IF statements to calculate the amount_owing, and
3 Accumulators for total_customers and total_amount_owing.

C Solution algorithm

```
Bill_gas_customers
        Print 'CUSTOMER USAGE FIGURES' heading
        Set total_customers to zero
        Set total_amount_owing to zero
        Read customer record
        DOWHILE more records
            IF usage ≤ 60 THEN
                amount_owing = usage * $2.00
            ELSE
                amount_owing = (60 * $1.75) + ((usage − 60) * $1.50)
            ENDIF
            Print customer_number, name, address, gas_usage, amount_owing
            Add amount_owing to total_amount_owing
            Add 1 to total_customers
            Read customer record
        ENDDO
        Print total_customers
        Print total_amount  owing
    END
```

Note that, in this example, there is:

• initial processing before the loop,
• processing of the current record within the loop, and
• final processing after exiting the loop.

6.2 CHAPTER SUMMARY

This chapter developed solution algorithms to eight typical programming problems. The approach to all eight problems followed the same path:

1 The problem was defined, using a defining diagram.
2 The control structures required were written down, along with any extra variables required.
3 The solution algorithm was produced, using pseudocode and the three basic control structures: sequence, selection and repetition.

It was noted that the solution algorithms mostly followed the same basic pattern, although the statements within the pattern were quite different. This pattern was first introduced in Chapter 5, as follows:

```
Process_sequential_file
        Initial processing
        Read first record
        DOWHILE more records exist
                Process this record
                Read next record
        ENDDO
        Final processing
    END
```

6.3 PROGRAMMING PROBLEMS

Construct a solution algorithm for the following programming problems. Your solution should contain:

- a defining diagram,
- a list of control structures required,
- a pseudocode algorithm, and
- a desk check of the algorithm.

1 Design an algorithm that will prompt for and receive your age in years and months and calculate and display your age in months. If the calculated months figure is more than 500, three asterisks should also appear beside the month figure. Your program is to continue processing until a sentinel of 999 is entered.

2 Design an algorithm that will prompt for and receive the measurement for the diameter of a circle, and calculate and display the area and circumference of that circle. Your program is to continue processing until a sentinel of 9999 is entered.

3 A file of student records contains name, gender (M or F), age (in years) and marital status (single or married) for each student. Design an algorithm that will read through the file and calculate the numbers of married men, single men, married women and single women. Print these numbers on a Student Summary Report. If any single men are over 30 years of age, print their names and ages on a separate Eligible Bachelors Report.

4   Design an algorithm that will read a file of employee records and produce a weekly report of gross earnings for those employees. Gross earnings are earnings before tax and other deductions have been deducted. Each input record contains the employee number, the hours worked and the hourly rate of pay. Each employee's gross pay is calculated as the product of the hours worked and the rate of pay. At the end of the report, print the total gross earnings for that week.

5   Design an algorithm that will read the same file as in Problem 4, and produce a weekly report of the net earnings for those employees. Net earnings are gross earnings minus deductions. Each employee has two deductions from their gross earnings each week: tax payable (15% of gross earnings) and medical levy (1% of gross earnings). Your report is to print the gross earnings, tax payable, medical levy and net earnings for each employee. At the end of the report, print the total gross earnings, total tax, total medical levy and total net earnings.

6   A parts inventory record contains the following fields:
    • record code, (only code 11 is valid)
    • part number (6 characters; 2 alpha and 4 numeric, e.g. AA1234),
    • part description, and
    • inventory balance.

    Design an algorithm that will read the file of parts inventory records, validate the record code and part number on each record, and print the details of all valid inventory records which have an inventory balance equal to zero.

7   Design a program that will read the same parts inventory file described in Problem 6, validate the record code and part number on each record, and print the details of all valid records whose part numbers fall within the values AA3000 and AA3999 inclusive. Also print a count of these selected records at the end of the parts listing.

8   Design a program that will produce the same report as in Problem 7, but in addition, print at the end of the parts listing, a count of all the records whose part number falls between AA3000 and AA3999, as well as a count of all records whose part numbers begin with the value 'AA'.

9   An electricity supply authority records the amount of electricity that each customer uses on an electricity usage file. This file consists of:
    (a) A header record (first record), which provides the total kilowatt hours used during the month, by all customers.
    (b) A number of detail records, each containing the customer number, customer name and electricity usage (in kilowatt hours) for the month.

    Design a solution algorithm that will read the electricity usage file and produce an electricity usage report showing the customer number, customer name, electricity usage and the amount owing. The amount owing is calculated at 11 cents for each kilowatt hour used, up to 200 hours, and 8 cents for each kilowatt hour used over 200 hours. The total electricity usage in kilowatt hours is also to be accumulated.
        At the end of the program compare the total electricity usage accumulated in the program with the value provided in the header record, and print an appropriate message if the totals are not equal.

10 Design an algorithm that will read a file of customer records, showing the total amount owing on his or her credit card, and produce a report showing the customer's minimum amount due. Each customer record contains the customer number, name, address, postcode and total amount owing. The minimum amount due is calculated on the total amount owing, as follows:

If the total amount owing is less than $5.00, the total amount owing becomes the minimum amount due. If the total amount owing is greater than $5.00, the minimum amount due is calculated to be one-quarter of the total amount owing, provided this resulting amount is not less than $5.00. If the resulting amount is less than $5.00, the minimum amount due is $5.00.

Array processing

Array of sunshine

OBJECTIVES

- To introduce arrays and the uses of arrays
- To develop pseudocode algorithms for common operations on arrays
- To illustrate the manipulation of single and two dimensional arrays

OUTLINE

7.1 ARRAY PROCESSING

Arrays are one of the most powerful programming tools available. They provide the programmer with a way of organising a collection of homogeneous data items (i.e. items that have the same type and the same length) into a single data structure. An array, then, is a data structure that is made up of a number of variables all of which have the same data type; for example, all the exam scores for a class of thirty mathematics students. By using an array, a single variable name such as 'scores' can be associated with all thirty exam scores.

The individual data items that make up the array are referred to as the elements of the array. Elements in the array are distinguished from one another by the use of an index or subscript, enclosed in parentheses, following the array name; for example: 'scores(3)'

The subscript indicates the position of an element within the array; so scores(3) refers to the third exam score, or third element of the array, scores, and scores(23) refers to the twenty-third exam score.

The subscript or index may be a number or a variable, and may then be used to access any item within the valid bounds of an array, for example:

scores (6), or
element (index)

Arrays are an internal data structure, i.e. they are required only for the duration of the program in which they are defined. They are a very convenient mechanism for storing and manipulating a collection of similar data items in a program, and a programmer should be familiar with the operations most commonly performed on them. Arrays are sometimes referred to as tables.

Operations on arrays

Arrays can be used:

- to load initial information into an array which is later required for processing,
- to process the elements of the array,
- to store the results of processing into the elements of an array, or
- to store information, which is then written to a report.

Thus, the most typical operations performed on arrays are:

- loading a set of initial values into the elements of an array,
- processing the elements of an array,
- searching an array, using a linear or binary search, for a particular element, and
- writing out the contents of an array to a report.

Usually, the elements of an array are processed in sequence, starting with the first element. This can be accomplished easily in pseudocode with either a DO loop or a DOWHILE loop.

Simple algorithms that manipulate arrays

The following algorithms involve the simple manipulation of arrays. Each algorithm can be written using a DO loop or a DOWHILE loop, as in the first example. In each algorithm, the contents of the array and the number of elements have been established and the subscript is named index.

Example 7.1 *Find the sum of the elements of an array*

In this example, each element of the array is accumulated into a variable called sum. When all elements have been added, the variable sum is printed. Algorithms using a DO loop and a DOWHILE loop have been provided.

```
Find_sum_of_elements                    (Using DO loop)
    Set sum to zero
    DO index = 1 to number_of_elements
        sum = sum + array (index)
    ENDDO
    Print sum
END
```

```
Find_sum_of_elements                    (Using DOWHILE loop)
    Set sum to zero
    Set index to 1
    DOWHILE index <= number_of_elements
        sum = sum + array (index)
        index = index + 1
    ENDDO
    Print sum
END
```

Example 7.2 *Find the mean (average) of the elements of an array*

In this example, each element of the array is accumulated into a variable called sum. When all elements have been added, the average of the elements is found using the formula average = sum / number of elements and is then printed. The algorithm uses a DO loop.

```
Find_element_average
    Set sum to zero
    DO index = 1 to number_of_elements
        sum = sum + array (index)
    ENDDO
    average = sum / number_of_elements
    Print average
END
```

Example 7.3 *Find the largest of the elements of an array*

In this example, the elements of an array are searched to determine which element is the largest. The algorithm starts by putting the first element of the array into the variable largest_element, and then looking at the other elements of the array to see if a larger value exists. The largest value is then printed.

```
Find_largest_element
      Set largest_element to array (1)
      DO index = 2 to number_of_elements
            IF array (index) > largest_element THEN
                  largest_element = array (index)
            ENDIF
      ENDDO
      Print largest_element
END
```

Example 7.4 *Find the smallest of the elements of an array*

In this example, the elements of an array are searched to determine the smallest element. The algorithm starts by putting the first element of the array into the variable smallest_element, then looking at the other elements of the array to see if a smaller value exists. The smallest value is then printed.

```
Find_smallest_element
      Set smallest_element to array (1)
      DO index = 2 to number_of_elements
            IF array (index) < smallest_element THEN
                  smallest_element = array (index)
            ENDIF
      ENDDO
      Print smallest_element
END
```

Example 7.5 *Find the range of the elements of an array*

In this example, the elements of an array are searched to determine the smallest and the largest elements. The algorithm starts by putting the first element of the array into the variables smallest_element and largest_element, then looks at the other elements to see if a smaller or larger value exists. The two values are then printed.

```
Find_range_of_elements
      Set smallest_element to array (1)
      Set largest_element to array (1)
      DO index = 2 to number_of_elements
            IF array (index) < smallest_element THEN
                  smallest_element = array (index)
            ELSE
                  IF array (index) > largest_element THEN
                        largest_element = array (index)
                  ENDIF
            ENDIF
      ENDDO
      Print the range as smallest_element followed by largest_element
END
```

7.2 INITIALISING THE ELEMENTS OF AN ARRAY

Because an array is an internal data structure, initial values must be placed into the array before any information can be retrieved from it. These initial values can be assigned to the elements of the array as constants, or they can be read into the array from a file.

Loading constant values into an array

This method should only be used when the data in the array is unlikely to be changed; for example, the names of the 12 months of the year. To initialise such an array, establish an array called month_table, which contains twelve elements all of the same size. Then assign the elements of the array with the names of the months, one by one, as follows:

```
Initialise_month_table
    month_table(1) = 'January '
    month_table(2) = 'February '
        :
        :
        :
    month_table(12) = 'December '
END
```

Note that each element of the array must be the size of the largest month, i.e. September, so the shorter month names must be padded with blanks.

Loading initial values into an array from an input file

Defining array elements as constants in a program is not recommended if the values change frequently, as the program will need to be changed every time an array element changes. Therefore a general procedure is required to read values into the elements of an array from an input file.

The reading of a series of values from a file into an array can be represented by a simple DOWHILE loop. The loop should terminate when either the array is full or the input file has reached end of file. Both these conditions can be catered for in the condition clause of the DOWHILE loop.

In the following pseudocode algorithm, values are read from an input file and assigned to the elements of an array, starting with the first element, until there are no more input values or the array is full. The array name is array, the subscript is index, and the maximum number of elements that the array can hold is placed in max_num_elements.

```
Read_values_into_array
        Set max_num_elements to required value
        Set index to zero
        Read first input value
        DOWHILE (input values exist) AND (index < max_num_elements)
                index = index + 1
                array (index) = input value
                Read next input value
        ENDDO
        IF (input values exist) AND index = max_num_elements THEN
                Print 'Too many input values for array'
        ENDIF
END
```

Note that the processing will terminate when either the input file has reached EOF or the array is full. An error message will be printed if there are more input data items than there are elements in the array.

Arrays of variable size

In some programs, the number of entries in an array can vary. In this case, a sentinel value (e.g. 9999) is used to mark the last element of the array, both in the initialising file of data items and in the array itself. The sentinel record will indicate the end of input records during initial processing and the last element of the array during further processing. The algorithm for loading values into an array of variable size must include a check to ensure that no attempt is made to load more entries into the array than there are elements, as in the following example:

```
Read_values_into_variable_array
        Set max_num_elements to required value
        Set index to zero
        Read first input value
        DOWHILE (input value NOT = 9999) AND (index < max_num_elements)
                index = index + 1
                array (index) = input value
                Read next input value
        ENDDO
        IF index < max_num_elements THEN
                index = index + 1
                array (index) = 9999
        ELSE
                Print 'Array size too small'
        ENDIF
END
```

Note that the processing will terminate when either the sentinel record has been read or the array is full. An error message will be printed if there are more input data items than there are elements in the array.

Paired arrays

Many arrays in business applications are paired; that is, there are two arrays that have the same number of elements. The arrays are paired because the elements in the first array correspond to the elements in the same position in the second array. For example, a sales number array can be paired with a sales name array. Both arrays would have the same number of elements, with corresponding sales numbers and sales names. When you have determined where in the sales number array a particular salesperson's number appears, retrieve the salesperson's name from the corresponding position in the sales name array. In this way, the salesperson's number and name can appear on the same report, without any extra keying.

In the following example, an algorithm has been designed to read a file of product codes and corresponding selling prices for a particular company and load them into two corresponding arrays, named product_codes and selling_prices. In the algorithm, the subscript is index, and the field max_num_elements contains the total number of elements in each array.

```
Read_values_into_paired_arrays
    Set max_num_elements to required value
    Set index to zero
    Read first input record
    DOWHILE (NOT EOF input record) AND (index < max_num_elements)
        index = index + 1
        product_codes (index) = input product_code
        selling_prices (index) = input selling_price
        Read next record
    ENDDO
    IF (NOT EOF input record) AND index = max_num_elements THEN
        Print 'Too many input values for arrays'
    ENDIF
END
```

7.3 SEARCHING AN ARRAY

A common operation on arrays is to search the elements of an array for a particular data item. The reasons for searching an array may be:

- to edit an input value, i.e. to check that it is a valid element of an array;
- to retrieve information from an array;
- to retrieve information from a corresponding element in a paired array.

When searching an array, it is an advantage to have the array sorted into ascending sequence, so that, when a match is found, the rest of the array does not have to be searched. If you find an array element that is equal to an input entry, a match has been found and the search can be stopped. Also, if you find an array element that is greater than an input entry, no match has been found and the search can be stopped. Note that if the larger entries of an array are searched more often than the smaller entries, it may be an advantage to sort the array into descending sequence.

An array can be searched using either a linear search or a binary search.

A linear search of an array

A linear search involves looking at each of the elements of the array, one by one, starting with the first element. Continue the search until either you find the element being looked for or you reach the end of the array. A linear search is often used to validate data items.

The pseudocode algorithm for a linear search of an array will require a program flag named element_found. This flag, initially set to false, will be set to true once the value being looked for is found, that is, when the current element of the array is equal to the data item being looked for. In the following algorithm, the data item being searched for is stored in the variable input_value, and max_num_elements contains the total number of elements in the array.

```
Linear_search_of_an_array
    Set max_num_elements to required value
    Set element_found to false
    Set index to 1
    DOWHILE (NOT element_found) AND (index <= max_num_elements)
        IF array (index) = input_value THEN
            Set element_found to true
        ELSE
            index = index + 1
        ENDIF
    ENDDO
    IF element_found THEN
        Print array (index)
    ELSE
        Print 'value not found', input_value
    ENDIF
END
```

A binary search of an array

When the number of elements in an array exceeds 25, and the elements are sorted into ascending sequence, a more efficient method of searching the array is a binary search.

A binary search locates the middle element of the array first, and determines if the element being searched for is in the first half or second half of the table. The search then points to the middle element of the relevant half table, and the comparison is repeated. This technique of continually halving the area under consideration is continued until the data item being searched for is found, or its absence is detected.

In the following algorithm, a program flag named element_found is used to indicate whether the data item being looked for has been found. The variable low_element indicates the bottom position of the section of the table being searched, and high_element indicates the top position. The maximum number of elements that the array can hold is placed in the variable max_num_elements.

The binary search will continue until the data item has been found, or there can be no more halving operations (i.e. low_element is not less than high_element).

```
Binary_search_of_an_array
      Set element_found to false
      Set low_element to 1
      Set high_element to max_num_elements
      DOWHILE (NOT element_found) AND (low_element < = high_element)
            index = (low_element + high_element) / 2
            IF input_value = array (index) THEN
                  Set element_found to true
            ELSE
                  IF input_value < array (index) THEN
                        high_element = index − 1
                  ELSE
                        low_element = index + 1
                  ENDIF
            ENDIF
      ENDDO
      IF element_found THEN
            Print array (index)
      ELSE
            Print 'value not found', input_value
      ENDIF
END
```

7.4 WRITING OUT THE CONTENTS OF AN ARRAY

The elements of arrays are often used as a series of accumulators of data, to be written to a report. Writing out the contents of an array involves starting with the first element of the array and continuing until all elements have been written. This can be represented by a simple DO loop or a DOWHILE loop.

In the following pseudocode algorithm, the name of the array is array, and the subscript is index. The number of elements in the array is represented by number_of_elements.

```
Write_values_of_array                    (using DO loop)
      DO index = 1 to number_of_elements
            Print array (index)
      ENDDO
END
```

```
Write_values_of_array                    (using DOWHILE loop)
      Set index to 1
      DOWHILE index < = number_of_elements
            Print array (index)
            index = index + 1
      ENDDO
END
```

7.5 PROGRAMMING EXAMPLES USING ARRAYS

Example 7.6 *Process_exam_scores*

Design a program that will <u>prompt</u> for and <u>receive</u> 18 examination scores from a mathematics test, <u>compute</u> the class average, and <u>display</u> all the scores and the class average to the screen.

A Defining diagram

Input	Processing	Output
18 exam scores	Prompt for scores Get scores Compute class average Display scores Display class average	18 exam scores class_average

B Control structures required

This is an example of a counted repetition loop, as we know that there are exactly 18 exam scores. The programmer will need to consider the following requirements:

- an array to store the exam scores, i.e. 'scores',
- an index to identify each element in the array,
- one DO loop to accept the scores, and
- another DO loop to display the scores to the screen.

C Solution algorithm

```
Process_exam_scores
    Set total_score to zero
    DO index = 1 to 18
        Prompt operator for score
        Get scores (index)
        total_score = total_score + scores(index)
    ENDDO
    Compute average_score = total_score / 18
    DO index = 1 to 18
        Display scores(index)
    ENDDO
    Display average_score
END
```

Example 7.7 *Process integer array*

Design an algorithm that will <u>read</u> an array of 100 integer values and <u>count</u> the number of integers in the array which are greater than the average value of all the integers in the array. The algorithm is to <u>display</u> the average integer value and the count of integers greater than the average.

A *Defining diagram*

Input	Processing	Output
100 integer values	Read integer values Compute integer average Compute integer count Display integer average Display integer count	integer_average integer_count

B *Control structures required*

- an array of integer values, i.e. numbers,
- a DO loop to calculate the average of the integers, and
- a DO loop to count the number of integers greater than the average.

C *Solution algorithm*

```
Process_integer_array
      Set integer_total to zero
      Set integer_count to zero
      DO index = 1 to 100
            integer_total = integer_total + numbers (index)
      ENDDO
      integer_average = integer_total / 100
      DO index = 1 to 100
            IF numbers (index) > integer_average THEN
                  add 1 to integer_count
            ENDIF
      ENDDO
      Display integer_average, integer_count
END
```

Example 7.8 *Validate sales number*

Design an algorithm that will <u>read</u> a file of sales transaction and <u>validate</u> the sales numbers on each record. As each sales record is read, the sales number on the record is to be verified against an array of 35 sales numbers. Any sales number not found in the array is to be <u>flagged</u> as an error.

A Defining diagram

Input	Processing	Output
sales records	Read sales records Validate sales numbers Print error message	error_message

B Control structures required

- a previously initialised array of sales numbers, i.e. sales_numbers,
- a DOWHILE loop to read the sales file
- a DOWHILE loop to perform a linear search of the array for the sales number, and
- a variable element_found that will stop the linear search process.

C Solution algorithm

```
Validate_sales_numbers
        Set max_num_elements to 35
        Read sales record
        DOWHILE sales records exist
                Set element_found to false
                Set index to 1
                DOWHILE (NOT element_found) AND (index <= max_num_elements)
                        IF sales_numbers (index) = input sales number THEN
                                Set element_found to true
                        ELSE
                                index = index + 1
                        ENDIF
                ENDDO
                IF element_found = false THEN
                        Print 'invalid sales number', input sales number
                ENDIF
                Read sales record
        ENDDO
    END
```

Example 7.9 Calculate_freight_charge

Design an algorithm that will <u>read</u> an input weight for an item to be shipped, <u>search</u> an array of shipping weights and <u>retrieve</u> a corresponding freight charge. In this algorithm, two paired arrays, each containing 6 elements, have been established and initialised. The array, shipping_weights, contains a range of shipping weights in grams, and the array, freight_charges, contains a corresponding array of freight charges in dollars, as follows.

Shipping weights (grams)	Freight charges ($)
1–100	3.00
101–500	5.00
501–1000	7.50
1001–3000	12.00
3001–5000	16.00
5001–9999	35.00

A Defining diagram

Input	Processing	Output
entry weight	Prompt for entry weight Get entry weight Search shipping weights array Compute freight charge Display freight charge	freight_charge error_message

B Control structures required

- two arrays, shipping_weights and freight_charges, already initialised
- a DOWHILE loop to search the shipping_weights array and hence retrieve the freight charge.

C Solution algorithm

```
Calculate_freight_charge
      Set max_num_elements to 6
      Set index to 1
      Prompt for entry weight
      Get entry weight
      DOWHILE (index <= max_num_elements)
            IF shipping_weights (index) < entry weight THEN
                  add 1 to index
            ENDIF
      ENDDO
      IF index <= max_num_elements THEN
            freight_charge = freight_charges (index)
            Display 'Freight charge is', freight_charge
      ELSE
            Display 'invalid shipping weight', entry weight
      ENDIF
END
```

7.6 TWO-DIMENSIONAL ARRAYS

So far, all algorithms in this chapter have manipulated one-dimensional arrays; that is, only one subscript is needed to locate an element in an array. In some business applications, there is a need for multidimensional arrays, where two or more subscripts are required to locate an element in an array. The following freight charges array is an example of a two-dimensional array, and is an extension of Example 7.9 above. It is a two-dimensional array because the calculation of the freight charges to ship an article depends on two values; the shipping weight of the article and the geographical area or zone to which it is to be shipped, namely zones 1 ,2, 3 or 4.

The range of shipping weights, in grams, is provided in the same one-dimensional array as in Example 7.9, as follows.

Shipping weights (grams)
1–100
101–500
501–1000
1001–3000
3001–5000
5001–9999

Freight charges ($)		(by shipping zone)	
1	2	3	4
2.50	3.50	4.00	5.00
3.50	4.00	5.00	6.50
4.50	6.50	7.50	10.00
10.00	11.00	12.00	13.50
13.50	16.00	20.00	27.50
32.00	34.00	35.00	38.00

In the freight charges array, any one of four freight charges may apply to a particular shipping weight, depending on the zone to which the shipment is to be delivered. Thus, the array is set out as having rows and columns, where the six rows represent the six shipping weight ranges, and the four columns represent the four geographical zones.

The number of elements in a two-dimensional array is calculated as the product of the number of rows and the number of columns, in this case, $6 \times 4 = 24$.

An element of a two-dimensional array is specified using the name of the array, followed by two subscripts, enclosed in parentheses, separated by a comma. The row subscript is specified first, followed by the column subscript. Thus an element of the above freight charges array would be specified as freight_charges (row_index, column_index). So, freight_charges (5, 3) refers to the freight charge listed in the array where the 5th row and the 3rd column intersect, i.e. a charge of $20.00.

Loading a two-dimensional array

A two-dimensional array is loaded in columns within row order, that is all the columns for row one are loaded before moving to row two and loading the columns for that row, and so on.

In the following pseudocode algorithm, values are read from an input file of freight charges and assigned to a two-dimensional freight_charges array. The array has six rows, representing the six shipping weight ranges, and four columns, representing the four geographical shipping zones, as in the above example.

The reading of a series of values from a file into a two-dimensional array can be represented by a DO loop (or DOWHILE loop) within a DOWHILE loop.

```
Read_values_into_array
      Set max_num_elements to 24
      Set row_index to zero
      Read input file
      DOWHILE (input values exist) AND (row_index < 6)
            row_index = row_index + 1
            DO column_index = 1 to 4
                  freight_charges (row_index, column_index) = input value
                  Read input file
            ENDDO
      ENDDO
      IF (input values exist) AND row_index = 6 THEN
            Print 'Array size too small'
      ENDIF
END
```

Searching a two-dimensional array

Search method 1

In the following pseudocode algorithm, the freight charges for an article are to be calculated by searching a previously initialised two-dimensional array. The input values for the algorithm are the shipping weight of the article, and the geographical zone to which it is to be shipped.

First the one-dimensional shipping_weights array is searched for the correct weight category (row_index) and then the two-dimensional freight_charges array is looked up using that weight category (row_index) and geographical zone (column_index).

```
Calculate_Freight_Charges
    Prompt for shipping_weight, zone
    Get shipping_weight, zone
    Set row_index to 1
    Set element_found to false
    DOWHILE (NOT element_found) AND (row_index <= 6)
        IF shipping_weights (row_index) < input shipping_weight THEN
            add 1 to row_index
        ELSE
            Set element_found to true
        ENDIF
    ENDDO
    IF row_index <= 6 THEN
        IF zone = (1 or 2 or 3 or 4) THEN
            freight_charge = freight_charges (row_index, zone)
        ELSE
            Display 'invalid zone', zone
        ENDIF
    ELSE
        Display 'invalid shipping weight', input shipping_weight
    ENDIF
    Display freight_charge
END
```

Search method 2

In the following algorithm, an input employee number is validated against a two-dimensional array of employee numbers, which has ten rows and five columns. The array is searched sequentially, by columns within rows, using two DOWHILE loops until a match is found. If no match is found, an error message is printed.

```
Search_employee_numbers
    Set row_index to 1
    Set employee_found to false
    Read input employee_number
    DOWHILE (NOT employee_found) AND (row_index <=10)
        Set column_index to 1
        DOWHILE (NOT employee_found) AND (column_index <= 5)
            IF employee_numbers (row_index, column_index) = input
                                            employee_number THEN
                Set employee_found to true
            ENDIF
            column_index = column_index + 1
        ENDDO
        row_index = row_index + 1
    ENDDO
    IF NOT employee_found THEN
        Print 'invalid employee number', input employee_number
    ENDIF
END
```

Writing out the contents of a two-dimensional array

To write out the contents of a two-dimensional array, write out the elements in the columns within a row, before moving on to the next row. This is represented in pseudocode by a DO loop within another DO loop.

In the following pseudocode algorithm, the elements of a two-dimensional array are printed to a report, by column within row, using two subscripts.

```
Write_values_of_array
        Set number_of_rows to required value
        Set number_of_columns to required value
        DO row_index = 1 to number_of_rows
            DO column_index = 1 to number_of_columns
                Print array (row_index, column_index)
            ENDDO
        ENDDO
END
```

7.7 CHAPTER SUMMARY

This chapter defined an array as a data structure made up of a number of variables or data items that all have the same data type and are accessed by the same name. The individual elements that make up the array are accessed by the use of an index or subscript beside the name of the array, for example, scores(3).

Algorithms were developed for the most common operations on arrays, namely:

- loading a set of initial values into the elements of an array,
- processing the elements of an array,
- searching an array, using a linear or binary search, for a particular element, and
- writing out the contents of an array to a report.

Programming examples using both one- and two-dimensional arrays were developed.

7.8 PROGRAMMING PROBLEMS

Construct a solution algorithm for the following programming problems. Your solution should contain:

- a defining diagram,
- a list of control structures required,
- a pseudocode algorithm, and
- a desk check of the algorithm.

1   Design an algorithm that will read an array of 200 characters and display to the screen a count of the occurrences of each of the five vowels (a, e, i, o, u) in the array.

2 Design an algorithm that will accept a person's name from the screen entered as surname, first name, separated by a comma. Your program is to display the name as first name, followed by three blanks, followed by the surname.

3 Design an algorithm that will prompt for and receive 10 integers from an operator at a terminal, and count the number of integers whose value is less than the average value of the integers. Your program is to display the average integer value and the count of integers less than the average.

4 Design an algorithm that will prompt for and receive up to 20 integers from an operator at a terminal and display to the screen the average of the integers. The operator is to input a sentinel of 999 after the required number of integers (up to 20) have been entered.

5 Design an algorithm that will read a file of student letter grades and corresponding grade points and load them into two paired arrays, as follows:

Letter grade	Grade points
A	12
B	9
C	6
D	3
F	0

Your program is to read each record on the file (which contains a letter grade followed by a grade point), validate the letter grade (which must be A, B, C, D, or F), check that the grade point is numeric, and load the values into the parallel arrays. Your program is to stop processing when the file reaches EOF or the arrays are full. Print an error message if there are more records on the file than elements in the array.

6 Design an algorithm that will read a file of student records containing the student's number, name, subject number and letter grade. Your program is to use the letter grade on the student record to retrieve the corresponding grade points for that letter grade from the paired arrays that were established in Problem 5. Print a report showing each student's number, name, subject number, letter grade and grade point. At the end of the report, print the total number of students and the grade point average (total grade points divided by the number of students).

7 Design an algorithm that will prompt for and receive an employee number from an operator at a terminal. Your program is to search an array of valid employee numbers to check that the employee number is valid, look up a parallel array to retrieve the corresponding employee name for that number, and display the name to the screen. If the employee number is not valid, an error message is to be displayed.

8 An employee file contains records that show an employee's number, name, job code and pay code. The job codes and pay codes are three-digit codes that refer to corresponding job descriptions and pay rates, as in the following tables:

Job code	Job description
A80	Clerk
A90	Word processor
B30	Accountant
B50	Programmer
B70	Systems analyst
C20	Engineer
C40	Senior engineer
D50	Manager

Pay code	Pay rate
01	$9.00
02	$9.50
03	$12.00
04	$20.00
05	$23.50
06	$27.00
07	$33.00

Your program is to read the employee file, use the job code to retrieve the job description from the job table, use the pay code to retrieve the pay rate from the pay rate table, and print for each record the employee's number, name, job description and pay rate. At the end of the report, print the total number of employees.

9   The ACME Oil and Gas Company needs a personnel salary report for its employees, showing their expected increase in salary for the next year. Each record contains the employee's number, name, gross salary, peer performance rating and supervisor performance rating. The percentage increase in salary to be applied to the gross salary is based on two factors: the peer performance rating and the supervisor performance rating, as specified in the following two-dimensional array:

Salary increase percentage table					
Peer performance rating	**Supervisor performance rating**				
	1	2	3	4	5
1	.013	.015	.017	.019	.021
2	.015	.017	.019	.021	.023
3	.017	.019	.021	.023	.027
4	.019	.021	.023	.025	.030
5	.021	.023	.025	.027	.040

Your program is to retrieve the percentage increase in salary, using the peer performance rating and the supervisor performance rating as indexes to look up the salary increase percentage table. Then calculate the new salary by applying the percentage increase to the gross salary figure. For each employee, print the employee's number, name, this year's gross salary and next year's gross salary. At the end of the report print the two total gross salary figures.

10. Fred's Auto Dealership requires a program that will calculate the sales discount to be applied to a vehicle, based on its year of manufacture and type. The discount is extracted from a two-dimensional table as follows: the year of manufacture of the vehicle is divided into six categories (1999, 1998, 1997, 1996, 1995, 1994), and the type of car is divided into five categories (mini, small, medium, full-size and luxury). No discount is given for a vehicle older than 1994.

Year of manufacture	Discount percentage				
	Mini	Small	Medium	Full-size	Luxury
	1	2	3	4	5
1999	.050	.055	.060	.065	.070
1998	.040	.045	.050	.055	.060
1997	.030	.035	.040	.045	.050
1996	.020	.025	.030	.035	.040
1995	.010	.015	.020	.025	.030
1994	.005	.010	.015	.020	.025

Your program is to read the vehicle file, which contains the customer number, customer name, make of car, year of manufacture, car type code (1, 2, 3, 4 or 5) and sales price. Use the year of manufacture and the car type code as indexes to retrieve the discount percentage from the discount percentage table. Then apply the discount percentage to the sales price to determine the discounted price of the vehicle. Print all vehicle details, including discounted price.

First steps in modularisation

Objectives

- To introduce modularisation as a means of dividing a problem into subtasks
- To present hierarchy charts as a pictorial representation of modular program structure
- To discuss intermodule communication, local and global variables, and the passing of parameters between modules
- To develop programming examples that use a simple modularised structure

Outline

8.1 MODULARISATION

Throughout the previous chapters, it has been emphasised that to design a solution algorithm, you must:

- define the problem;
- write down the control structures required to reach a solution; and
- devise a solution algorithm, which uses a combination of sequence, selection and repetition control structures.

Many solution algorithms have been presented, and all have been relatively simple; that is, the finished algorithm has been less than one page in length. As programming problems increase in complexity, however, it becomes more and more difficult to consider the solution as a whole. Given a complex problem, you often will not be able to see initially what the solution might be.

You must first identify the major tasks to be performed in the problem, then divide the problem into sections that represent those tasks. These sections can be considered subtasks or functions. Once the major tasks in the problem have been identified, the programmer may then need to look at each of the subtasks and identify within them further subtasks, and so on. This process of identifying first the major tasks, then further subtasks within them, is known as top-down design or functional decomposition.

By using this top-down design methodology, the programmer is adopting a modular approach to program design. That is, each of the subtasks or functions will eventually become a module within a solution algorithm or program. A module, then, can be defined as a section of an algorithm that is dedicated to a single function. The use of modules makes the algorithm simpler, more systematic, and more likely to be free of errors. Since each module represents a single task, the programmer can develop the solution algorithm task by task, or module by module, until the complete solution has been devised.

Modularisation is the process of dividing a problem into separate tasks, each with a single purpose. Top-down design methodology allows the programmer to concentrate on the overall design of the algorithm without getting too involved with the details of the lower level modules. Another benefit of top-down design is that separate modules, once identified and written, are easily understood, can be reused, and can be independently modified if necessary.

The modularisation process

The division of a problem into smaller subtasks, or modules, is a relatively simple process. When you are defining the problem, write down the activities or processing steps to be performed. These activities are then grouped together to form more manageable tasks or functions, which will eventually form modules. The emphasis when defining the problem must still be to concentrate on the tasks or functions that need to be performed. Each function will be made up of a number of activities, all of which contribute to the performance of a single task.

A module must be large enough to perform its task, and must include only the operations that contribute to the performance of that task. It should have a single entry, and a single exit with a top-to-bottom sequence of instructions. The name of the module should describe the work to be done as a single specific function. The convention of naming a module by using a verb, followed by a two-word object, is particularly important here, as it helps to identify the separate task or function that the module has been designed to perform. Also, the careful naming of modules using this convention makes the algorithm and resultant code easier to follow. For example, typical module names might be:

```
Print_page_headings
Calculate_sales_tax
Validate_input_date
```

By using meaningful module names such as these, you can automatically describe the task that the module has been designed to perform, and anyone reading the algorithm can easily see what the module is supposed to do.

The mainline

Since each module performs a single specific task, a mainline routine must provide the master control that ties all the modules together and coordinates their activity. This program mainline should show the main processing functions, and the order in which they are to be performed. It should also show the flow of data and the major control structures. The mainline should be easy to read, be of manageable length and show sound logic structure. Generally, you should be able to read a pseudocode mainline, and see exactly what it is being done in the program.

Let us now look at two algorithms, introduced in Chapter 4, whose solutions will be much simpler once modularisation is used.

Example 8.1 *Read three characters*

Design a solution algorithm that will prompt a terminal operator for three characters, accept those characters as input, sort them into ascending sequence and output them to the screen. The algorithm is to continue to read characters until 'XXX' is entered.

A *Defining diagram*

Input	Processing	Output
char_1	Prompt for characters	char_1
char_2	Accept three characters	char_2
char_3	Sort three characters	char_3
	Output three characters	

B Initial solution algorithm

```
Read_three_characters
        Prompt the operator for char_1, char_2, char_3
        Get char_1, char_2, char_3
        DOWHILE NOT (char_1 = X AND char_2 = X AND char_3 = X)
                IF char_1 > char_2 THEN
                        temp = char_1
                        char_1 = char_2
                        char_2 = temp
                ENDIF
                IF char_2 > char_3 THEN
                        temp = char_2
                        char_2 = char_3
                        char_3 = temp
                ENDIF
                IF char_1 > char_2 THEN
                        temp = char_1
                        char_1 = char_2
                        char_2 = temp
                ENDIF
                Display to the screen char_1, char_2, char_3
                Prompt operator for char_1, char_2, char_3
                Get char_1, char_2, char_3
        ENDDO
    END
```

This solution looks cumbersome and awkward, so it is an ideal candidate for modularisation as follows:

C Solution algorithm using a module

One of the processing steps in the defining diagram is to 'sort three characters'. In the algorithm above, this was converted into three separate IF statements in the mainline. The mainline could have been simplified considerably if these three IF statements were put into a separate module called Sort_three_characters and the module was called by the mainline when required. The module would then perform the single specific task of sorting the three characters into ascending sequence. The solution algorithm would now look like this:

```
Read_three_characters
        Prompt the operator for char_1, char_2, char_3
        Get char_1, char_2, char_3
        DOWHILE NOT (char_1 = X AND char_2 = X AND char_3 = X)
                Sort_three_characters
                Display to the screen char_1, char_2, char_3
                Prompt operator for char_1, char_2, char_3
                Get char_1, char_2, char_3
        ENDDO
    END
```

```
Sort_three_characters
    IF char_1 > char_2 THEN
        temp = char_1
        char_1 = char_2
        char_2 = temp
    ENDIF
    IF char_2 > char_3 THEN
        temp = char_2
        char_2 = char_3
        char_3 = temp
    ENDIF
    IF char_1 > char_2 THEN
        temp = char_1
        char_1 = char_2
        char_2 = temp
    ENDIF
END
```

The solution algorithm now consists of two modules; a mainline module called Read_three_characters and a submodule called Sort_three_characters. When the mainline wants to pass control to its submodule, it simply names that module. Control will then pass to the called module, and when the processing in that module is complete, the module will pass control back to the mainline. The resultant mainline is simple and easy to read. The mainline and its module should now be represented in a hierarchy chart.

8.2 HIERARCHY CHARTS OR STRUCTURE CHARTS

After the tasks have been grouped into functions or modules, present these modules graphically in a diagram. This diagram is known as a hierarchy chart, as it shows not only the names of all the modules but also their hierarchical relationship to each other.

A hierarchy chart may also be referred to as a structure chart or a visual table of contents. The hierarchy chart uses a tree-like diagram of boxes; each box represents a module in the program and the lines connecting the boxes represent the relationship of the modules to others in the program hierarchy. The chart shows no particular sequence for processing the modules; only the modules themselves in the order in which they first appear in the algorithm.

At the top of the hierarchy chart is the controlling module, or mainline. On the next level are the modules that are called directly from the mainline; that is the modules immediately subordinate to the mainline. On the next level are the modules that are subordinate to the modules on the first level, and so on. This diagrammatic form of hierarchical relationship appears similar to an organisational chart of personnel within a large company.

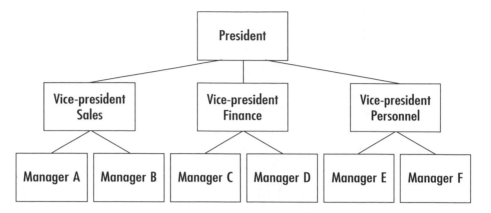

The mainline will pass control to each module when it is ready for that module to perform its task. The controlling module is said to invoke or call the subordinate module. The controlling module is, therefore, referred to as the calling module, and the subordinate module the called module. On completion of its task, the called module returns control to the calling module.

The hierarchy chart for Example 8.1 would be relatively simple. It would show a calling module, (Read_three_characters) and a called module, (Sort_three_characters) as follows:

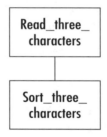

8.3 COMMUNICATION BETWEEN MODULES

When designing solution algorithms, you should consider not only the breaking up of the problem into modules but also the flow of information between the modules. The fewer and simpler the communications between modules, the easier it is to understand and maintain one module without reference to other modules. This flow of information, called intermodule communication, can be accomplished by the scope of the variable (local or global data) or the passing of parameters.

Scope of a variable

The scope of a variable is the portion of a program in which that variable has been defined and to which it can be referred. If a list is created of all the modules in which a variable can be referenced, that list defines the scope of the variable. Variables can be global, where the scope of the variable is the whole program, and local, where the scope of the variable is simply the module in which it is defined.

Global data

When information or data uses the same variable name in both the calling module and the called modules of a program, the data is known as global data, and the scope of the variable is the whole program because the data can be accessed by every module in the program.

All data, however, does not need to be global.

Local data

Variables that are defined within a subordinate module are called local variables. These local variables are not known to the calling module, nor to any other module. The scope of a local variable is simply the module in which it is defined. Using local variables can reduce what is known as program side effects.

Side effects

A side effect is a form of cross-communication of a module with other parts of a program. It occurs when a subordinate module alters the value of a global variable inside a module. Side effects are not necessarily detrimental. However, they do tend to decrease the manageability of a program. A programmer should be aware of their impact.

If a program is amended at any time by a programmer other than the person who wrote it, a change may be made to a global variable. This change could cause side effects or erroneous results because the second programmer is unaware of other modules, which also alter that global variable.

Passing parameters

Another method of intermodule communication is the passing of parameters or arguments between modules. Parameters are simply data items transferred from a calling module to its subordinate module at the time of calling. When the subordinate module terminates and returns control to its caller, the values in the parameters are transferred back to the calling module.

When a calling module calls a subordinate module in pseudocode, it must consist of the name of the called module with a list of the parameters to be passed to the called module enclosed in parentheses, for example:

Print_page_headings (page_count, line_count)

The called module will have, following its name, a list of parameters that it expects to receive from the calling module. The names that the respective modules give to their parameters need not be the same (although it helps readability if they are) but their number, type and order must be identical.

Parameters may have one of three functions:

1   To pass information from a calling module to a subordinate module. The subordinate module would then use that information in its processing, but would not need to communicate any information back to the calling module.
2   To pass information from a subordinate module to its calling module. The calling module would then use that parameter in subsequent processing.

3 To fulfil a two-way communication role. Information may be passed by the calling module to a subordinate module, where it is amended in some fashion, then passed back to the calling module.

These parameters which pass between modules can be incorporated into a hierarchy chart or structure chart using the following symbols:

For data parameters   For status parameters

Data parameters contain the actual variables or data items which will be passed between modules.

Status parameters act as program flags and should contain just one of two values: true or false. These program flags or switches are set to true or false, according to a specific set of conditions. They are then used to control further processing.

When designing modular programs, the programmer should avoid using data parameters to indicate status as well, because this can affect the program in two ways:

1 It may confuse the reader of the program because a variable has been over-loaded; i.e. it has been used for more than one purpose; and
2 It may cause unpredictable errors when the program is amended at some later date, as the maintenance programmer may be unaware of the dual purpose of the variable.

8.4 USING PARAMETERS IN PROGRAM DESIGN

Let us look again at Example 8.1 and change the solution algorithm so that parameters are used to communicate between modules.

Example 8.2 *Read three characters*

Design a solution algorithm that will prompt a terminal operator for three characters, accept those characters as input, sort them into ascending sequence, and output them to the screen. The algorithm is to continue to read characters until 'XXX' is entered.

A Defining diagram

Input	Processing	Output
char_1	Prompt for characters	char_1
char_2	Accept three characters	char_2
char_3	Sort three characters	char_3
	Output three characters	

B Group the activities into modules

The activities can be grouped into two main functions:

1   Read_three_characters
2   Sort_three_characters

The module Read_three_characters will send the three input characters to its subordinate module, Sort_three_characters, in the form of parameters. The module Sort_three_characters will then sort the three characters and send these sorted values back to the mainline module as parameters.

C Construct a hierarchy chart

The hierarchy chart can show not only the modules and their relationship to each other, but also the parameters that are to be passed between the modules. It is up to the programmer to decide if parameters are to be included in the hierarchy chart.

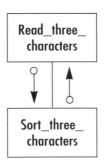

char_1
char_2
char_3

D Establish the logic of the solution algorithm using pseudocode (mainline and subordinate module)

```
Read_three_characters
      Prompt the operator for char_1, char_2, char_3
      Get char_1, char_2, char_3
      DOWHILE NOT (char_1 = X AND char_2 = X AND char_3 = X)
            Sort_three_characters (char_1, char_2, char_3)
            Output to the screen char_1, char_2, char_3
            Prompt operator for char_1, char_2, char_3
            Get char_1, char_2, char_3
      ENDDO
END

Sort_three_characters (char_1, char_2, char_3)
      IF char_1 > char_2 THEN
            temp = char_1
            char_1 = char_2
            char_2 = temp
      ENDIF
      IF char_2 > char_3 THEN
            temp = char_2
            char_2 = char_3
            char_3 = temp
      ENDIF
      IF char_1 > char_2 THEN
            temp = char_1
            char_1 = char_2
            char_2 = temp
      ENDIF
END
```

Note that the module Read_three_characters specifies three parameters when calling the module Sort_three_characters, and the module Sort_three_characters names its three parameters in the heading line of the module. The names of the parameters are the same in the calling list and the called list, but they do not have to be.

Variable sharing by using global variables is very efficient in terms of memory usage. However, the use of global variables means that called modules are not really portable or independent. As a result, when considering intermodule communication, use the passing of parameters between modules in preference to global variables.

8.5 STEPS IN MODULARISATION

Top-down modular design is really quite simple if the following steps are performed every time you are presented with a programming problem:

1. Define the problem by dividing it into its three components: input, output, and processing. The processing component should consist of a list of activities to be performed.
2. Group the activities into subtasks or functions to determine the modules that will make up the program. Remember that a module is one section of a program dedicated to the performance of a single function. Note that not all the activities may be identified at this stage. Only the modules of the first level of the hierarchy chart may be identified, with other more subordinate modules developed later.
3. Construct a hierarchy chart to illustrate the modules and their relationship to each other. Once the structure (or organisation) of the program has been developed, the order of processing of the modules can be considered. Intermodule communication and the passing of parameters can also be considered at this step.
4. Establish the logic of the mainline of the algorithm in pseudocode. This mainline should contain some initial processing before the loop; some processing within the loop; and some final processing after exiting the loop. It should contain calls to the major processing modules of the program, and should be easy to read and understand.
5. Develop the pseudocode for each successive module in the hierarchy chart. The modularisation process is complete when the pseudocode for each module on the lowest level of the hierarchy chart has been developed.
6. Desk check the solution algorithm. This is achieved by first desk checking the mainline, then each subordinate module in turn.

8.6 PROGRAMMING EXAMPLES USING MODULES

The solution algorithms to the following programming examples will be developed using the six steps in modularisation, introduced in section 8.5.

Example 8.3 *Calculate employee's pay*

A program is required by a company to <u>read</u> an employee's number, pay rate and the number of hours worked in a week. The program is then to <u>compute</u> the employee's weekly pay and <u>print</u> it along with the input data. The program is to continue reading employee details until there are no more records on the file.

According to the company's rules, no employee may be paid for more than 60 hours per week, and the maximum hourly rate is $25.00 per hour. If more than 35 hours are worked, payment for the overtime hours worked is calculated at time and a half. If the hours worked field or the hourly rate field is out of range, the input data and an appropriate message are to be <u>printed</u> and the employee's weekly pay is not to be calculated.

A Define the problem

Input	Processing	Output
emp_no pay_rate hrs_worked	Read employee details Validate input fields Calculate employee pay Print employee details	emp_no pay_rate hrs_worked emp_weekly_pay error_message

B Group the activities into modules

The activities can be grouped into three main functions

1 Compute_employee_pay   **(mainline)**
2 Validate_input_fields
3 Calculate_employee_pay

C Construct a hierarchy chart

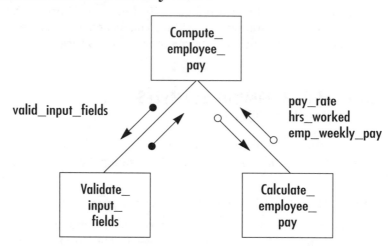

If you write the solution algorithm as three separate modules, the readability of the solution will improve dramatically. The mainline will invoke its subordinate modules and pass parameters to them when it wants to pass control to them. Similarly, when processing in the called modules is complete, control will pass back to the calling module. By breaking the tasks into smaller, more manageable modules, the programmer can concentrate on the main logic of the mainline, leaving the details of the lower level modules till later.

The parameter valid_input_fields will pass between the mainline and its subordinate module Validate_input_fields as a flag to check if the input fields are valid. The parameters pay_rate, hrs_worked and emp_weekly_pay will pass between the mainline and the subordinate module Calculate_employee_pay.

D Establish the logic of the mainline of the algorithm, using pseudocode

```
Compute_employee_pay
      Set valid_input_fields to true
      Read emp_no, pay_rate, hrs_worked
      DOWHILE more records
            Validate_input_fields (valid_input_fields)
            IF valid_input_fields THEN
                  Calculate_employee_pay (pay_rate, hrs_worked, emp_weekly_pay)
                  Print emp_no, pay_rate, hrs_worked, emp_weekly_pay
            ELSE
                  set valid_input_fields to true
            ENDIF
            Read emp_no, pay_rate, hrs_worked
      ENDDO
END
```

E Develop the pseudocode for each successive module in the hierarchy chart

```
Validate_input_fields (valid_input_fields)
      Set error_message to blank
      IF pay_rate > $25 THEN
            error_message = 'Pay rate exceeds $25.00'
            Print emp_no, pay_rate, hrs_worked, error_message
            valid_input_fields = false
      ENDIF
      IF hrs_worked > 60 THEN
            error_message = 'Hours worked exceeds limit of 60'
            Print emp_no, pay_rate, hrs_worked, error_message
            valid_input_fields = false
      ENDIF
END

Calculate_employee_pay (pay_rate, hrs_worked, emp_weekly_pay)
      IF hrs_worked < = 35 THEN
            emp_weekly_pay = pay_rate * hrs_worked
      ELSE
            overtime_hrs = hrs_worked – 35
            overtime_pay = overtime_hrs * pay_rate * 1.5
            emp_weekly_pay = (pay_rate * 35) + overtime_pay
      ENDIF
END
```

F Desk check the solution algorithm

The desk checking of an algorithm with modules is no different to the method developed for our previous examples.

1 Create some valid input test data.
2 List the output that the input data is expected to produce.
3 Use a desk check table to walk the data through the mainline of the algorithm to ensure that the expected output is achieved.

In this example, the two subordinate modules are relatively simple. Validate_input_fields contains two IF statements and Calculate_employee_pay contains just one IF statement. In this case there is no need to desk check the modules individually as they can be desk checked at the same time as the mainline. However, if a module contains logic that is particularly complicated, a separate desk check table should be drawn up for that module as well as the mainline module.

(i) Input data

Three test cases will be used to test the algorithm.

Record	hrs_worked	pay_rate
emp 1	20	$35.00
emp 2	20	$40.00
emp 3	30	$65.00
EOF		

(ii) Expected results

emp 1	20	$35.00	$700.00
emp 2	20	$40.00	$850.00
emp 3	30	$65.00	Pay rate exceeds $25.00
emp 3	30	$65.00	Hours worked exceeds limit of 60

(iii) Desk check table

Only the processing steps of the mainline of the algorithm will be written down in the desk check table. When a call is made to a module, all the processing steps in that module will be recorded on one line of the desk check table. By doing this, the internal logic of each module is checked at the same time as the mainline.

Statement	valid_ input_ fields	hrs_ worked	pay_ rate	DO-WHILE OK?	error_ message	emp_ weekly_ pay	ovt_ hrs	ovt_ pay
Initialise	true							
Read		20	$35					
DOWHILE				yes				
Validate_input_fields					blank			
IF								
Calculate_emp_pay						$700		
Print		print	print			print		
Read		20	$40					
DOWHILE				yes				
Validate_input_fields					blank			
IF								
Calculate_emp_pay						$850	5	$150
Print		print	print			print		
Read		30	$65					
DOWHILE				yes				
Validate_input_fields	false	print	print		invalid pay			
	false	print	print		invalid hours			
IF	true							
Read		EOF	EOF					
END								

Example 8.4 *Produce orders report*

The Acme Spare Parts Company wants to produce an orders report from its product orders file. Each record on the file contains the product number of the item ordered, the product description, the number of units ordered, the retail price per unit, the freight charges per unit; and the packaging costs per unit.

The output report is to contain headings and column headings as specified in the following chart:

	ACME SPARE PARTS		PAGE xx
	ORDERS REPORT		
PRODUCT	PRODUCT	UNITS	TOTAL AMOUNT
NO	DESCRIPTION	ORDERED	DUE
xxxx	xxxxxxxxxxx	xxx	xxxxx
xxxx	xxxxxxxxxxx	xxx	xxxxx

Each detail line is to contain the product number, description, number of units ordered and the total amount due for the order. There is to be an allowance of 45 detail lines per page.

The amount due for each product is the number of units ordered times the retail price of the unit. A discount of 10% is allowed on the amount due for all orders over $100.00. The freight charges and packaging costs per unit must be added to this resulting value to determine the total amount due.

A Define the problem

Input	Processing	Output
Order record	Print headings as required	main headings
• prod_number	Read order records	column headings
• prod_description	Calculate amount due	page number
• no_of_units	Calculate discount	detail lines
• retail_price	Calculate freight charge	• prod_number
• freight_charge	Calculate packaging	• prod_description
• packaging_cost	Print order details	• no_of_units
	Compute page increments	• total_amount_due

B Group the activities into modules

The activities in the processing component can be grouped into two functions or modules as follows:

1 'Print headings as required' can become a module. This is an example of a module that will be created because it is reusable. That is, the module will be called whenever the report needs to skip to a new page. A page headings module is a standard requirement of most report programs. The name of this module will be Print_page_headings.

2 The four processing steps

   calculate amount due,
   calculate discount,
   calculate freight charge, and
   calculate packaging

can be grouped together because they all contribute to the performance of a single task to calculate the total_amount due. It is this total_amount_due which is required on each detail line of the report. The name of this module will be Calculate_total_amount_due to describe its function.

C   Construct a hierarchy chart

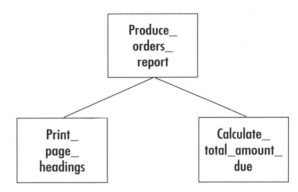

This diagram illustrates the structure of the algorithm. The main controlling module, or mainline, is called Produce_orders_report. The mainline will call on two subordinate modules, namely Print_page_headings and Calculate_total_amount_due, as required. When the mainline calls on a module, it will pass control to that module. All the processing steps in that module will then be executed before control returns to the mainline. For simplicity, parameters passed between modules have not been indicated on the hierarchy chart, but will appear in the pseudocode algorithm.

D Establish the logic of the mainline of the algorithm, using pseudocode

The mainline will require:

1   A DOWHILE loop to control the repetition,
2   Calls to its two subordinate modules,
3   A page accumulator for the page heading routine, and
4   A line counter to record the number of detail lines printed on each page.

```
Produce_orders_report
       Set page_count to zero
       Set line_count to zero
       Print_page_headings (line_count)
       Read order record
       DOWHILE more records
             IF line_count > 45 THEN
                   Print_page_headings (line_count)
             ENDIF
             Calculate_total_amount_due (order record, total_amount_due)
             Print prod_number, prod_description, no_of_units, total_amount_due
             Add 1 to line_count
             Read order record
       ENDDO
END
```

E Develop pseudocode for each successive module in the hierarchy chart

1 The pseudocode for Print_page_headings is standard for a page heading routine that will increment the page counter, print a series of headings and reset the line counter. The parameter line_count is passed between the calling and called modules.

```
Print_page_headings (line_count)
      Add 1 to page_count
      Print main heading 'ACME SPARE PARTS'
      Print heading 'ORDERS REPORT'
      Print column headings 1
      Print column headings 2
      Print blank line
      Set line_count to zero
END
```

2 The pseudocode for the module 'Calculate_total_amount_due' will compute the total amount due using a series of intermediate calculations. The required fields on the order record are passed to the called module, which calculates the total amount due, then returns this total_amt_due to the calling module.

```
Calculate_total_amount_due (order record, total_amt_due)
      amount_due = no_of_units * retail_price
      IF amount_due > $100.00 THEN
            discount = amount_due * 0.1
      ELSE
            discount = zero
      ENDIF
      amount_due = amount_due − discount
      freight_due = freight_charge * no_of_units
      packaging_due = packaging_charge * no_of_units
      total_amount_due = amount_due + freight_due + packaging_due
END
```

F Desk check the solution algorithm

As before, to desk check an algorithm with modules you must:

1 Create some valid input test data.
2 List the output that the input data is expected to produce.
3 Use a desk check table to walk the data through the mainline of the algorithm to ensure that the expected output is achieved.

In this example, the two subordinate modules consist merely of a series of sequential statements. There is no need to desk check the modules individually, as they can be desk checked at the same time as the mainline. However, if a module contains logic that is particularly complicated, a separate desk check table should be drawn up for that module as well as the mainline module.

(i) Input data

Three test cases will be used to test the algorithm. To test for correct page skipping, we would temporarily reduce the line limit from 45 to a conveniently small number, e.g. 2.

Record	prod_ no	prod_ description	no_of_ units	retail_ price	freight_ charge	packaging_ charge
1	100	rubber hose	10	1.00	0.20	0.50
2	200	steel pipe	20	2.00	0.10	0.20
3	300	steel bolt	100	3.00	0.10	0.20
EOF						

(ii) Expected results

```
                        ACME SPARE PARTS              PAGE 1
                          ORDERS REPORT

      PRODUCT             PRODUCT              UNITS        TOTAL AMOUNT
        NO               DESCRIPTION          ORDERED          DUE

       100              Rubber hose             10           $17.00
       200              Steel pipe              20           $46.00
       300              Steel bolt             100          $300.00
```

(iii)   Desk check table

Only the processing steps of the mainline of the algorithm will be written down in the desk check table. When a call is made to a module, all the processing steps in that module will be recorded on one line of the desk check table. By doing this, you can check the internal logic of each module at the same time as the mainline.

Statement	DO-WHILE OK?	page_counter	line_counter	prod_no	no_of_units	retail_price	freight_charge	packaging_charge	total_amount_due
Initialise		0							
Print_page_headings		1							
Initialise			0						
Read				100	10	1.00	0.20	0.50	
DOWHILE	yes								
IF									
Calculate									17.00
Print				print	print				print
Add			1						
Read				200	20	2.00	0.10	0.20	
DOWHILE	yes								
IF									
Calculate									46.00
Print				print	print				print
Add			2						
Read				300	100	3.00	0.10	0.20	
DOWHILE	yes								
IF									
Calculate									300.00
Print				print	print				print
Add			3						
Read				EOF					
DOWHILE	no								
END									

8.7 CHAPTER SUMMARY

This chapter introduced a modular approach to program design. A module was defined as a section of an algorithm that is dedicated to the performance of a single function. Top-down design was defined as the process of dividing a problem first into the major tasks and then into further subtasks within those major tasks until all the tasks have been identified. Programming examples were provided showing the benefits of using modularisation.

Hierarchy charts were introduced as a method of illustrating the structure of a program that contains modules. Hierarchy charts show the names of all the modules and their hierarchical relationship to each other.

Intermodule communication was defined as the flow of information or data between modules. Local and global variables were introduced, along with the scope of a variable and the side effects of using only global data.

The passing of parameters was introduced as a form of intermodule communication and a method of representing parameters on a structure chart was devised.

The steps in modularisation that a programmer must follow were listed. These were: define the problem; group the activities into subtasks or functions; construct a hierarchy chart; establish the logic of the mainline, using pseudocode; develop the pseudocode for each successive module in the hierarchy chart; and desk check the solution algorithm.

Programming examples using these six steps in modularisation were then developed in pseudocode.

8.8 PROGRAMMING PROBLEMS

Construct a solution algorithm for the following programming problems. To obtain your final solution you should:

- define the problem,
- group the activities into modules (also consider the data that each module requires),
- construct a hierarchy chart,
- establish the logic of the mainline using pseudocode,
- develop the pseudocode for each successive module in the hierarchy chart, and
- desk check the solution algorithm.

1 Design an algorithm that will prompt for and accept an employee's annual salary, and calculate the annual income tax due on that salary. Income tax is calculated according to the following table and is to be displayed on the screen.

Portion of salary	Income tax rate (%)
$0 to $5000	0%
$5000 to $10 000	6%
$10 000 to $20 000	15%
$20 000 to $30 000	20%
$30 000 to $40 000	25%
$40 000 and above	30%

Your program is to continue to process salaries until a salary of zero is entered.

2 Design an algorithm that will prompt for and accept four numbers, sort them into ascending sequence and display them to the screen. Your algorithm is to include a module called Order_two_numbers which is to be called from the mainline to sort two numbers at a time.

3 Design an algorithm that will prompt for and accept a four-digit representation of the year (e.g. 1999). Your program is to determine if the year provided is a leap year and print a message to this effect on the screen. Also print a message on the screen if the value provided is not exactly four numeric digits. Continue processing until a sentinel of 0000 is entered.

4 The members of the board of a small university are considering voting for a pay increase for their 25 faculty members. They are considering a pay increase of 8%. However, before doing so, they want to know how much this pay increase will cost. Design an algorithm that will prompt for and accept the current salary for each of the faculty members, then calculate and display their individual pay increases. At the end of the algorithm, print the total faculty payroll before and after the pay increase, and the total pay increase involved.

5 Design an algorithm that will produce an employee payroll register from an employee file. Each input employee record contains the employee number, employee's gross pay, income tax, union dues, and other deductions. Your program is to read the employee file and print a detail line for each employee record showing employee number, gross pay, income tax, union dues, other deductions and net pay. Net pay is calculated as gross pay – income tax – union dues – other deductions. At the end of the report, print the total net pay for all employees.

6 Design an algorithm that will produce an inventory report from an inventory file. Each input inventory record contains the item number, open inventory amount, amount purchased and amount sold. Your program is to read the inventory file and print a detail line for each inventory record showing item number, open inventory amount, amount purchased, amount sold and final inventory amount. The final inventory amount is calculated as opening inventory amount + purchases – sales. At the end of the report, print the total open inventory amount, the total amount purchased, the total amount sold and the total final inventory amount.

7 Design an algorithm that will produce a savings account balance report from a customer savings accounts file. Each input savings accounts record contains the account number, balance forward, deposits (sum of all deposits), withdrawals (sum of all withdrawals) and interest earned. Your program is to read the savings account file and print a detail line for each savings account record showing account number, balance forward, deposits, withdrawals, interest earned and final account balance. The final account balance is calculated as balance forward + deposits – withdrawals + interest. A heading is to appear at the top of each page and allowance is to be made for 45 detail lines per page. At the end of the report, print the total balances forward, total deposits, total withdrawals, total interest earned and total final account balances.

8 Design an algorithm that will read a file of sales volume records and print a report showing the sales commission owing to each salesperson. Each input record contains salesperson number, name and their volume of sales for the month. The commission rate varies according to sales volume as follows:

On sales volume ($) of	Commission rate (%)
$0.00–$199.99	5%
$200.00–$999.99	8%
$1000.00–$1999.99	10%
$2000.00 and above	12%

The calculated commission is an accumulated amount according to the sales volume figure. For example, the commission owing for a sales volume of $1200.00 would be calculated as follows:

Commission = (200 * 5%) + ((1000 – 200) * 8%) + ((1200 – 1000) * 10%))

Your program is to print the salesperson's number, name, volume of sales and calculated commission, with the appropriate column headings.

9 Design an algorithm that will prompt for and receive your current cheque book balance, followed by a number of financial transactions. Each transaction consists of a transaction code and a transaction amount. The transaction code can be a deposit ('D') or a cheque ('C'). Your program is to add each deposit transaction amount to the balance and subtract each cheque transaction amount. After each transaction is processed, a new running balance is to be displayed on the screen, with a warning message if the balance becomes negative. When there are no more transactions, a 'Q' is to be entered for transaction code to signify the end of the data. Your algorithm is then to display the initial and final balances, along with a count of the number of cheques and deposits processed.

10 At Olympic diving competition level, ten diving judges award a single mark (with one decimal place) for each dive attempted by a diving competitor. This mark can range from 0 to 10. Design an algorithm that will receive a score from the ten judges and calculate the average score. The screen should display the following output:

Judge	1	2	3	4	5	6	7	8	9	10
Mark	6.7	8.1	5.8	7.0	6.6	6.0	7.6	6.1	7.2	7.0
Score for the dive		6.81								

Further modularisation, cohesion and coupling

Objectives

- To further develop modularisation using a more complex problem
- To introduce cohesion as a measure of the internal strength of a module
- To introduce coupling as a measure of the extent of information interchange between modules

Outline

9.1 STEPS IN MODULARISATION

In Chapter 8, the six steps to be followed when using top-down modular design to develop a solution algorithm for a problem were listed as follows:

1 Define the problem by dividing it into its three components: input, output and processing. The processing component should consist of a list of activities to be performed.
2 Group the activities into subtasks or functions to determine the modules that will make up the program. Remember that a module is one section of a program dedicated to the performance of a single function. Note that not all the activities may be identified at this stage. Only the modules of the first level of the hierarchy chart may be identified, with other more subordinate modules developed later.
3 Construct a hierarchy chart to illustrate the modules, and their relationship to each other. Once the structure (or organisation) of the program has been developed, you can consider the order of processing of the modules. Intermodule communication and the passing of parameters can also be considered at this step.
4 Establish the logic of the mainline of the algorithm in pseudocode. This mainline should contain some initial processing before the loop; some processing within the loop; and some final processing after exiting the loop. It should contain calls to the major processing modules of the program, and should be easy to read and understand.
5 Develop the pseudocode for each successive module in the hierarchy chart. The modularisation process is complete when the pseudocode for each module on the lowest level of the hierarchy chart has been developed.
6 Desk check the solution algorithm. This is achieved by first desk checking the mainline, and then each subordinate module in turn.

This chapter develops a solution algorithm for a more complex problem, that is, a problem which, when divided into submodules, has more than one level in the hierarchy chart.

Example 9.1 *Calculate vehicle registration costs*

A program is required to calculate and print the registration cost of a new vehicle that a customer has ordered.

The program is to be interactive. That is, all the input details will be provided at a terminal on the salesperson's desk. The program will then calculate the related costs and return the information to the screen.

The input details required are:

Owner's name
Vehicle make
Vehicle model
Weight (in kg)
Body type (sedan or wagon)
Private or business code ('P' or 'B')
Wholesale price of vehicle

A federal tax is also to be paid. This is calculated at the rate of $2.00 for each $100.00, or part thereof, of the wholesale price of the vehicle.

The vehicle registration cost is calculated as the sum of the following charges:

Registration fee	$27.00	
Tax levy	PRIVATE	5% of wholesale price
	BUSINESS	7% of wholesale price
Weight tax	PRIVATE	1% of weight (converted to $)
	BUSINESS	3% of weight (converted to $)
Insurance premium	PRIVATE	1% of wholesale price
	BUSINESS	2% of wholesale price

The program is to calculate the total registration charges for the vehicle plus federal tax, and is to print all the relevant information on the screen as follows:

Vehicle make:
Vehicle model:
Body type:
Registration fee:
Tax levy:
Weight tax:
Insurance premium:
Total registration charges:
Federal tax:
Total amount payable:

(Total amount payable = total registration charges + federal tax.)

The program is to process registration costs until an owner's name of 'XXX' is entered. None of the other entry details will be required after the value 'XXX' has been entered.

A Define the problem

Input	Processing	Output
owners_name	Get input details	vehicle_make
vehicle_make	Calculate tax_levy	vehicle_model
vehicle_model	Calculate weight_tax	body_type
weight	Calculate insurance_premium	registration_fee
body_type	Calculate total_registration_costs	tax_levy
usage_code	Calculate federal_tax	weight_tax
wholesale_price	Calculate total_amount_payable	insurance_premium
	Display details to screen	total_registration_charges
		federal_tax
		total_amount_payable

B Group the activities into modules

The activities in the processing component can be grouped into three main functions, as follows:

1   Get input details.
    There are a number of input fields to read from the screen, so a module can be created to perform this function. The name of the module will be Get_vehicle_details. Note that the read from the screen of the owner's name must be separate, as it is the entry of 'XXX' in this field that will cause the repetition to cease.

2   Display details to screen.
    Similarly, there are a number of output fields to display onto the screen, so a module can be created to perform this function. The name of this module will be Display_registration_details.

3   The following activities in the processing section of the algorithm all contribute to the performance of a single task: to calculate the total amount payable. The name of this module will be Calculate_total_amount_payable.

    - calculate tax_levy,
    - calculate weight_tax,
    - calculate insurance_premium,
    - calculate total_registration_charges,
    - calculate federal_tax, and
    - calculate total_amount_payable.

    To aid readability this model can be divided into two smaller tasks, Calculate_federal_tax and Calculate_total_registration. The module Calculate_total_amount_payable will call these two modules as required to perform those functions.

C Construct a hierarchy chart

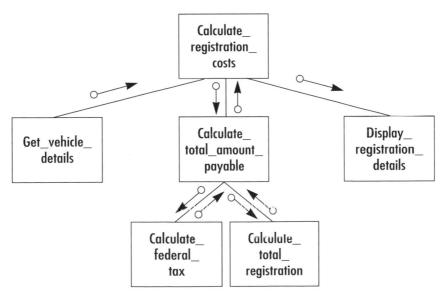

The hierarchy chart illustrates the structure that the algorithm will take. The mainline is called Calculate_registration_costs. It will call three subordinate modules: Get_vehicle_details, Calculate_total_amount_payable and Display_registration_details. The module Calculate_total_amount_payable will also call two modules to help perform its task: Calculate_federal_tax and Calculate_total_registration.

D Establish the logic of the mainline of the algorithm using pseudocode

The mainline will require:

1 A DOWHILE loop to process the repetition; and
2 Calls to the modules as required.

```
Calculate_registration_costs
    Read owners_name
    DOWHILE owners_name NOT = 'XXX'
        Get_vehicle_details (vehicle details)
        Calculate_total_amount_payable (registration details, total_amount_payable)
        Display_registration_details (vehicle details, registration details,
                                        total_amount_payable)
        Read owners_name
    ENDDO
END
```

The mainline appears to be very simple. It consists of a Read before the loop, calls to its three subordinate modules within the loop, and a Read just before the end of the loop. By reading the algorithm, you can easily understand the processing of the program because of the modular nature of the algorithm and the careful choice of module names.

E Develop the pseudocode for each successive module in the hierarchy chart

1 Get_vehicle_details is a module that prompts for and reads the required fields. The owner's name is read separately in the mainline.

```
Get_vehicle_details (vehicle details)
    Get vehicle_make
    Get vehicle_model
    Get weight
    Get body_type
    Get usage_code
    Get wholesale_price
END
```

2 Calculate_total_amount_payable is a module which calls two other modules.

```
Calculate_total_amount_payable (registration details, total_amount_payable)
    Calculate_federal_tax (vehicle details, federal_tax)
    Calculate_total_registration (vehicle details, registration details)
    total_amount_payable = federal_tax + total_registration_charges
END
```

3   Calculate_federal_tax contains the steps required to calculate the federal tax. The federal tax is payable at the rate of $2.00 for each $100.00 or part thereof of the wholesale price of the car. (A variable called tax_units is used to count the number of whole $100 units.)

```
Calculate_federal_tax (vehicle details, federal_tax)
      Set tax_units = zero
      DOWHILE wholesale_price > $100
            wholesale_price = wholesale_price − 100
            increment tax_units by 1
      ENDDO
      federal_tax = (tax_units + 1) * $2.00
END
```

4   Calculate_total_registration contains all the processing required to calculate the total registration costs. The total cost of registration is the sum of the registration fee, tax levy, weight tax and insurance premium.

```
Calculate_total_registration (vehicle details, registration details)
      registration_fee = $27.00
      IF usage_code = 'P' THEN
            tax_levy = wholesale_price * 0.05
            weight_tax = weight * 0.01
            insurance_premium = wholesale_price * 0.01
      ELSE
            tax_levy = wholesale_price * 0.07
            weight_tax = weight * 0.03
            insurance_premium = wholesale_price * 0.02
      ENDIF
      total_registration_charges = registration_fee + tax_levy +
            weight_tax + insurance_premium
END
```

5   Display_registration_details is a module which displays the required output onto the screen.

```
Display_registration_details (vehicle details, registration details, total_amount_payable)
      Display vehicle_make,
      Display vehicle_model,
      Display body_type
      Display registration_fee
      Display tax_levy
      Display weight_tax
      Display insurance_premium
      Display total_registration_charges
      Display federal_tax
      Display total_amount_payable
END
```

When a program is modularised in this fashion, the pseudocode for each successive module becomes very simple.

F Desk check the solution algorithm

(i) Input data:

As there are two branches in the logic of the program, two test cases should be sufficient to test the algorithm. Only the relevant input fields will be provided.

Record	weight	usage_code	wholesale_price
1	1000	P	30 000
2	2000	B	20 000
XXX			

(ii) Expected Results:

	Record 1	Record 2
Registration fee	27.00	27.00
Tax levy	1500.00	1400.00
Weight tax	10.00	60.00
Insurance premium	300.00	400.00
Total registration charges	1837.00	1887.00
Federal tax	600.00	400.00
Total amount payable	2437.00	2287.00

(iii) Desk Check Table:

The desk checking will be of the main processing steps of the mainline. When a call to a module is made, all the processing steps of the module are recorded on one line of the desk check table. This, in effect, checks both the mainline logic and the modules at the same time.

Statement	owners_ name	DOWHILE OK?	Weight	Usage_ code	wholesale_ price	federal_ tax	total_ registra- tion	total_ amount_ payable
Initialise								0
Read	1							
DOWHILE		yes						
Get			1000	P	30 000			
Calculate						600	1837	2437
Display						yes	yes	yes
Read	2							
DOWHILE		yes						
Get			2000	B	20 000			
Calculate						400	1887	2287
Display						yes	yes	yes
Read	XXX							
DOWHILE		no						
END								

9.2 MODULE COHESION

A module has been defined as a section of an algorithm that is dedicated to the performance of a single function. It contains a single entry and a single exit, and the name chosen for the module should describe its function.

Programmers often need guidance in determining what makes a good module. Common queries are 'How big should a module be?', 'Is this module too small?' or 'Should I put all the read statements in one module?'

There is a method you can use to remove some of the guesswork when establishing modules. You can look at the cohesion of the module. Cohesion is a measure of the internal strength of a module, i.e. how closely the elements or statements of a module are associated with each other. The more closely the elements of a module are associated, the higher the cohesion of the module. Modules with high cohesion are considered good modules, because of their internal strength.

Edward Yourdon and Larry Constantine[1] established seven levels of cohesion and placed them in a scale from the weakest to the strongest.

Cohesion level	Cohesion attribute	Resultant module strength
Coincidental	Low Cohesion	Weakest
Logical		
Temporal		
Procedural	↓	↓
Communicational		
Sequential		
Functional	High Cohesion	Strongest

Each level of cohesion in the table will be discussed in this chapter, and pseudocode examples which illustrate each level will also be provided.

Coincidental cohesion

The weakest form of cohesion a module can have is coincidental cohesion. It occurs when elements are collected into a module simply because they happen to fall together. There is no meaningful relationship between the elements at all, and so it is difficult to concisely define the function of the module.

Fortunately, these type of modules are rare in today's programming practice. They typically used to occur as a result of one of the following conditions:

- an existing program may have been arbitrarily segmented into smaller modules because of hardware constrictions on the operation of the program;
- existing modules may have been arbitrarily subdivided to conform to a badly considered programming standard (for example, each module should have no more than 50 program statements);

---

[1] Edward Yourdon & Larry Constantine, *Structured Design: Fundamentals of a Discipline of Computer Program and System Design.* Prentice-Hall, 1979.

- a number of existing modules may have been combined into one module either to reduce the number of modules in a program or to increase the number of statements in a module to a particular minimum number.

With continually increasing storage capacity and speed of execution, modules that are forced to contain unrelated elements for the above reasons occur only rarely.

Here is a pseudocode example of a module which has coincidental cohesion:

```
File_processing
        Open employee updates file
        Read employee record
        Print_page_headings
        Open employee master file
        Set page_count to one
        Set error_flag to false
END
```

Notice that the instructions within the module have no meaningful relationship to each other.

Logical cohesion

Logical cohesion occurs when the elements of a module are grouped together according to a certain class of activity. That is, the elements fall into some general category because they all do the same kind of thing.

An example might be a module that performs all the read statements for three different files: a sort of 'Read_all_files' module. In such a case the calling module would need to indicate which of the three files it required the called module to read, by sending a parameter.

A module such as this is slightly stronger than a coincidentally cohesive module, because the elements are, at least, somewhat related. However, logically cohesive modules are usually made up of a number of smaller, independent sections, which should exist independently rather than be combined together because of a related activity. Often when a module such as this is called, only a small subset of the elements within the module will be executed.

A pseudocode example for a 'Read_all_files' module might look like this:

```
Read_all_files (file_code)
        CASE of file_code
        1 :   Read customer transaction record
              IF not EOF
                      increment customer_transaction_count
              ENDIF
        2 :   Read customer master record
              IF not EOF
                      increment customer_master_count
              ENDIF
        3 :   Read product master record
              IF not EOF
                      increment product_master_count
              ENDIF
        ENDCASE
END
```

Notice that the three Read instructions in this module perform three separate functions.

Temporal cohesion

Temporal cohesion occurs when the elements of a module are grouped together because they are related by time. Typical examples are initialisation and finalisation modules, where elements are placed together because they perform certain housekeeping functions at the beginning or end of a program.

A temporally cohesive module can be considered a logically cohesive module, where time is the related activity. However, it is slightly stronger than a logically cohesive module because most of the elements in a time-related module are executed each time the module is called. Usually, however, the elements are not all related to the same function.

A pseudocode example of a temporally cohesive module might look like this:

```
Initialisation
       Open transaction file
       Issue prompt 'Enter todays date — DDMMYY'
       Read todays_date
       Set transaction_count to zero
       Read transaction record
       IF not EOF
               increment transaction_count
       ENDIF
       Open report file
       Print_page_headings
       Set report_total to zero
END
```

Notice that the elements of the module perform a number of functions.

Procedural cohesion

Procedural cohesion occurs when the elements of a module are related because they operate according to a particular procedure. That is, the elements are executed in a particular sequence so that the objectives of the program are achieved. As a result, the modules contain elements related more to program procedure than to program function.

A typical example of a procedurally cohesive module is the mainline of a program. The elements of a mainline are grouped together because of a particular procedural order.

The weakness of procedurally cohesive modules is that they cut across functional boundaries. That is, the procedure may contain only part of a function at one level, but at the same time may contain multiple functions at a lower level, as in the pseudocode example below:

```
Read_student_records_and_total_student_ages
    Set number_of_records to zero
    Set total_age to zero
    Read student record
    DOWHILE more records exist
        Add age to total_age
        Add 1 to number_of_records
        Read student record
    ENDDO
    Print number_of_records, total_age
END
```

Note that the use of the word 'and' in the module name indicates that this module performs more than one function.

Communicational cohesion

Communicational cohesion occurs when the elements of a module are grouped together because they all operate on the same (central) piece of data. Communicationally cohesive modules are commonly found in business applications because of the close relationship of a business program to the data it is processing. For example, a module may contain all the validations of the fields of a record; or all the processing required to assemble a report line for printing.

Communicational cohesion is acceptable because it is data related. It is stronger than procedural cohesion because of its relationship with the data, rather than the control-flow sequence.

The weakness of a communicationally cohesive module lies in the fact that usually a combination of processing for a particular piece of data is performed, as in this pseudocode example:

```
Validate_product_record
    IF transaction_type NOT = '0' THEN
        error_flag = true
        error_message = 'invalid transaction type'
        Print_error_report
    ENDIF
    IF customer_number is NOT numeric THEN
        error_flag = true
        error_message = 'invalid customer number'
        Print_error_report
    ENDIF
    IF product_no = blanks
    OR product_no has leading blanks THEN
        error_flag = true
        error_message = 'invalid product no'
        Print_error_report
    ENDIF
END
```

Sequential cohesion

Sequential cohesion occurs when a module contains elements that depend on the processing of previous elements. That is, it might contain elements in which the output data from one element serves as input data to the next. Thus, a sequentially cohesive module is like an assembly line: a series of sequential steps perform successive transformations of data.

Sequential cohesion is stronger than communicational cohesion because it is more problem oriented. Its weakness lies only in the fact that the module may perform multiple functions or fragments of functions.

Here is a pseudocode example of a sequentially cohesive module:

```
Process_purchases
      Set total_purchases to zero
      Get number_of_purchases
      DO loop_index = 1 to number_of_purchases
            get purchase
            add purchase to total_purchases
      ENDDO
      sales_tax = total_purchases * sales_tax_percent
      amount_due = total_purchases + sales_tax
END
```

Note that this module first calculates total_purchases and then uses the variable total_purchases in the subsequent calculation of amount_due.

Functional cohesion

Functional cohesion occurs when all the elements of a module contribute to the performance of a single specific task. The module can be easily named by a single verb followed by a two-word object.

Mathematically oriented modules are a good example of functional cohesion, as the elements making up the module form an integral part of the calculation.

A pseudocode example of a functionally cohesive module is the module Calculate_sales_tax:

```
Calculate_sales_tax
      IF product is sales tax exempt THEN
            sales_tax = 0
      ELSE
            IF product_price < $50.00 THEN
                  sales_tax = product_price * 0.25
            ELSE
                  IF product_price < $100.00 THEN
                        sales_tax = product_price * 0.35
                  ELSE
                        sales_tax = product_price * 0.5
                  ENDIF
            ENDIF
      ENDIF
END
```

Summary of cohesion levels

When designing a program's structure, you should try to form modules that have a single problem-related function. If functional cohesion is achieved, the modules will be more independent, easier to read and understand, and more maintainable than modules with lesser cohesion.

In some cases it is not easy to construct a program where every module has functional cohesion. Some modules may contain lower levels of cohesion, or even a combination of types of cohesion. This may not be a problem. However, it is important that you can recognise the various cohesion levels and justify a module with a lower cohesion in a particular set of circumstances.

Your prime consideration is to produce modules and programs that are easy to understand and modify. The higher the cohesion of the modules, the more likely you have achieved this aim.

9.3 MODULE COUPLING

When designing a solution algorithm, look not only at the cohesion of modules but also at the flow of information between modules. You should aim to achieve module independence, i.e. modules that have fewer and simpler connections with other modules. These connections are called interfaces or couples.

Coupling is a measure of the extent of information interchange between modules. Tight coupling implies large dependence on the structure of one module by another. Because there are a higher number of connections, there are many paths along which errors can extend into other parts of the program.

Loose coupling is the opposite of tight coupling. Modules with loose coupling are more independent and easier to maintain.

Glenford Myers[1] devised a coupling scale similar to Yourdon and Constantine's cohesion scale.

Coupling level	Coupling attribute	Resultant module design quality
Common	Tight coupling	poorest
External	↓	↓
Control		
Stamp	↓	↓
Data	Loose coupling	best

The five levels of coupling are listed in a scale from the poorest module design quality to the best. Each of the levels of coupling will be discussed and pseudocode examples which illustrate each level will be provided. Note that these levels of coupling are not definitive. They are merely the coupling levels that Glenford Myers believes can exist in modular programs.

---

[1] Glenford Myers, *Composite Structured Design*. Van Nostrand Reinhold, 1978.

Common coupling

Common coupling occurs when modules reference the same global data structure. (A data structure is a collection of related data items, such as a record or an array.) When modules experience common coupling, a global data structure is shared by the modules.

This means that the data can be accessed and modified by any module in the program, which can make the program difficult to read.

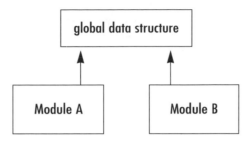

The following pseudocode example shows two modules that experience common coupling because they access the same global data structure (the customer record):

```
A    Read_customer_record
            Read customer record
            IF EOF THEN
                    set EOF_flag to true
            ENDIF
     END

B    Validate_customer_record
            IF customer_number is NOT numeric THEN
                    error_message = 'invalid customer number'
                    Print_error_report
            ENDIF
            :
            :
     END
```

External coupling

External coupling occurs when two or more modules access the same global data variable.

It is similar to common coupling except that the global data is an elementary data item, rather than a data structure. Because the global data has a simpler structure, external coupling is considered to be looser than common coupling.

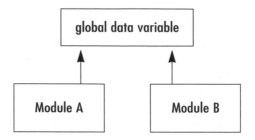

The following pseudocode example shows two modules that exhibit external coupling because they share the same global data item (sales_tax).

```
A    Calculate_sales_tax
            IF product is sales exempt THEN
                        sales_tax = 0
                ELSE
                    IF product_price < $50.00 THEN
                            sales_tax = product_price * 0.25
                                :
                                :
                ENDIF
            END

B    Calculate_amount_due
        :
        :
        amount_due = total_amount + sales_tax
    END
```

Control coupling

Control coupling occurs when a module passes another module a control variable that is intended to control the other module's logic. These control variables are referred to as program flags, or switches and are passed between modules in the form of parameters.

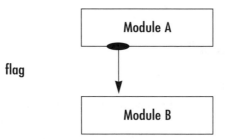

The weakness of control coupled modules is that the passing of the control field between modules implies that one module is aware of the internal logic of the other.

The following pseudocode example shows two modules that are logically cohesive because of the passing of the control parameter (input_code):

```
A    Process_input_code
            Read input_code
            Choose_appropriate_action (input_code)
            :
            :
     END

B    Choose_appropriate_action (input_code)
            CASE OF input_code
            1 : Read employee record
            2 : Print_page_headings
            3 : Open employee master file
            4 : Set page_count to zero
            5 : error_message = 'Employee number not numeric'
            ENDCASE
     END
```

Stamp coupling

Stamp coupling occurs when one module passes a non-global data structure to another module. The non-global data structure is passed in the form of a parameter

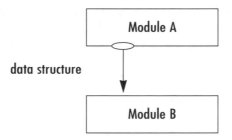

Stamp-coupled modules demonstrate loose coupling and offer good module design quality. The only relationship between the two modules is the passing of the data structure between them; there is no need for either module to know the internal logic of the other.

The following pseudocode example shows two modules that are stamp coupled because of the passing of the data structure current_record.

```
A    Process_transaction_record
            :
            :
            IF transaction record is for a male THEN
                    Process_male_student (current_record)
            ELSE
                    Process_female_student (current_record)
            ENDIF
            :
            :
     END
```

```
B     Process_male_student (current_record)
            increment male_student_count
            IF student_age > 21 THEN
                    increment mature_male_count
            ENDIF
            :
            :
      END
```

Data coupling

Data coupling occurs when a module passes a non-global data variable to another module. It is similar to stamp coupling except that the non-global data variable is an elementary data item, not a data structure.

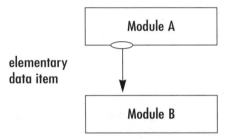

Modules that are data coupled demonstrate the loosest coupling and offer the best module design qualities. The only relationship between the two modules is the passing of one or more elementary data items between them.

The following pseudocode example shows two modules that are data coupled because they pass the elementary data items total_price and sales_tax.

```
A     Process_customer_record
            :
            :
            Calculate_sales_tax (total_price, sales_tax)
            :
      END

B     Calculate_sales_tax (total_price, sales_tax)
            IF total_price < $10.00 THEN
                    sales_tax = total_price * 0.25
            ELSE
                    IF total_price < $100.00 THEN
                            sales_tax = total_price * 0.3
                    ELSE
                            sales_tax = total_price * 0.4
                    ENDIF
            ENDIF
      END
```

A summary of coupling levels

When designing solution algorithms, you should aim towards module independence and a minimum of information interchange between modules.

If the programming language allows it, try to uncouple each module from its surroundings by:

1 Passing data to a subordinate module in the form of parameters, rather than using global data, and
2 Writing each subordinate module as a self-contained unit that can accept data passed to it; operate on it without reference to other parts of the program; and pass information back to the calling module, if required.

However, your prime consideration must be to produce modules and programs that are easily understood and modified. If the chosen programming language offers only global data, the fact that the program has been well designed will minimise the effects of tight coupling.

9.4 CHAPTER SUMMARY

This chapter revised the six steps to be followed when using top-down modular design to develop a solution to a typical programming problem. A solution algorithm using three levels of modularisation in its hierarchy chart was then developed.

Cohesion and coupling were introduced and must be considered when designing modular programs. A program that has been well designed has modules which are independent, easy to read and easily maintained. Such modules are likely to exhibit high cohesion and loose coupling.

Cohesion is a measure of the internal strength of a module. The higher the cohesion, the better the module. Seven levels of cohesion were given and each level was discussed, with a pseudocode example provided.

Coupling is a measure of the extent of information interchange between modules. The fewer the connections between the modules, the more loosely they are coupled, offering good module design quality. Five levels of coupling were given and each level was discussed, with a pseudocode example provided.

9.5 PROGRAMMING PROBLEMS

Construct a solution algorithm for the following programming problems. To obtain your final solution you should:

- define the problem,
- group the activities into modules (also consider the data which each module requires),
- construct a hierarchy chart,
- establish the logic of the mainline using pseudocode,
- develop the pseudocode for each successive module in the hierarchy chart, and
- desk check the solution algorithm.

1 Design an algorithm that will produce a reorder list of products from a product inventory file. Each input product record contains the item number, the quantity on hand for the item, the quantity on order, the minimum

inventory level for that item, and an obsolete code ('X' if the item is obsolete, blank if it is not).

Your program is to read the product file and determine which items are to be reordered. An item is to be reordered if it is not obsolete and if the quantity of the item currently on hand, plus the amount on order, is less than its minimum inventory level. Print a detail line for each item to be reordered, listing the item number, quantity on hand, quantity on order, and minimum inventory level. Print headings and column headings at the top of each page, allowing for 45 detail lines per page, and at the end of the report, the total number of items to be reordered.

2 Design an algorithm that will produce a list of selected student names from a student file. Each input student record contains the student's number, the student's name, the number of semester hours the student is currently taking, and the age of the student.

Your program is to read the student file and prepare a list of names of all full-time students (students taking 12 or more semester hours) who are 30 years of age or older. If a student appearing on the list is taking more than 20 semester hours, place three asterisks after the student's name. Print a detail line for each student selected, listing student number, student name, age and number of semester hours. Print headings and column headings at the top of each page, allowing for 45 detail lines per page, and at the end of the report, the total number of selected students.

3 Design an algorithm that will produce a list of selected customers from a customer file. Each input record contains the customer's name, current monthly sales and year-to-date sales. Each time the program is run, a parameter record containing a dollar amount is read in as the first record in the file.

Your program is to read the parameter record, followed by the customer file, and prepare a list of customers whose purchases total at least $10 000 in the current month. Customers should also be included in the list if their year-to-date sales are at least as great as the amount read in as a parameter.

Print a detail line for each customer, listing customer's name, current monthly sales, year-to-date sales and the parameter amount. Print headings and column headings at the top of each page, allowing for 45 detail lines per page, and at the end of the report, the total number of selected customers.

4 Design an algorithm that will produce a tax report from an employee income file. Each input record contains the employee number and the employee's taxable income. There is one record for each employee.

Your program is to read the employee income file and calculate the tax owing on that employee's taxable income, according to the following table:

Taxable income	Tax payable
$0–$15 000	20% of taxable income
$15 000–$29 999	$3000 + 30% of amount greater than $15 000
$30 000–$49 999	$7500 + 40% of amount greater than $30 000
$50 000–$74 999	$15 500 + 50% of amount greater than $50 000
$75 000 and above	$28 000 + 75% of amount greater than $75 000

Print a detail line for each employee, listing the employee number, taxable income and tax payable. Print headings and column headings at the top of each page, allowing for 45 detail lines per page, and at the end of the report, the total taxable income and total tax payable.

5 Design an algorithm that will create a data validation edit report from an inventory file. Each field on the inventory record is to be validated as follows:

Field	Format
Stock number	numeric
Item number	numeric (1–5000)
Description	alphanumeric
Quantity on hand	numeric (500–999)
Quantity on order	numeric (500–999)
Price per unit	numeric (10–1000)
Inventory re-order level	numeric (50–500)

If a field is found to be in error, print a line in the data validation edit report showing the stock number, the item number and an appropriate message, as indicated in the diagram below. There may be multiple messages for the one record. Print headings and column headings at the top of each page, allowing for 45 detail lines per page.

Data Validation Edit Report		
Stock number	Item number	Message
00742	4003	Quantity on hand out of range
00853	5201	Quantity on order out of range
00932	1007	Price per unit not numeric
00932	1007	Reorder level not valid

6 Design an algorithm that will produce a list of successful applicants who have applied at the local Riff Raff department store for credit. Each input record contains the applicant's name, employment status, years in current job (if any), years at current residence, monthly wages, amount of non-mortgage debt, and number of children.

Your program is to read the applicant's file and determine whether or not each applicant will be granted credit. The store grants credit to a person who has worked in the same job for more than one year, as well as someone who is employed and has lived in the same location for at least two years. However, if a person owes more than two month's wages in non-mortgage debt or has more than six children, credit is denied.

Print a detail line for each applicant, listing the applicant's name and whether or not that applicant has been granted credit. Print headings and column headings at the top of each page, allowing for 45 detail lines per page, and at the end of the report, the total number of successful applicants.

7 Design an algorithm that will calculate the percentage discount allowed on a customer's purchase, from a customer file. Each input record contains the customer's number, the customer's name, the class code and, for wholesale customers, the number of units purchased and the distance from the warehouse. The class code contains either 'R' for retail customers or 'W' for wholesale customers. The end-of-file of the input file is denoted by a customer number of 99999.

Your program is to read the customer file and determine the percentage discount, if any, on a customer's purchase, according to the following guidelines. Retail customers get no discount. Wholesale customers who purchase fewer than 10 units also receive no discount. A 10% discount is given to wholesale customers who purchase at least 10 but fewer than 30 units, and are within 50 kilometres of the distributor's warehouse. If a wholesale customer purchases between 10 and 30 units but is more than 50 kilometres away, only a 5% discount is allowed. Wholesale customers who purchase 30 or more units receive a 15% discount if they are within 50 kilometres of the warehouse. If they are more than 50 kilometres away, they only get a 10% discount.

Print a detail line for each customer, listing the customer number, customer name, class code, number of units purchased and the percentage discount (if any) to be applied on a customer's purchases.

Print headings and column headings at the top of each page, allowing for 45 detail lines per page.

8 The Tidy Phones telephone company's charges file contains records for each call made by its Metroville subscribers during a month. Each record on the file contains the subscriber's name, subscriber's phone number, phone number called, distance from Metroville of the number called (in kilometres), and the duration of the call (in seconds).

Design a program that will read the Tidy Phones charges file and produce a Telephone Charges Report, as follows.

		TIDY PHONES TELEPHONE CHARGES	PAGE: XX
SUBSCRIBER NAME	SUBSCRIBER NUMBER	PHONE NUMBER CALLED	COST OF CALL
XXXX	XXXXXXXXXX	XXX-XXXX	999.99
XXXX	XXXXXXXXXX	XXX-XXXX	999.99
		TOTAL REVENUE	9999.99

The cost of each call is calculated as follows:

Distance from Metroville	Cost ($)/minute
less than 25 km	0.35
$25 \leq km < 75$	0.65
$75 \leq km < 300$	1.00
$300 \leq km \leq 1000$	2.00
greater than 1000 km	3.00

Main headings and column headings are to appear as printed on the report with an allowance of 45 detail lines per page. The total revenue line is to print three lines after the last detail line.

9 Design an algorithm that will produce a payroll register from an employee file. Each input record contains the employee number, the hours worked that week, and the rate of pay.

Your program is to read the employee file, and for each employee number, look up a table of employee numbers and names to retrieve the employee's name. The table contains about a hundred entries, and is in sequence of employee number with the number 9999 used as a sentinel to mark the end of the table. If the employee number cannot be found in the table, a message is to print on the report and no more processing is to be performed for that record. The gross pay for each employee is also to be calculated as hours worked times rate of pay.

Print a detail line for each employee, listing the employee's number, employee's name, hours worked, rate of pay and gross pay. Print headings and column headings at the top of each page, allowing for 45 detail lines per page, and at the end of the report, the total number of employees and total gross pay.

10 The Mitre 11 hardware outlets require an inventory control program which is to accept order details for an item, and generate a shipping list and a back order list.

Design an interactive program that will conduct a dialogue on the screen for the input values, and print two reports as required. The screen dialogue is to appear as follows:

ENTER Item No.	99999
Quantity on hand	999
Order quantity	999
Order number	999999

If an item number does not have precisely five digits, an error message is to appear on the screen. If the quantity on hand is sufficient to meet the order (order quantity <= quantity on hand), one line is to be printed on the shipping list. If the quantity on hand is insufficient to meet the order (order quantity > quantity on hand), the order is to be filled partially by whatever stock is available. For this situation, one line should appear on the shipping list with the appropriate number of units shipped (quantity on hand) and a message 'Order partially filled'. An entry for the balance of the order (order quantity – quantity on hand) is to be printed on the back order list.

If the quantity on hand is zero, the message 'Out of stock' is to appear on the shipping list, and an entry for the full order quantity is to be printed on the back order list.

Your program is to continue to process inventory orders, until a value of zero is entered for the item number.

Report layouts for the shipping list and back order list are as follows:

```
                    MITRE-11 HARDWARE                PAGE xx
                    INVENTORY CONTROL
                      SHIPPING LIST
   ORDER              ITEM              UNITS          MESSAGE
    NO                 NO              SHIPPED
   999999             99999             999              —
   999999             99999             999              —
```

```
                    MITRE-11 HARDWARE                PAGE xx
                    INVENTORY CONTROL
                      BACK ORDER LIST
      ORDER              ITEM           BACK ORDER
       NO                 NO               QTY
      999999             99999            999
      999999             99999            999
```

10

CHAPTER

General algorithms for common business problems

Objectives

*   To provide general pseudocode algorithms to four common business applications. Topics covered are:
    *   report generation with page break
    *   single-level control break
    *   multiple-level control break
    *   sequential file update

Outline

10.1 PROGRAM STRUCTURE

The aim of this chapter is to present a number of general pseudocode solutions to a selection of typical programming problems. All of the features covered in the previous nine chapters have been incorporated into these solutions, with the result that each solution offers a sound modular structure with highly cohesive modules.

Throughout this book, reference has been made to a general solution algorithm for the processing of sequential files. This algorithm is a skeleton solution, and in pseudocode looks like this:

```
Process_sequential_file
        Initial processing
        Read first record
        DOWHILE more records exist
                Process this record
                Read next record
        ENDDO
        Final processing
    END
```

This basic solution algorithm forms the framework for almost all commercial business programs. It does not include processing for page headings, control breaks, total lines or special calculations. However, you can easily incorporate these requirements by expanding this general solution.

This general solution algorithm can also be modularised:

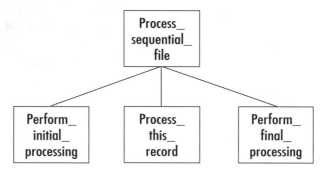

The mainline module would now look like this:

```
Process_sequential_file
        Perform_initial_processing
        Read first record
        DOWHILE more records exist
                Process_this_record
                Read next record
        ENDDO
        Perform_final_processing
    END
```

The module Process_this_record can be extended, as required, for the processing of a particular programming problem. We will use this basic program structure to develop solution algorithms to four common business programming applications.

10.2 REPORT GENERATION WITH PAGE BREAK

Most reports require page heading lines, column heading lines, detail lines and total lines. Reports are also required to skip to a new page after a predetermined number of detail lines have been printed.

A typical report might look like this:

	GLAD RAGS CLOTHING COMPANY		
12/5/93	CURRENT ACCOUNT BALANCES		PAGE: 1
CUSTOMER NUMBER	CUSTOMER NAME	CUSTOMER ADDRESS	ACCOUNT BALANCE
12345	Sporty's Boutique	The Mall, Redfern	300.50
12346	Slinky's Nightwear	245 Picnic Road, Pymble	400.50
		Total customers on file	200
		Total customers with balance owing	150
		Total balance owing	4300.00

Our general solution algorithm for processing a sequential file can be extended by the addition of new modules that cater for these report requirements, as follows:

A Hierarchy chart

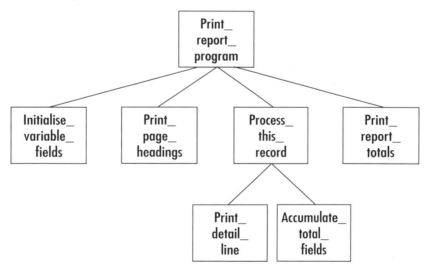

Once the hierarchy chart has been established, the solution algorithm can be developed in pseudocode.

B Solution algorithm

Mainline

```
Print_report_program
        Initialise_variable_fields
        Print_page_headings
        Read first record
        DOWHILE more records exist
                IF linecount > max_detail_lines THEN
                        Print_page_headings
                ENDIF
                Process_this_record
                Read next record
        ENDDO
        Print_report_totals
END
```

Subordinate modules

```
1    Initialise_variable_fields
                set accumulators to zero
                set pagecount to zero
                set linecount to zero
                set max_detail_lines to required value
        END
2    Print_page_headings
                increment pagecount
                print heading lines
                print column heading lines
                print blank line (if required)
                set linecount to zero
        END
3    Process_this_record
                Perform necessary calculations (if any)
                Print_detail_line
                Accumulate_total_fields
        END
4    Print_detail_line
                prepare detail line
                print detail line
                increment linecount
        END
5    Accumulate_total_fields
                increment accumulators as required
        END
6    Print_report_totals
                prepare total line(s)
                print total line(s)
        END
```

This general pseudocode solution can now be used as a framework for any report program which requires page breaks.

10.3 SINGLE-LEVEL CONTROL BREAK

Printed reports that also produce control break total lines are very common in business applications. A control break total line is a summary line for a group of records that contain the same record key. This record key is a designated field on each record, and is referred to as the control field. The control field is used to identify a record or a group of records within a file. A control break occurs each time there is a change in value of the control field. Thus, control break total lines are printed each time a control break is detected.

Reports that print control break totals can be categorised as being either single-level or multiple-level control break reports depending on whether there is one control field or more than one control field.

Here is a single-level control break report.

MULTI-DISK COMPUTER COMPANY
SALES REPORT BY SALESPERSON

12/05/99					PAGE: 1
SALESPERSON NUMBER	SALESPERSON NAME	PRODUCT NUMBER	QTY SOLD	PRICE	EXTENSION AMOUNT
1001	Mary Smith	1032	2	10.00	20.00
		1033	2	20.00	40.00
		1044	2	30.00	60.00
		Sales total for Mary Smith			120.00
1002	Jane Brown	1032	2	10.00	20.00
		1045	1	35.00	35.00
		Sales total for Jane Brown			55.00
		Report sales total			175.00

Note that a control break total line is printed each time the salesperson number changes.

There are two things you must consider when designing a control break program:

1 The file to be processed must have been sorted into control field sequence. (In the example above the file was sorted into ascending sequence of salesperson number.) If the file has not been sorted, erroneous results will occur.
2 Each time a record is read from the input file, the control field on the current record must be compared with the control field on the previous record. If the control fields are different a control break total line must be printed for the previous set of records, i.e. before the current record is processed.

The general solution algorithm, which was developed for a Report Generation program, can be extended by the addition of two new modules to incorporate a single-level control break. These modules are named Print_control_total_line and Reset_control_totals.

A Hierarchy chart

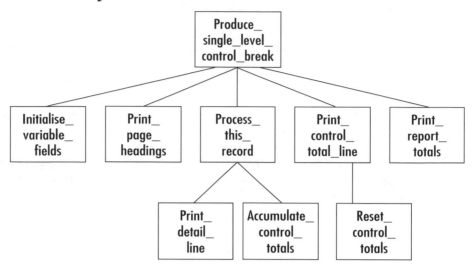

All control break report programs will require the following variables:

1   A variable named this_control_field which will hold the control field of the record just read.
2   A variable named prev_control_field which will hold the control field of the previous record. (To cater for the first record, the statements after the first Read statement will set the new control field to both the variables this_control_field and prev_control_field.)
3   One or more variables to accumulate the control break totals.
4   One or more variables to accumulate the report totals.

B Solution algorithm

```
Mainline
    Produce_single_level_control_break
            Initialise_variable_fields
            Print_page_headings
            Read first record
            this_control_field = control field
            prev_control_field = control field
            DOWHILE more records exist
                    IF this_control_field NOT = prev_control_field THEN
                            Print_control_total_line
                            prev_control_field = this_control_field
                    ENDIF
                    IF linecount > max_detail_lines THEN
                            Print_page_headings
                    ENDIF
                    Process_this_record
                    Read next record
                    this_control_field = control field
            ENDDO
            Print_control_total_line
            Print_report_totals
        END
```

There are four points in this mainline algorithm that are essential for a control break program to function correctly:

1 Each time a new record is read from the file, the new control field is assigned to the variable this_control_field.
2 When the first record is read, the new control field is assigned to both the variables this_control_field and prev_control_field. This will prevent the control totals printing before the first record has been processed.
3 The variable prev_control_field is updated as soon as a change in the control field is detected.
4 After the end of the file has been detected, the module Print_control_total_line is called. This will then print the control break totals for the last record or set of records.

Subordinate modules

1   Initialise_variable_fields
      set control total accumulators to zero
      set report total accumulators to zero
      set pagecount to zero
      set linecount to zero
      set max_detail_lines to required value
   END
2   Print_page_headings
      increment pagecount
      print heading lines
      print column heading lines
      print blank line (if required)
      set linecount to zero
   END
3   Process_this_record
      Perform necessary calculations (if any)
      Print_detail_line
      Accumulate_control_totals
   END
4   Print_control_total_line
      prepare control total line
      print control total line
      print blank line (if required)
      increment linecount
      Reset_control_totals
   END
5   Print_report_totals
      prepare report total line
      print report total line
   END
6   Print_detail_line
      prepare detail line
      print detail line
      increment linecount
   END

```
7    Accumulate_control_totals
         increment control total accumulators
     END
8    Reset_control_totals
         add control total accumulators to report total accumulators
         set control total accumulators to zero
     END
```

Notice that when a control total line is printed, the module Reset_control_totals is called. This module will add the control totals to the report totals and reset the control totals to zero for the next set of records. This generation solution algorithm can now be used as a framework for any single-level control break program.

10.4 MULTIPLE-LEVEL CONTROL BREAK

Often reports are required to produce multiple-level control break totals. For instance, the Sales Report produced in section 10.3 may require sales totals for each salesperson in the company as well as sales totals for each department within the company.

The Monthly Sales Report might then look like this:

MULTI-DISK COMPUTER COMPANY
12/05/99   SALES REPORT BY SALESPERSON   PAGE: 1

DEPT	SALESPERSON NUMBER	SALESPERSON NAME	PRODUCT NUMBER	QTY SOLD	PRICE	EXTENSION AMOUNT
01	1001	Mary Smith	1032	2	10.00	20.00
			1033	2	20.00	40.00
			1044	2	30.00	60.00
		Sales total for Mary Smith				120.00
	1002	Jane Brown	1032	2	10.00	20.00
			1045	1	35.00	35.00
		Sales total for Jane Brown				55.00
		Sales total for Dept 01				175.00
02	1050	Jenny Ponds	1033	2	20.00	40.00
			1044	2	30.00	60.00
		Sales total for Jenny Ponds				100.00
		Sales total for Dept 02				100.00
		Report sales total				275.00

Note that a control break total line is printed each time the salesperson number changes, and each time the department number changes. Thus, there are two control fields in this file: salesperson number and department number.

The concepts that applied to a single-level control break program also apply to a multiple-level control break program:

1 The input file must be sorted into control field sequence. When there is more than one control field, the file must be sorted into a sequence of minor control field within major control field. (To produce the Sales Report, the Sales File must have been sorted into salesperson number within department number.)

2 Each time a record is read from the file, the control field on the current record must be compared with the control field of the previous record. If the minor control field has changed, the control totals for the previous minor control field must be printed. If the major control field has changed, the control totals for the previous minor control field and major control field must be printed.

The general solution algorithm which was developed for a single-level control break program can be extended by the addition of two new modules to incorporate a two-level control break. If three control breaks were required, another two modules would be added to the solution algorithm, and so on.

The names of the modules that produce the control totals have been changed slightly, so that they indicate which level of control break has occurred. These new module names are: Print_minor_control_totals, Print_major_control_totals, Reset_minor_control_totals, and Reset_major_control_totals.

A Hierarchy chart

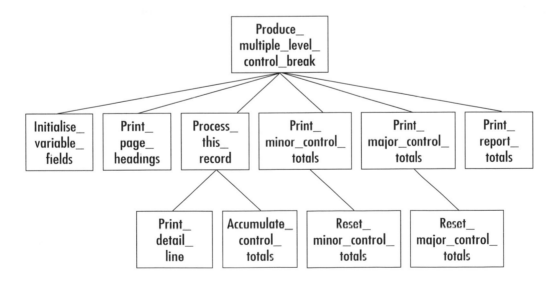

B Solution algorithm

```
Mainline
    Produce_multiple_level_control_break
            Initialise_variable_fields
            Print_page_headings
            Read first record
            this_minor_control_field = minor control field
            prev_minor_control_field = minor control field
            this_major_control_field = major control field
            prev_major_control_field = major control field
            DOWHILE more records exist
                IF this_major_control_field NOT = prev_major_control_field THEN
                        Print_minor_control_totals
                        prev_minor_control_field = this_minor_control_field
                        Print_major_control_totals
                        prev_major_control_field = this_major_control_field
                ELSE
                        IF this_minor_control_field NOT = prev_minor_control_field THEN
                            Print_minor_control_totals
                            prev_minor_control_field = this_minor_control_field
                        ENDIF
                ENDIF
                IF linecount > max_detail_lines THEN
                        Print_page_headings
                ENDIF
                Process_this_record
                Read next record
                this_minor_control_field = minor control field
                this_major_control_field = major control field
            ENDDO
            Print_minor_control_totals
            Print_major_control_totals
            Print_report_totals
    END
```

The points to be noted in this mainline are:

1   Each time a new record is read from the input file, the new control fields are assigned to the variables this_minor_control_field and this_major_control_field.

2   When the first record is read, the new control fields are assigned to both the current and previous control field variables. This will prevent control totals printing before the first record has been processed.

3   After the end of the input file has been detected, the two modules Print_minor_control_totals and Print_major_control_totals will be called. This will then print control totals for the last minor control field record, or set of records, and the last major control field set of records.

Subordinate modules

1　Initialise_variable_fields
　　　　set minor control total accumulators to zero
　　　　set major control total accumulators to zero
　　　　set report total accumulators to zero
　　　　set pagecount to zero
　　　　set linecount to zero
　　　　set max_detail_lines to required value
　　END
2　Print_page_headings
　　　　increment pagecount
　　　　print heading lines
　　　　print column heading lines
　　　　print blank line (if required)
　　　　set linecount to zero
　　END
3　Process_this_record
　　　　Perform necessary calculations (if any)
　　　　Print_detail_line
　　　　Accumulate_control_totals
　　END
4　Print_minor_control_totals
　　　　prepare minor control total line
　　　　print minor control total line
　　　　print blank line (if required)
　　　　increment linecount
　　　　Reset_minor_control_totals
　　END
5　Print_major_control_totals
　　　　prepare major control total line
　　　　print major control total line
　　　　print blank line (if required)
　　　　increment linecount
　　　　Reset_major_control_totals
　　END
6　Print_report_totals
　　　　prepare report total line
　　　　print report total line
　　END
7　Print_detail_line
　　　　prepare detail line
　　　　print detail line
　　　　increment linecount
　　END
8　Accumulate_control_totals
　　　　increment minor control total accumulators
　　END

```
9   Reset_minor_control_totals
          add minor control total accumulators to major control total accumulators
          set minor control total accumulators to zero
    END
10  Reset_major_control_totals
          add major control total accumulators to report total accumulators
          set major control total accumulators to zero
    END
```

Because the solution algorithm has simple design and good modular structure, the processing of intermediate control field breaks as well as major and minor control field breaks can be handled easily. The solution algorithm would simply require the addition of two new modules: Print_intrmed_control_totals and Reset_intrmed_control_totals. The IF statement in the mainline would then be expanded to include this extra condition, as follows:

```
IF this_major_control_field NOT = prev_major_control_field THEN
      Print_minor_control_totals
      prev_minor_control_field = this_minor_control_field
      Print_intrmed_control_totals
      prev_intrmed_control_field = this_intrmed_control_field
      Print_major_control_totals
      prev_major_control_field = this_major_control_field
ELSE
      IF this_intrmed_control_field NOT = prev_intrmed_control_field THEN
            Print_minor_control_totals
            prev_minor_control_field = this_minor_control_field
            Print_intrmed_control_totals
            prev_intrmed_control_field = this_intrmed_control_field
      ELSE
            IF this_minor_control_field NOT = prev_minor_control_field THEN
                  Print_minor_control_totals
                  prev_minor_control_field = this_minor_control_field
            ENDIF
      ENDIF
ENDIF
```

This pseudocode algorithm can now be used to process any multiple-level control break program.

10.5 SEQUENTIAL FILE UPDATE

Sequential file updating is a very common batch processing application. It involves updating a master file by the application of update transactions on a transaction file. Both files are sequential. A new master file that incorporates the update transactions is produced. Usually, audit reports and error reports are also printed.

A system flow chart of a sequential update program would look like this:

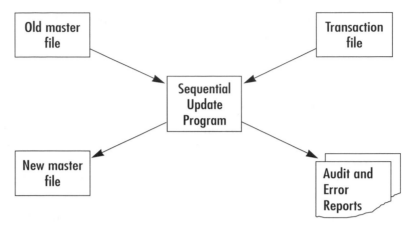

System concepts

1   Master file

A master file is a file that contains permanent and semi-permanent information about the data entities it contains. The records on the master file are in sequence, according to a key field (or fields) on each record. For example, a customer master file may contain the customer's name, address, phone number, credit rating and current balance, and may be in sequence of customer name.

2   Transaction file

A transaction file contains all the data and activities that are included on the master file. If the transaction file has been designed specifically to update a master file, there are usually three types of update transactions on this file. These are transactions to:

- add a new record,
- update or change an existing record, and
- delete an existing record.

For example, a customer transaction file might contain transactions that are intended to add a new customer record, change some data on an existing customer record, or delete a customer record on the customer master file. The transaction file is also in sequence according to the same key field as the master record.

3   Audit report

An audit report is a detailed list of all the transactions that were applied to the master file. It provides an accounting trail of the update activities that take place, and is used for control purposes.

4 Error report

An error report is a detailed list of errors that occurred during the processing of the update. Typical errors might be the attempted update of a record that is not on the master file, or the addition of a record that already exists. This error report will require some action to confirm and correct the identified errors.

Sequential update logic

The logic of a sequential update program is more difficult than the other problems encountered, because there are two sequential input files. Processing involves reading a record from each of the input files and comparing the keys of the two records. As a result of this comparison, processing falls generally into three categories:

1   If the transaction record key is less than the old master record key, the transaction is probably an add transaction. The details on the transaction record should be put into master record format, and the record should be written to the new master file. Another record should then be read from the transaction file.
2   If the transaction record key is equal to the old master record key, the transaction is probably an update or delete transaction. If the transaction is an update, the master record should be amended to reflect the required changes. If the transaction is a delete, the master record should not be written to the new master file. Another transaction record should then be read from the transaction file.
3   If the transaction record key is greater than the old master record key, there is no matching transaction for that master record. In this case the old master record should be written unchanged to the new master file and another record read from the old master file.

Sequential update programs also need to include logic that will handle multiple transaction records for the same master record, and the possibility of transaction records that are in error. The types of transaction record errors that can occur are:

1   An attempt to add a new master record when a record with that key already exists on the master file.
2   An attempt to update a master record when there is no record with that key on the master file.
3   An attempt to delete a master record when there is no record with that key on the master file.
4   An attempt to delete a master record when the current balance is not equal to zero.

Balance line algorithm

The logic of the sequential update program has fascinated programmers for many years. Authors have offered many solutions to the problem, but none of these has been a truly general solution. Most solutions have been designed around a specific programming language.

A good general solution algorithm written in pseudocode was presented by Barry Dwyer in a paper entitled 'One More Time — How to Update a Master File'[1]. This algorithm has been referred to as the balance line algorithm. It handles multiple transaction records for the one master record as well as the possibility of transaction record errors.

A modularised version of the balance line algorithm is presented in this chapter. It introduces the concept of a current record. The current record is the record that is currently being processed, ready for updating and writing to the new master file. The current record is established when the record keys on the two files are compared. The current record will be the record that has the smaller record key. Its format will be that of a new master record.

Thus, if the transaction record key is less than the old master key, the current record will be made up of the fields on the transaction record. If the transaction record key is equal to or greater than the old master record key, the old master record will become the current record.

The current record will remain the current record until there are no more transactions to be applied to that record. It will then be written to the new master file, and a new current record will be established.

Another variable, current_record_status, is used as a program flag to indicate whether or not the current record is available for processing. If the current_record_status is active, the current record has been established and is available for updating or writing out to the new master file. If the current_record_status is inactive, the current record is not available to be updated or written to the new master file, e.g. the current record may have been marked for deletion.

The processing of the two files will continue until end_of_job has been reached. Each_of_job will occur when both the input files have no more data to be processed. Since it is not known which file will reach end of file (EOF) first, the record key of each file will be set to a high value when EOF is reached. When the record key of one of the files is high, the other file will continue to be processed, as required, until the record key on that file is assigned the same high value. End_of_job occurs when the record keys on both the files is the same high value.

Let us now establish a general solution algorithm for a sequential update program. The logic provided will also include the printing of the audit and error reports.

---

[1] Barry Dwyer, 'One More Time — How to Update a Master File'. *Comm. ACM*, Vol. 124, No. 1, January 1981.

A Hierarchy chart

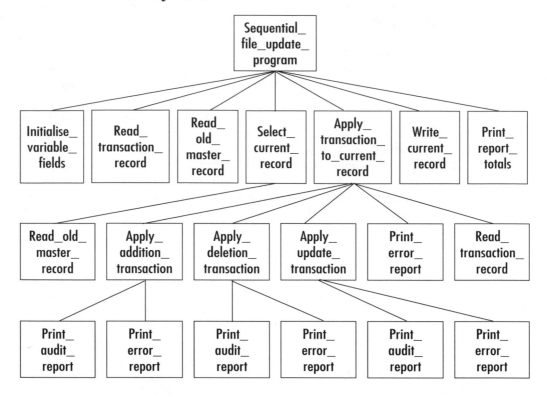

B Solution algorithm

Mainline

```
Sequential_file_update_program
        Initialise_variable_fields
        Read_transaction_record
        Read_old_master_record
        set current_record_status to 'inactive'
        DOWHILE NOT end_of_job
            Select_current_record
            DOWHILE transaction_record_key = current_record_key
                Apply_transaction_to_current_record
            ENDDO
            IF current_record_status = 'active' THEN
                Write_current_record
                set current_record_status to 'inactive'
            ENDIF
        ENDDO
        Print_report_totals
    END
```

Subordinate modules

1　Initialise_variable_fields
　　　　set total_transaction_records to zero
　　　　set total_old_master_records to zero
　　　　set total_new_master_records to zero
　　　　set total_error_records to zero
　　　　set end_of_job to false
　　END

2　Read_transaction_record
　　　　Read transaction record
　　　　IF NOT EOF THEN
　　　　　　increment total_transaction_records
　　　　ELSE
　　　　　　set transaction_record_key to high value
　　　　　　IF old_master_record_key = high value THEN
　　　　　　　　set end_of_job to true
　　　　　　ENDIF
　　　　ENDIF
　　END

3　Read_old_master_record
　　　　Read old master record
　　　　IF NOT EOF THEN
　　　　　　increment total_old_master_records
　　　　ELSE
　　　　　　set old_master_record_key to high value
　　　　　　IF transaction_record_key = high value THEN
　　　　　　　　set end_of_job = true
　　　　　　ENDIF
　　　　ENDIF
　　END

4　Select_current_record
　　　　IF transaction_record_key < old_master_record_key THEN
　　　　　　set up current record with transaction record fields
　　　　ELSE
　　　　　　set up current record with old master record fields
　　　　　　set current_record_status to 'active'
　　　　　　Read_old_master_record
　　　　ENDIF
　　END

5　Apply_transaction_to_current_record
　　　　CASE OF transaction_type
　　　　　　addition : Apply_addition_transaction
　　　　　　deletion : Apply_deletion_transaction
　　　　　　update : Apply_update_transaction
　　　　　　other : error_message = 'invalid transaction type'
　　　　　　　　　　Print_error_report
　　　　ENDCASE
　　　　Read_transaction_record
　　END

6   Write_current_record
         write current record to new master file
         increment total_new_master_records
     END
7   Print_report_totals
         print total_transaction_records
         print total_old_master_records
         print total_new_master_records
         print total_error_records
     END
8   Apply_addition_transaction
         IF current_record_status = 'inactive' THEN
             set current_record_status to 'active'
             Print_audit_report
         ELSE
             error_message = 'Invalid addition; record already exists'
             Print_error_report
         ENDIF
     END
9   Apply_deletion_transaction
         IF current_record_status = 'active' THEN
             set current_record_status to 'inactive'
             Print_audit_report
         ELSE
             error_message = 'Invalid deletion, record not on master file'
             Print_error_report
         ENDIF
     END
10   Apply_update_transaction
         IF current_record_status = 'active' THEN
             apply required change(s) to current record
             Print_audit_report
         ELSE
             error_message = 'Invalid update, record not on master file'
             Print_error_report
         ENDIF
     END
11   Print_audit_report
         print transaction details on audit report
         CASE OF transaction_type
             addition : print 'record added'
             deletion : print 'record deleted'
             update : print 'record updated'
         ENDCASE
     END
12   Print_error_report
         print transaction details on error report
         print error_message
         increment total_error_records
     END

Note that end_of_job is reached when the transaction_record_key = high value AND the old_master_record_key = high value. This pseudocode algorithm can now be used to process any sequential file update report.

10.6 CHAPTER SUMMARY

The aim of this chapter was to develop general pseudocode algorithms to four common business applications. The applications covered were:

- report generation with page break,
- single-level control break,
- multiple-level control break, and
- sequential file update.

In each section, the application was discussed, a hierarchy chart was developed, and a general solution algorithm was presented in pseudocode. These solution algorithms can be used when writing programs which incorporate any of the above applications.

10.7 PROGRAMMING PROBLEMS

Using the sample solution algorithms provided in this chapter, design a solution algorithm for the following programming problems. Your solution should contain:

- a defining diagram,
- a hierarchy chart,
- a pseudocode algorithm, and
- a desk check of the solution.

1 Design an algorithm to produce a list of customers from the Glad Rags Clothing Company's customer master file. Each record on the customer master file contains the customer's number, name, address (street, city, state, and postcode), and the customer's account balance.

Your program is to read the customer master file and print a report of all customers whose account balance is greater than zero. Each detail line is to contain the customer's number, name, address and account balance. Print headings and column headings at the top of each page, allowing for 35 detail lines per page, and at the end of the report, the total customers on file, the total customers with balance owing, and the total balance owing, as follows:

```
                    GLAD RAGS CLOTHING COMPANY
XX/XX/XX                CURRENT ACCOUNTS BALANCES              PAGE: XX

CUSTOMER      CUSTOMER      ADDRESS                           ACCOUNT
NUMBER        NAME                                            BALANCE

XXXXX         XXXXXXXXXX    XXXXXXXXXXXXXXXXXXXX              9 999.99
XXXXX         XXXXXXXXXX    XXXXXXXXXXXXXXXXXXXX              9 999.99
  :               :                   :                          :
                            Total customers on file               999
                            Total customers with balance owing    999
                            Total balance owing              99 999.99
```

2 Design an algorithm to produce a sales commission report from a company's sales file. Each record on the sales file contains the salesperson's number, name and sales amount.

Your program is to read the sales file, calculate the sales commission according to the following table, and print a sales commission report.

Sales range	Commission(per cent)
$0–$499.99	No commission
$500.00–$749.99	2%
$750.00 and above	3%

Each detail line is to contain the salesperson's number, sales amount, commission rate and total commission. Print headings and column headings at the top of each page, allowing for 35 detail lines per page, and at the end of the report, the total commission, as follows.

```
                    SALES COMMISSIONS                        PAGE: XX
SALESPERSON   SALESPERSON     SALES       COMMISSION    COMMISSION
NUMBER        NAME            AMOUNT       RATE
XXXXX         XXXXXXXXXXXXX   99 999.99    x%                999.99
XXXXX         XXXXXXXXXXXXX   99 999.99    x%                999.99
                                          TOTAL COMMISSION  9999.99
```

3 Design an algorithm that will create a validation report from a customer sales file. Each field on the sales record is to be validated as follows:

Field	Format
Customer number	numeric
Customer name	alphanumeric
Street	alphanumeric
Town	alphanumeric
Postcode	numeric
Phone	alphanumeric
Fax	alphanumeric
Balance due	numeric
Credit limit	numeric (0–$1000)

If a field is found to be in error, print a line on the validation report showing the customer number, name, address (street, town, postcode) and an appropriate message, as indicated in the diagram below. There may be multiple messages for the one record. Print headings and column headings at the top of each page, allowing for 45 detail lines per page.

VALIDATION REPORT
CUSTOMER SALES FILE   PAGE: XX

CUSTOMER NUMBER	CUSTOMER NAME	ADDRESS	MESSAGE
xxxxx	xxxxxxxxxxxxx	xxxxxxxxxxxxx	POST CODE NOT NUMERIC
xxxxx	xxxxxxxxxxxxx	xxxxxxxxxxxxx	CREDIT LIMIT INVALID

4 The Multi-Disk computer company requires a single-level control break program to produce a sales report by salesperson from their sales file. Design an algorithm that will read the sales file and create the sales report as shown below.

   Each record on the sales file contains the salesperson's number, name, the product number of the product sold, the quantity sold and the price of the product. There may be more than one record for each salesperson, depending on the products sold that month. The sales file has been sorted into ascending sequence of salesperson number.

   Your program is to read the sales file sequentially, calculate the extension amount (price * quantity sold) for each product sold and print a detail line for each record processed. Control total lines showing the sales total for each salesperson are to be printed on change of salesperson number. Print headings and column headings at the top of each page, allowing for 40 detail lines per page.

MULTI-DISK COMPUTER COMPANY
XX/XX/XX   **SALES REPORT BY SALESPERSON**   PAGE: XX

SALESPERSON NUMBER	SALESPERSON NAME	PRODUCT NUMBER	QTY SOLD	PRICE	EXTENSION AMOUNT
xxxx	xxxxxxxxxx	xxxx	99	999.99	9 999.99
		xxxx	99	999.99	9 999.99
		xxxx	99	999.99	9 999.99
		Sales total for xxxxxxxxx			99 999.99
		Report sales total			999 999.99

5 The same sales file as described in Problem 4 exists, with the addition of a further field, the department number. The sales file has been sorted into ascending sequence of salesperson number within department number. Print the same sales report, with the additional requirement of printing a sales total line on change of department number, as well as on change of salesperson number.

   Print the report details as per the following sales report: headings and column headings at the top of each page, allowing for 40 detail lines per page.

		MULTI-DISK COMPUTER COMPANY				
XX/XX/XX		SALES REPORT				PAGE: XX

DEPT	SALESPERSON NUMBER	SALESPERSON NAME	PRODUCT NUMBER	QTY SOLD	PRICE	EXTENSION AMOUNT
xx	xxxx	xxxxxxxxxx	xxxx	99	999.99	9 999.99
			xxxx	99	999.99	9 999.99
			xxxx	99	999.99	9 999.99
			Sales total for xxxxxxxxxx			99 999.99
			Sales total for Dept xx			999 999.99
			Report sales total			9999 999.99

6 ABC University requires a single-level control break program to produce a lecturer information report by lecturer from the university's course file. Design an algorithm that will read the course file and create the lecturer information report as shown below.

Each record on the course file contains details of a lecturer's teaching load; that is, the lecturer's number, name, the course number of the course being taught, the credit hours for that course and the class size. There may be more than one record for each lecturer, depending on the number of courses he or she teaches. The course file has been sorted into ascending sequence of lecturer number.

Your program is to read the course file sequentially, calculate the lecturer's contact hours ((class size/50)* credit hours), and produce the lecturer information report. On change of lecturer number print control total lines showing the total contact hours for each lecturer. Print headings and column headings at the top of each page, allowing for 40 detail lines per page.

ABC UNIVERSITY
LECTURER INFORMATION REPORT

LECTURER NUMBER	LECTURER NAME	COURSE NUMBER	CREDIT HOURS	CLASS SIZE	CONTACT HOURS
xxxx	xxxxxxxxxx	xxxxx	x	xxx	xxx
		xxxxx	x	xxx	xxx
		xxxxx	x	xxx	xxx
		CONTACT HOURS FOR LECTURER xxxx			x xxx
		CONTACT HOURS FOR UNIVERSITY			xx xxx

7 The same course file as described in Problem 6 exists, with the addition of a further field, the university department number. The course file has been sorted into ascending sequence of lecturer number within department number. Print the same lecturer information report, with the additional requirement of printing a total contact hours line on change of department number, as well as on change of lecturer number.

Print the report details as per the following lecturer information report. Print headings and column headings at the top of each page, allowing for 40 detail lines per page.

ABC UNIVERSITY
LECTURER INFORMATION REPORT

DEPARTMENT NUMBER	LECTURER NUMBER	LECTURER NAME	COURSE NUMBER	CREDIT HOURS	CLASS SIZE	CONTACT HOURS
xxx	xxxx	xxxxxxxxxx	xxxxx	x	xxx	xxx
			xxxxx	x	xxx	xxx
		CONTACT HOURS FOR LECTURER xxxx				x xxx
	xxxx	xxxxxxxxxx	xxxxx	x	xxx	xxx
			xxxxx	x	xxx	xxx
		CONTACT HOURS FOR LECTURER xxxx				x xxx
		CONTACT HOURS FOR DEPARTMENT xxx				x xxx
		CONTACT HOURS FOR UNIVERSITY				xx xxx

8 The same course file as described in Problem 7 exists, with the addition of a further field, the college number. The course file has been sorted into ascending sequence of lecturer number within department number within college number. The same lecturer information report is to be printed, with the additional requirement of printing a total contact hours line on change of college number, as well as on change of department number and on change of lecturer number.

Print the report details as per the following lecturer information report. Print headings and column headings at the top of each page, allowing for 40 detail lines per page.

ABC UNIVERSITY
LECTURER INFORMATION REPORT

COLLEGE NUMBER	DEPT NUMBER	LECTURER NUMBER	LECTURER NAME	COURSE NUMBER	CREDIT HOURS	CLASS SIZE	CONTACT HOURS
xxxxx	xxx	xxxx	xxxxxxxxxx	xxxxx	x	xxx	xxx
			xxxxx	x	xxx	xxx	
			CONTACT HOURS FOR LECTURER xxxx				xxx
			CONTACT HOURS FOR DEPARTMENT xxx				x xxx
	xxx	xxxx	xxxxxxxxxx	xxxxx	x	xxx	xxx
			xxxxx	x	xxx	xxx	
			CONTACT HOURS FOR LECTURER xxxx				xxx
			CONTACT HOURS FOR DEPARTMENT xxx				x xxx
			CONTACT HOURS FOR COLLEGE xxxxx				xx xxx
			CONTACT HOURS FOR UNIVERSITY				xx xxx

9 The XYZ Bank requires a program to sequentially update its savings account master file. A sequential file of update transactions is to be used as the input transaction file, along with the customer master file.

The customer master file contains the customer's account number, and the balance forward amount. The customer transaction update file contains three types of records, as follows:

(i) Deposit records containing a record code of 'D', the account number and the amount of a deposit.

(ii) Withdrawal records containing a record code of 'W', the account number and the amount of a withdrawal.

(iii) Interest records containing a record code of 'I', the account number and the amount of interest earned.

There is a deposit record for each deposit a customer made, a withdrawal record for each withdrawal and an interest record if interest was credited during the period. The updating process consists of adding each deposit or interest to the balance forward amount on the master record, and subtracting each withdrawal.

Both files have been sorted into account number sequence. There can be multiple update transactions for any one savings account master record and a new savings account master file is to be created.

If a transaction record is in error, the transaction details are to be printed on the transaction error report, with one of the following messages:

'invalid deposit, account number not on file'
'invalid withdrawal, account number not on file'
'invalid interest record, account number not on file'

10 The Yummy Chocolates confectionery company requires a program to sequentially update its customer master file. A sequential file of update transactions is to be used as the input transaction file, along with the customer master file.

The customer master file contains the customer number, customer name, customer address (street, city, state and postcode) and account balance. The customer transaction file contains the same fields, as well as a transaction code of 'A' (add), 'D' (delete) and 'U' (update).

Both files have been sorted into customer number sequence. There can be multiple update transactions for any one customer master record and a new customer master file is to be created.

Transaction records are to be processed as follows:

(i) If the transaction record is an 'Add', the transaction is to be written to the new customer master file.

(ii) If the transaction record is a 'Delete', the old master record with the same customer number is not to be written to the new customer master file.

(iii) If the transaction record is an update, the old master record with the same customer number is to be updated as follows:

if customer name is present, update customer name
if street is present, update street
if town is present, update town
if state is present, update state
if postcode is present, update postcode
if balance paid is present, subtract balance paid from account balance on old customer master record.

As each transaction is processed, print the transaction details on the customer master audit report, with the message, 'record added', 'record deleted' or 'record updated' as applicable.

If a transaction record is in error, the transaction details are to be printed on the customer update errors report, with one of the following messages:

'invalid addition, customer already exists'
'invalid deletion, customer not on file'
'invalid update, customer not on file'.

Object-oriented design

Information hiding

OBJECTIVES

- To introduce object-oriented design
- To define objects, classes, attributes, methods and information hiding
- To list the steps required to create an object-oriented design to a problem

OUTLINE

11.1 INTRODUCTION TO OBJECT-ORIENTED DESIGN

In this book, program design has concentrated on *what* a program has to do. This is said to be a *procedural* approach to design and programming because it involves identifying and organising the *processes* in the problem solution.

Procedural design has been found to have some limitations when very large systems are developed and maintained by a large team of developers. Even if they are structured and modular, large procedural systems can still become extremely complicated and difficult to understand. Developers are not always aware of work being performed on the system by other members of the development team. As a result, the same blocks of code are sometimes duplicated in different parts of the system, when ideally they should occur once only, and remain available to be reused. It can become difficult to trace and use efficiently the data being used by different processes in large procedural systems. Object-oriented programming and design is emerging as an important technique for business programming because of its suitability for building large systems.

Object-oriented design asks that we interact with the problem in much the same way that we interact with our world — we treat it as a set of separate objects that perform actions and relate to each other. An object-oriented program is a set of interacting *objects* rather than a set of functions.

In object-oriented design you need to identify the *data* in the objects as well as the *processes* or *actions* that can be performed on that data. Remember that in procedural design you needed merely to identify the *processes*.

Objects are said to *encapsulate* (enclose in a capsule) their data and the processes that act on those data. Objects, then, are like 'black boxes' to the outside world. The internal code that creates and maintains objects can exist independently from the rest of the system. This means that objects can be used in several places in one system or across several systems at the same time. The code inside an object can be easily maintained without interfering with the rest of the system. Conversely, changes to the rest of the system will not affect the object.

Objects

An object can be considered as a container for a set of data and the operations that need to be performed on it. An object has the following properties:

- It has a *name* that is unique for the lifetime of the object
- It has data in the form of a set of characteristics or *attributes*, each of which has a value at any given point in time
- There is a set of operations or *methods* that can be performed on the data
- It is an instance (example) of a *class*

Consider a real-world object, such as a car. Each car object has a *name* in the form of its licence plate and has *attributes* to describe it: make, model, number of doors, body length, engine size and colour. Cars also have *methods*, things that they can do: stop, turn, accelerate and brake.

In a computer program an object's attributes are the properties or characteristics that describe it. Each object of the same type will have an identical set of attributes, but the attributes of one object may contain different data values from those of another object.

Consider an object-oriented payroll program used to calculate the pay for each of the employees in a business. Each employee has an identifying employee number, and may have varying rates of pay and hours of work. For each employee's pay to be processed the program will use a TimeSheet object with a unique name, such as timeSheet12345, and with attributes of empNumber, payRate and hoursWorked, which will have the values relevant to each employee.

Methods

Objects receive messages from other objects, asking them to perform services or operations. Thus, each object has a number of *methods* or set of operations, sometimes called procedures or functions, which perform these services. The purpose of the payroll program is to calculate the individual pay for each employee as well as to determine the overall wages bill. Each TimeSheet object in the payroll program will have methods such as calculatePay( ) which are identical to those contained in all other TimeSheet objects.

Methods can manipulate the values stored in an object's attributes, but can only act on the data inside the object or on values passed to the object. In other words, the data inside any object can only be affected by that object's methods.

As you can see from the examples given, object names, attributes and methods should be assigned meaningful names.

Classes and objects

An object is created from a template or pattern, called a *class*, which defines the basic attributes and the methods available to objects of that class. When an object is created, it is given a unique name and a copy of all the attributes and methods from its class. The process of creating objects from classes is called *instantiation*, and an object is described as an *instance,* or example, of its class. Many objects can be instantiated from a class, each containing the same attributes, but not necessarily storing the same values in those attributes.

Constructors

The process of instantiating an object from the class template is performed by a special method, or set of instructions, known as a *constructor*. Until the constructor is called, no object exists. As each object is created, it receives its own copy of all the attributes and methods for its class. The constructor puts actual values into the attributes.

Every class should have a default constructor that initialises the class attributes. The constructor may:

- have no parameters, in which case a new object is assigned all the default values for its attributes, or
- may have parameters that initialise the attributes with those particular values.

Classes can be progressively created from other classes by copying (or *inheriting*) attributes and methods from the base (or parent) classes. Each generation can have its own set of methods and attributes in addition to those it has *inherited.*

For example, in a Banking program, an Account class is created to manage customer accounts. The class Account includes attributes such as accountName and balance, as well as methods such as deposit and withdraw money. There are different type of accounts so a new class called Cheque Account inherits all of the features of Account but adds some special features such as clearanceFee and chequeBook. The features of the template class, which are retained by Cheque Account, are obtained by *inheritance*.

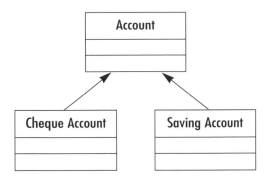

Every ChequeAccount object that is created by the program contains all the properties and methods of the Account class as well as the extra features of the ChequeAccount class. A request to print the value of uncleared cheques may be serviced by a ChequeAccount object but would be meaningless to a SavingsAccount object. A ChequeAccount object may have additional attributes to store information about cheque books.

A SavingsAccount object may have methods to calculate interest and add over-the-counter withdrawal fees, neither of which would be required in the Account or ChequeAccount classes.

Information hiding

In object-oriented design each object can be regarded as a 'black box' whose internal workings are hidden from all other objects. This principle of information hiding simplifies the use of objects, because the rest of the system does not need to know how they are structured or how they perform their operations.

The goal of information hiding is to make the object as robust and independent as possible. It ensures that attribute values cannot be accidentally changed by other parts of the system, and carefully controls the interactions that the object has with other objects.

Public and private methods

An object's methods, or set of operations, can be *public* or *private*.

The *public* methods of an object are those producing services requested by other objects. Objects must be able to communicate and interact with the rest of the program, and this communication is achieved by the passing of *messages*. A message is a function call or method call made by one object to a method in another object. In order to produce the required services the called object's method may need to receive information from the calling object. These inputs and outputs are received and sent as parameters, enclosed in parentheses, after the name of the public method.

For example, in a Banking program, the deposit( ) method of an account object will need to receive the deposit amount, in the form of a parameter, for example, deposit (depositAmount), to be able to perform its service of updating the account balance. The method deposit( ), then, is a public method.

Other methods, *private* methods, are needed to perform the internal operations in an object and cannot be accessed directly from outside the object.

Similarly, an object's attributes may be private, or invisible, to the rest of the system, or they may be public. Public attributes are not desirable, as their use can lead to unintended side effects. In describing methods and attributes as private or public, we are describing their *visibility* to the system. It is important to determine the visibility of methods and attributes at design time.

To illustrate the concept of visibility, consider our real-world car object. Some of the car's methods, such as choke( ) or setSeatHeight( ), are private, because they are an internal operation of the actual car. Others are necessarily public, and help the object interact with external systems such as the brakeLight( ) or soundHorn( ) methods. Consider the potential problems that might arise if the accelerate( ) or brake( ) method in one car changed the velocity attribute in a neighbouring car.

11.2 STEPS IN CREATING AN OBJECT-ORIENTED SOLUTION

The steps in creating an OO solution are:

- Identify the objects and the methods to be performed
- Determine the relationship between the objects
- Design the algorithms for the methods, using structured design
- Develop the mainline algorithm.

To start your object-oriented design, read the problem definition carefully, looking for nouns and noun phrases. These may translate into the *objects* in the program. To identify the *methods*, or operations, look closely at the verbs that describe the actions performed by the nouns. List the objects and their operations in an Object Table to create a framework from which to refine a model.

Using the four steps for creating an OO solution to a problem, let's look at Example 8.3, which was developed in Chapter 8, using top-down design.

Example 11.1 *Calculate employee's pay*

Create a program that will read employee data from a file and, for each employee, compute the employee's pay, which should then be printed together with the input data. Employee data consists of an employee number, pay rate and the number of hours worked in a week. The program is to continue reading employee details until there are no more records in the file.

According to the company's rules, no employee may be paid for more than 60 hours per week. The maximum hourly rate is $25.00 per hour. If more than 35 hours are worked, payment for the overtime hours worked is calculated at time and a half. If the hours worked or the hourly rate is out of the accepted range, the input data and an appropriate message are to be printed and the employee's weekly pay is not to be calculated.

Step 1: Identify the objects and the methods to be performed

First, just as if you were using a top-down approach to define a problem, underline the nouns and adjectives relevant to the problem in the problem statement.

This will begin to reveal the possible classes, the objects which will be derived from these classes, and their associated attributes. With the nouns and adjectives and adjective-noun phrases underlined, the problem statement would look like this:

> Create a program that will read employee data from a file and, for each <u>employee</u>, compute the <u>employee's pay,</u> which should then be printed together with the input data. Employee data consists of an <u>employee</u> <u>number,</u> <u>pay rate</u> and the <u>number of hours worked in a week.</u> The program is to continue reading employee details until there are no more records in the file.
>
> According to the company's rules, no employee may be paid for more than 60 hours per week. The maximum hourly rate is $25.00 per hour. If more than 35 hours are worked, payment for the <u>overtime hours worked</u> is calculated at time and a half. If the hours worked or the hourly rate is out of the accepted range, the input data and an appropriate <u>message</u> are to be printed and the employee's weekly pay is not to be calculated.

You can see that the word <u>employee</u> is used as a noun in the first sentence, but as an adjective describing <u>pay,</u> <u>number,</u> <u>pay rate</u> and <u>number of hours worked</u> in the second sentence. This indicates that employee is an object with attributes, or properties, of number, pay rate and hours worked. But do these attributes really define an employee in the real world? In fact, they more closely define the contents of a time sheet, so the object will be named TimeSheet.

In the second paragraph, <u>pay</u> is calculated from pay rate and hours worked. Therefore it is a 'derived' value and is not necessarily an attribute. Likewise, <u>overtime hours</u> and <u>message</u> are not always necessary for the existence of a TimeSheet object, so you can omit them from the object definition.

Not all of the nouns and adjectives in the problem statement are vital to the solution. For example, you do not need to underline the words *company's rules* or *program*.

Using meaningful names, these components can be set up in an object table as follows:

Object	Attributes	Methods
TimeSheet	empNumber payRate hoursWorked	

Now establish the methods, or set of operations, for each object by underlining the verbs and verb phrases relevant to the problem in the problem statement.

Create a program that will read employee data from a file and, for each employee, compute the employee's pay, which should then be printed together with the input data. Employee data consists of an employee number, pay rate and the number of hours worked in a week. The program is to continue reading employee details until there are no more records in the file.

According to the company's rules, no employee may be paid for more than 60 hours per week. The maximum hourly rate is $25.00 per hour. If more than 35 hours are worked, payment for the overtime hours worked is calculated at time and a half. If the hours worked or the hourly rate is out of the accepted range, the input data and an appropriate message are to be printed, and the employee's weekly pay is not to be calculated.

Begin by identifying the visible or public operations. Notice that the verb phrases read employee data, print the pay and print the input data are operations in which the TimeSheet object will interact with system objects external to itself, so will be visible, or public, methods.

Next, look for the private or invisible operations. The words compute the employee's pay indicates that a private method is required to calculate the pay amount. Clearly, before the pay is calculated, the object will need to validate the inputs internally, so this also becomes a private method.

As we define the object's methods by distinguishing these operations, we can also begin to identify the messages that the methods may need in order to perform their functions. The messages will be shown in parentheses in the same way that parameters are shown for modules. The methods, preceded by + (plus), if they are public methods, and − (minus), if they are private methods, can now be added to the object table.

The *constructor* is a set of operations that creates an object by providing initial values to an object's attributes. It is a private method taken as implicit for each class, so it does not appear in the object table. We will assume that all of the attributes are private at this stage.

Object	Attributes	Methods
TimeSheet	empNumber payRate hoursWorked	+ readTimeSheet(validInput) + printTimeSheet( ) − validateInput(validInput) − calculatePay( ) + printPay( )

You may have noticed the empty parentheses ( ) at the end of some of the method names. Although in this example we have identified the parameter, validInput, which returns a message to indicate if the input data is valid, at this stage of defining our problem it is usually too early to be able to identify all the external information that will be needed by the methods. Convention dictates that we still insert empty parentheses after the method names to clearly distinguish them from attributes. You may find that when you design the method algorithms, you will have to insert parameters inside the parentheses of some method algorithm names.

At this point, some important differences between object-oriented and procedural approaches become clear. In the procedural approach you define what the program has to do; data is independent of the procedures that use it. Data is passed into and between procedures when and where it is required, so must be carefully scheduled and managed, along with the procedures that use it. This requires the designer and programmer to be familiar with all parts of the system that may access or process data used in the section they are working on.

In the object-oriented approach we are only interested in the service the object is providing and the information we must supply to the object so that it can do its work. Once an object is instantiated, its data and procedures are available for the rest of the program to access as necessary. Designers and programmers building other objects only need to know of an object's existence, services it may be able to provide and the inputs it requires to produce those services.

In this example, the TimeSheet object provides the service of printing the weekly pay and printing the TimeSheet details. In order to provide that service, it needs TimeSheet details supplied to it, in the form of employee number, hours worked, and pay rate. It is this 'black box' nature of objects that allows many programmers to work on one large system.

Step 2: Determine the relationship between the objects

The object table developed from the problem statement has only one type of object, so in this first example there is no relationship to define. Object-oriented design using multiple classes is developed in Chapter 12.

Step 3: Design the algorithms for the methods, using structured design

Each method in the object table requires a step-by-step description of the instructions that will produce the required behaviour. Each algorithm should start with the name of the method and finish with an END statement. It should use correct indentation and follow the rules of structured design.

Public methods

When the object performs the task of reading TimeSheet data from the file, it brings all of the needed data inside the scope of the newly created object. The object also takes responsibility for validating the data. The external program, which calls the object, is not concerned about how the data is validated, but it does need to know whether it is valid or not. Therefore the readTimeSheet( ) method must not only call a method to validate the data but it must return a parameter telling the world outside the object if the data is valid.

```
readTimeSheet(validInput)
        Set validInput to true
        Read empNumber, payRate, hoursWorked
        validateInput(validInput)
END
```

Most objects have a method that will print or display the current values of its attributes.

```
printTimeSheet( )
        Print empNumber, payRate, hoursWorked
END
```

The public method printPay( ) calls the private method calculatePay( ), which returns a parameter, weeklyPay, which can then be printed.

```
printPay( )
        calculatePay(weeklyPay)
        Print weeklyPay
END
```

Private methods

The private method, validateInput( ), validates the input data and returns a parameter, validInput, which contains a message indicating if the input data is valid or not. To follow good design practice, the values for the maximum hourly rate, the normal working hours and the maximum payable hours have been represented by the constants shown in upper case.

```
validateInput(validInput)
        Set errorMessage to blank
        IF payRate > MAX_PAY THEN
            errorMessage = "Pay rate exceeds $25.00"
            Print errorMessage
            validInput = false
        ENDIF
        IF hoursWorked > MAX_HOURS THEN
            errorMessage = "Hours worked exceeds limit of 60"
            Print errorMessage
            validInput = false
        ENDIF
END
```

The private method, calculatePay( ), calculates the weekly pay for each employee.

```
calculatePay(weeklyPay)
        IF hoursWorked <= NORM_HOURS THEN
            weeklyPay = payRate * hoursWorked
        ELSE
            overtimeHours = hoursWorked − NORM_HOURS
            overtimePay = overtimeHours * payRate * 1.5
            weeklyPay = (payRate * NORM_HOURS) + overtimePay
        ENDIF
END
```

Step 4: Develop the mainline algorithm

The final step is to develop a mainline that, like the mainline in a procedural program, ties the objects together and coordinates their activities.

Before the mainline is written, however, an algorithm for the constructor must be designed. The constructor is designed to instantiate, or create, a new TimeSheet object, and provide default values to its attributes. It is given the name of the object, in this case, TimeSheet.

```
TimeSheet( )
        Set empNumber to "Unknown"
        Set payRate to 0.0
        Set hoursWorked to 0
    END
```

The constructor is invoked in the mainline of the program with the pseudocode:

```
Create timeSheet as new TimeSheet( )
```

When there is more than one object instantiated from a class, it is important that the program can identify exactly which copy of a method it should be using when a method call is made. This is managed by using a special notation in which the object's name is placed in front of the method, separated by the 'dot operator'. For example, the printPay( ) method owned by timeSheet is referred to as timeSheet.printPay( ).

Note that the mainline algorithm includes the use of this notation, by which the visible or public methods are accessed by other parts of the program. Because the private methods are not publicly accessible they are not used with the dot operator.

```
computePay
        Set validInput to true
        Create timeSheet as new TimeSheet( )
        timeSheet.readTimeSheet(validInput)
        DOWHILE more records
                timeSheet.printTimeSheet( )
                IF validInput THEN
                        timeSheet.printPay( )
                ENDIF
                timeSheet.readTimeSheet(validInput)
        ENDDO
    END
```

The steps in object-oriented design are not always followed sequentially. As this example shows, sometimes a step can be completely omitted. However, as you have seen in procedural design, the same steps may have to be repeated and refined several times before the design is complete. The mainline algorithm may need to be developed at the same time as the other method algorithms, rather than waiting until all the method algorithms have been designed.

11.3 PROGRAMMING EXAMPLE USING OBJECT-ORIENTED DESIGN

Example 11.2 *Print student results*

Design a class to manage student results in a subject. Each student is identified by a unique student number. During the course of the subject each student completes three assignments representing 40% of the final mark but each scored out of 100, and an examination, also scored out of 100 marks. The final mark is calculated by multiplying the sum of the assignments by 0.133 and the examination by 0.6 and adding the two products together. The class will allow a user to update an assignment mark or an examination mark, and to print the final mark along with the student number for each student.

Step 1: *Identify the objects and methods to be performed*

To commence the design, underline the nouns and noun phrases to identify the objects and their attributes.

> Design a class to manage <u>student results</u> in a subject. Each <u>student</u> is identified by a <u>unique student number</u>. During the course of the subject each student completes <u>three</u> <u>assignments</u> representing 40% of the final mark but each scored out of 100, and <u>an examination</u>, also scored out of 100 marks. The <u>final mark</u> is calculated by multiplying the sum of the assignments by 0.133 and the examination by 0.6 and adding the two products together. The class will allow a user to update an assignment mark or an examination mark, and to print the final mark along with the student number for each student.

In the example it is apparent that a <u>student</u> object will be needed, with attributes of <u>unique student number</u>, <u>three assignments</u>, and <u>an examination</u>. There is no need to make final mark an attribute because it can be derived from the attributes above.

Now underline the verb and verb phrases to identify the methods, or operations, the object needs to perform.

> Design a class to <u>manage student results</u> in a subject. Each student is identified by a unique student number. During the course of the subject each student completes three assignments representing 40% of the final mark but each scored out of 100, and an examination, also scored out of 100 marks. The <u>final mark is</u> <u>calculated</u> by multiplying the sum of the assignments by 0.133 and the examination by 0.6 and adding the two products together. The class will allow a user to <u>update an assignment mark</u> or <u>an</u> <u>examination mark</u>, and to <u>print the final mark</u> along with the student number for each student.

The underlined verbs and verb phrases indicate that there are three public or visible methods, namely <u>update assignment mark</u>, <u>update examination mark</u> and the <u>print the final mark</u>, and one private method, <u>calculate final mark</u>. The input score must also be <u>validated</u> before it can be used in the calculations, so another private method to validate the score is required. The object table can now be drawn.

Object	Attributes	Methods
Student	studentNumber asstOne asstTwo asstThree examScore	+ updateAsst(asstNum, result) + updateExam(result) − validateScore( ) − calculateFinalMark( ) + printFinalMark( )

Step 2: Determine the relationships between the objects

There is only one object in the solution, so you can move to the next step.

Step 3: Design the algorithms for the methods, using structured design

Public methods

An algorithm is required for each method in the object table. The public method, updateAsst( ) method, requires that two parameters be passed to it: the assignment number and the result for the assignment. The result, passed as a parameter, will be validated by the private method, validateScore( ), before being used by the method.

```
updateAsst(asstNum, result)
    validateScore(validInput, result)
    IF validInput THEN
        CASE OF asstNum
            1: asstOne = result
            2: asstTwo = result
            3: asstThree = result
        OTHERWISE
            Report invalid assignment number error
        END CASE
    ENDIF
END
```

Similarly, the public method updateExam( ) will require the examination result to be passed to it. This result will also be validated by validateScore( ) before being used.

```
updateExam(result)
    validateScore(validInput, result)
    IF validInput THEN
        examScore = result
    ENDIF
END
```

The results will be printed by the method, printFinalMark( ), which calls the private method calculateFinalMark( ) to calculate the final mark before printing.

```
printFinalMark( )
        calculateFinalMark(finalMark)
        Print studentNumber, finalMark
END
```

Private methods

The assignment and examination results can be tested for range in validateScore( ) to ensure that no invalid scores are passed to the methods that use them. This method will return a message, validInput, which indicates if the input score is valid.

```
validateScore(validInput, result)
        Set validInput to true
        IF (result < 0 OR result >100) THEN
                Set validInput to false
                Report invalid result error
        ENDIF
END
```

The private method, calculateFinalMark( ), will calculate the final mark and return this value in a parameter.

```
calculateFinalMark(finalMark)
        finalMark = (asstOne + asstTwo + asstThree) * 0.133
        finalMark = finalMark + (examScore * 0.6)
END
```

Step 4: Develop the mainline algorithm

The problem definition stated that a <u>class</u> be designed rather than a program. This is a common task in object-oriented programming. Rather than develop a mainline algorithm that might drive an entire program, we will write a simple Test class, called testStudent, to allow the trialling of the Student class. This Test class will simply test that all the methods in the student class work correctly, so that it can be used later in the development of the system.

A constructor for the Student class, named Student, also needs to be developed to create the Student object and initialise the studentNumber attribute. The remaining attributes (asstOne, asstTwo, asstThree and examScore) will be set to default values in this constructor.

```
Student(studentNumber)
        set asstOne to 0
        set asstTwo to 0
        set asstThree to 0
        set examScore to 0
END
```

Note that the value of studentNumber is passed as a parameter to the constructor, which will create a Student object with the pseudocode:

```
Create student as new Student(studentNumber)
```

The Student class can now be trialed, using the Test class, testStudent:

```
testStudent( )
      Set studentNumber to 111555
      Set result to 80
      Set asstNum to 2
      Create student1 as new Student(studentNumber)
      Set studentNumber to 222000
      Create student2 as new Student(studentNumber)
      student1.printFinalMark( )
      student2.printFinalMark( )
      student1.updateAsst(asstNum, result)
      Set result to 95
      Set asstNum to 1
      student2.updateAsst(asstNum, result)
      student1.printFinalMark( )
      student2.printFinalMark( )
END
```

11.4 INTERFACE AND GUI OBJECTS

An interface is a device in a program that connects the user's responses to the computer's actions. Many popular programming languages provide a graphical user interface (GUI), which enables the programmer to select the elements of the program's user interface from a pre-existing range of options. These languages are call 'visual' languages, and include Visual Basic, Visual C and Visual J. Java also shares these features. The user interface options may include windows, buttons, menus, boxes to hold text, drop-down lists and many more. Once they are created, the programmer tailors the interface elements to suit the needs of the program. While some of the programs that provide GUIs are not strictly object oriented in their internal functioning, the interfaces are, and OOD approaches should be used in their design.

Each user interface element provided in the visual languages is an object with attributes and methods. The size, shape, colour, heading labels and modality of a window or form object on a screen are *attributes* defined by the programmer when the code for the program is written. The way the window behaves in response to events which may come from the user, the program or the system that the program is running on, is defined by the window's *methods* the programmer has chosen to use.

Example 11.3 *Library locater interface*

Consider a program that supplies users with the location of a book in a library, based on its call number. The library stores materials from 000 to 250 on the ground level, from 251 to 700 on the first level and from 701 onwards on the second level. The user will need to provide information to the program about the call number of the book he or she is seeking.

In the algorithm this menu may appear as a case statement or as a nested decision structure. In a visual language the inputs for these decision structures can be expressed in at least two possible ways: the user can be asked to enter a choice using text, or select from a series of menu buttons or option or radio buttons.

In the first instance, the program will have to test for invalid inputs and report them with error messages, because the user who types a call number into an input area could potentially make an error. This option requires that the designer prepare algorithms for error trapping and the programmer write the corresponding code. The advantage of this approach is that a specific location on the correct floor can be provided with fewer inputs from the user or with fewer objects to populate the screen.

In the second approach, there is no invalid input possible. The top-level algorithm will still be a complex decision structure that calls separate modules for each choice, but the decision structure will be expressed as a window containing objects that represent the menu choices. The user will select an option that matches his or her requirements and the correct location is displayed.

To design the user interface, first create an interface object table that differs slightly from the earlier object tables. Because the purpose here is <u>interface design</u> rather than <u>program design</u>, at this point you can ignore methods and concentrate on the appearance of the screen objects. The interface object table will allow you to specify which objects will appear and what the starting values of some of their attributes will be. The interface object table for the sample problem could begin like this:

Object	Attributes	Methods
Window	Caption	"Library Locater"
	BackColor	grey
Box 1	BackColor	green
Button 1	Caption	"000–005"
Button 2	Caption	"005–120"
. . .	. . .	. . .
Box 2	BackColor	yellow
. . .	. . .	. . .
Box 3	BackColor	blue
. . .	. . .	. . .
Button n	Caption	"Quit"

The second step is to plan the interface layout, mapping each of the objects in the table onto a screen. This can be done on paper or on screen according to the tools that you have available. Using this table to set the captions and back colours, one possible interface could be:

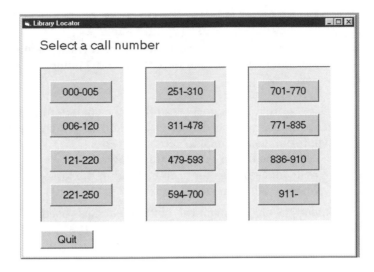

Procedural algorithms that use repetition structures often need to test for sentinel values. In the library locater example, the selection structure will occur inside a loop that is terminated when the user selects the "Quit" option. Although the repetition algorithm will look like many procedural algorithms with a sentinel value of "Quit", the code that is produced will potentially include no repetition structures. With thoughtful interface design, the user does not have to type in a sentinel value to leave the program. The exit condition can be represented as one of the options on the screen.

Having gone to the trouble to design the algorithm for a programmer to implement, don't overlook the interface design. The choices of interface design can have a significant impact on the complexity of your algorithm and the way your algorithm is implemented in the programming language.

11.5 CHAPTER SUMMARY

Object-oriented design is a fundamentally different process to procedural design. Instead of decomposing the problem into functions, the problem is broken up into the objects in the system, and the attributes and methods for each object are identified.

Objects encapsulate their data and methods, and can be regarded as 'black boxes' for the purposes of large system design. Objects are instantiated from classes that are templates defining the attributes and methods for objects of the type, but individual objects of the same type may store different data values in their attributes. The methods and attributes that are accessible by external objects are described as public, and the those which are internal to the object are private.

Interface design for visual programming languages uses object-oriented design principles. Interface objects have methods and attributes. The choice of interface design can reduce the complexity of both an algorithm and the resulting program.

11.6 PROGRAMMING PROBLEMS

1 A parts inventory file contains inventory records each with the fields:
- part number(6 characters, 2 alpha and 4 numeric eg. AA1234)
- part description
- inventory balance.

Design a program that will read the file, validate the part number for each record and print the details of all valid inventory records that have an inventory balance equal to zero.
a Design the object table for this program.
b Write an algorithm for each method in the table.
c Write an algorithm for a mainline.

2 Expand the algorithm for the TestStudent class used in Example 11.2 so that it tests all of the methods and attributes in the Student class.

3 Design a class that calculates and prints the balance owed by each customer of a phone company during the billing period. Phone calls are charged at 25c per minute and charges are added to the balance as the phone calls are completed. The constructor will set the balance owing to zero. Private methods will be needed to calculate the call charges as they are added and to update the balance following the calculation. Use a public method to add a new call to the balance.
a Design the object table for this class.
b Write an algorithm for each method in the table.
c Write an algorithm for a Test class that tests all methods and attributes.

4 Write an object-oriented design for a program that will prompt for and receive the diameter of a circle, and calculate and display the circumference and the area of that circle.
a Design the object table for this class.
b Write an algorithm for each method.
c Write an algorithm for a circle Test class.

5 Design a class to manage a share portfolio. Share holdings are identified by the company name, the number of shares purchased, the date of the purchase, the cost per share and the current price per share. You must be able to calculate the value of current shares, the profit or loss made on the stock purchase and be able to sell the shares.
a Design the object table for this class.
b Write an algorithm for each method.
c Write an algorithm for a Test class.

6 Write an algorithm for a default constructor for the Share class in Problem 5.

7 A library needs a program to keep track of the current loans. Each book has a title, an ISBN, an author, publisher, publication date, call number and a unique accession number. Library patrons have a unique user code, name, street address, postcode and an overdue balance that can be changed when a fine is imposed or when a fine is paid. The balance can be printed, as well as the user code and the patron's name and phone number. When a loan is made, the patron's user code and the loan item's accession number are recorded, as well as the date borrowed and the due date. When a loan

is overdue, a fine of $1 per day is charged to the borrower's overdue balance.

Design one or more classes that could be used by this program. Create the object table and write the method algorithms for all methods. Treat each class you design as though it has no relationship to the other classes.

8 Design the interface for a program that will prompt a user for his or her astrological sign and display the current prediction for the user. Prepare the interface object table and the interface layout.

9 In the Programming Problems Section of Chapter 8, read Problem 9 and design an interface for the program. Prepare the interface object table and the interface layout.

10 In the Programming Problems Section of Chapter 9, read Problem 10 and design the screen interface for the program. Prepare the interface object table and the interface layout. Explain how the interface design may impact on the algorithm for this problem.

12

CHAPTER

More object-oriented design

OBJECTIVES

- To introduce the concept of multiple classes, polymorphism and method overriding in object-oriented design
- To describe relationships between classes
- To develop an object-oriented solution to a complex problem

OUTLINE

12.1 OBJECT-ORIENTED DESIGN WITH MULTIPLE CLASSES

Since the advantage of object-oriented programming languages is their usefulness in constructing large programs, it would be very unusual for a program to make use of only one class. In designing programs that use multiple classes, we need to consider not only the individual class design but the relationships between the classes and therefore between the objects that are instantiated from those classes. It is also useful to understand how classes can evolve.

Notations

Object-oriented approaches have taken a long time to mature as design and programming methodologies. Three popular methods for representing OO design were developed by James Rumbaugh, Grady Booch and Ivar Jacobson. These methods were not only different in the ways they represent the designs, but also in the underlying theories of object behaviours and interaction. Recently a fourth notation called UML, standing for Unified Modelling Language, has emerged from the work of Rumbaugh, Booch and Jacobsen. The notation in this chapter is based on a simplified UML standard.

UML allows a designer to represent the relationship between classes as well as between objects. There are many points of similarity between these two design standards. This chapter will introduce some of the UML graphical notation used to design classes and their relationships.

Relationships between classes

When more than one class is used in a program, there can be one of three possible relationships between any two of the classes.

1 The simplest relationship is between two classes that are independent of each other in the program but perhaps able to use the services each provides.
2 A class may be related to another class by inheritance, when it receives all of the attributes and methods from its parent, but is given a unique name as well as its own extra attributes and methods.
3 A class may need another class as part of itself in order to be able to function at all.

For example, a Car class and a Garage class are independent although a car may sometimes need to use garage services, such as parking. A car is also a type of Road Vehicle and has inherited attributes that are shared by all road vehicles, such as make and model, and methods such as stop( ), turn( ) and accelerate( ). A car also has added attributes that are particular to cars, such as licence plate number, and methods, such as centralLock( ). A car contains an engine. So every object of the Car class needs to contain an object of the Engine class to be able to work effectively, and an object of the Engine class has little use outside its vehicle. These relationships can be shown graphically.

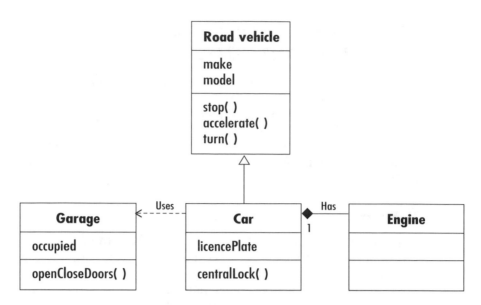

Using UML notation, the open-headed arrow between Road Vehicle and Car shows that Car is a type of Road Vehicle. The filled-diamond headed line and the number 1 between Car and Engine shows that an engine can only exist as part of a car and any engine can belong to only one car. (If the diamond had been empty, the engine object may be able to exist without a car.) The dashed open arrow between Car and Garage indicates that a Car class object can use the services of a Garage object.

Polymorphism

Polymorphism, meaning many-shaped, describes the use of methods of the same name for a variety of purposes. Extending the car example, the bicycle is another type of road vehicle that inherits all the attributes and methods of a car. But accelerate( ) for a car is quite different from accelerate( ) for a bicycle. Both need the method, but it is achieved in quite different ways for objects of each type. The car and the bicycle classes will each need to provide its own definition of accelerate( ) to be complete. This is an example of polymorphism.

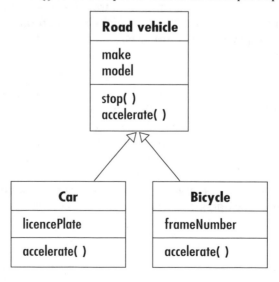

Method overriding occurs when a parent class provides a method, but the inheriting child class defines its own version of that method. The accelerate( ) method in the Car object is different from the accelerate( ) method in the Bicycle object, although it has the same name. Therefore, whenever the accelerate( ) method is called for by an object, such as Car or Bicycle, the version of the method residing inside that particular object will be used. In other words, the method in a sub-class will *override* the method in the base class.

In another type of polymorphism, *overloading*, several methods in a single class can have the same name. To differentiate between the methods, each method must have a different number of parameters or arguments. For example, a bicycle class may have two versions of the stop( ) method; such as stop(handbrake) and stop(handbrake, footbrake). When a call is made to the method, stop( ), the number of arguments is evaluated and the correct stop( ) method invoked.

12.2 PROGRAMMING EXAMPLE WITH MULTIPLE CLASSES

In Chapter 11, Example 11.1, the problem definition required only one class. The problem can now be extended so that it more closely resembles a real application. The additional information for the problem definition follows the second paragraph.

Example 12.1 *Calculate employee's pay*

Create a program that will read employee data from a file and, for each employee, compute the employee's pay, which should then be printed together with the input data. Employee data consists of an *employee type*, employee number, pay rate and the number of hours worked in a week. The program is to continue reading employee details until there are no more records in the file.

According to the company's rules, no employee may be paid for more than 60 hours per week. The maximum hourly rate is $25.00 per hour. If more than 35 hours are worked, payment for the overtime hours worked is calculated at time and a half. If the hours worked or the hourly rate are out of the accepted range, the input data and an appropriate message are to be printed and the employee's weekly pay is not to be calculated.

Most employees are paid according to these procedures, but two additional categories of employees are paid differently.

- Programmers can work on one or more projects. They do not earn overtime, but they are entitled to a $50 bonus for each week for each project that is running ahead of schedule. (An existing Projects class has a method, called earlyProjects(empNumber), that returns the number of projects for which that particular employee deserves a bonus.)
- Sales representatives earn commissions of $200.00 if their weekly sales exceed $19 999.99, and $100.00 if their sales are in the range of $10 0000 to $19 999.99. (An existing Sales class has a method, called getSales (empNumber), that returns the dollar and cents value of the total sales for that representative for that week.)

The field in the input file representing information about the employee type contains the character 'E' for all employees, except programmers and sales representatives, which have the input fields of 'P' and 'R' respectively.

Another part of the program (yet to be designed) maintains a permanent record of employee status, including personal details (such as name and address), and sick leave and annual leave history. Employees will be accessed by employee number. Every week, the weekly pay for each employee should be added to that employee's year-to-date pay amount. The only part of this program to be designed at this stage is the update of the year-to-date pay amount.

Notice that the problem definition refers to two existing classes, Projects and Sales. Since these objects already exist, they can be used in this program as well as in other programs that may need them. This is the principle of object reuse.

Step 1: Identify the objects and the methods to be performed

With a complex problem, this step involves a process of identification, development and refinement, until you are satisfied with the design of the object table. To simplify this process, the problem definition in this example will be divided into three parts: the original problem; the next three paragraphs; and the final two paragraphs. The objects, attributes and methods will be identified and refined in three stages.

Stage 1

1.1 TimeSheet Class

An object table has already been developed for the original problem. The TimeSheet Class was developed for Example 11.1 in Chapter 11, as follows:

Object	Attributes	Methods
TimeSheet	empNumber payRate hoursWorked	+ readTimeSheet(validInput) + printTimeSheet( ) − validateInput(validInput) − calculatePay( ) + printPay( )

Stage 2

To identify the classes and objects for the *new* parts of the problem, we need to underline the relevant nouns and adjectives in the next section of the problem statement, as follows:

> Most <u>employees</u> are paid according to these procedures, but two additional categories of employees are paid differently.

- Programmers can work on one or more projects. They do not earn overtime, but they are entitled to a $50.00 bonus for each week for each project that is running ahead of schedule. (An existing Projects class has a method, called earlyProjects(empNumber), which returns the number of projects for which that particular employee deserves a bonus.)
- Sales representatives earn commissions of $200.00 if their weekly sales exceed $19 999.99, and $100.00 if their sales are in the range of $10 0000 to $19 999.99. (An existing Sales class has a method, called getSales (empNumber), that returns the dollar and cents value of the total sales for that representative for that week.)

1.2 Programmer and sales representative TimeSheet classes

Objects and attributes

Looking at the above nouns and noun phrases, Programmers and Sales representatives are types of employees, with additional payroll calculations, so we know that they are objects, and probably TimeSheet objects.

A programmer isn't paid overtime, but earns a bonus, so bonus becomes an attribute of Programmer TimeSheet.

A sales representative produces weekly sales, so sales becomes an attribute of Sales Representative TimeSheet. He or she also earns a commission, but this is calculated, so it need not become an attribute.

There is already an existing class called Projects( ). The Projects class can be considered a 'black box', charged with the responsibility of informing a Programmer's TimeSheet object of the number of projects that deserve a bonus.

Similarly, there is an existing class called Sales( ). This class is also considered a black box, charged with the responsibility of returning the dollar and cents value of the total sales for the sales representative.

Methods

To establish the methods, or set of operations, for each new object, the verbs and verb phrases relevant to the problem are underlined.

Most employees are paid according to these procedures, but two additional categories of employees are paid differently.

- Programmers can work on one or more projects. They do not earn overtime, but they are entitled to a $50.00 bonus for each week for each project that is running ahead of schedule. (An existing Projects class has a method, earlyProjects (empNumber), that returns the number of projects for which that particular employee deserves a bonus.)
- Sales representatives earn commissions of $200.00 if their weekly sales exceed $19 999.99 and $100.00 if their sales are in the range of $10 0000 to $19 999.99. (An existing Sales class has a method, getSales(empNumber), which returns the dollar and cents value of the total sales for that representative for that week.)

Public methods

For a programmer, the existing Projects class and its method, earlyProjects( ) will handle the operations: <u>work on one or more projects</u>, <u>entitled to a bonus</u>, <u>running ahead of schedule</u>, and <u>deserves a bonus</u>. A method is required for the ProgrammerTimeSheet object to receive a value for the number of projects that deserve a bonus from the Projects class. This method will be a public method, called setBonus( ), where the prefix *set* indicates that the value of the attribute, bonus, will be altered. Remember that the value of an object's attributes cannot be altered except by the object's own methods.

Similarly, for a sales representative, the existing Sales class and its method getSales( ) will handle the operation: <u>returns the dollar and cents value of the total sales</u>. A method is required for the SalesRepTimeSheet to receive a value for the total sales received each week by a sales representative from the Sales class. This public method will be called setSales( ), where the prefix set indicates that the value of the attribute, sales, will be altered.

Private methods

Each sales representative will <u>earn commission</u>, so a private method, called calculateCommission( ), is required for the SalesRepTimeSheet. The verb <u>exceed</u>, and its related information, is useful in the algorithm to calculate the commission, but does not contribute to the class and object development stage.

We can now extend the object table, adding the new classes, their attributes and methods. The double colon between the class names shows that they are derived from the TimeSheet class and inherit the attributes of that class. The shaded areas for the Projects class and Sales class, indicate that the design is already complete for these parts of the program.

Object	Attributes	Methods
TimeSheet	empNumber payRate hoursWorked	+ readTimeSheet(validInput) + printTimeSheet( ) − validateInput(validInput) − calculatePay( ) + printPay( )
TimeSheet::ProgrammerTimeSheet TimeSheet::SalesRepTimeSheet	bonus sales	+ setBonus(projects) + setSales(sales) − calculateCommission( )
Projects Sales		+ earlyProjects(empNumber, numBonus) + getSales(empNumber, Sales)

We can also represent the hierarchical relationship between these classes (and the objects that will be instantiated from them) graphically:

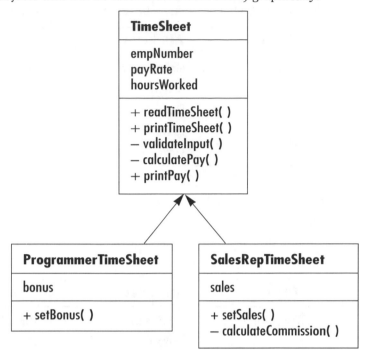

Stage 3

Now let's look at the last two paragraphs in the problem definition. The noun phrases have been underlined to help identify the objects and their attributes, and the verb phrases have been double underlined to identify the methods for each object.

> The field in the input file representing information about the employee type contains the character 'E' for all employees except programmers and sales representatives, which have the input fields of 'P' and 'R' respectively.
>
> Another part of the program (yet to be designed) maintains a permanent record of employee status, including personal details (such as name and address), and sick and annual leave history. Employees will be accessed by employee number. Every week, the weekly pay for each employee should be added to that employee's year-to-date pay amount. The only part of this program to be designed at this stage is the update of the year-to-date pay amount.

1.3 Employee Class

The first paragraph contains information about employee data that is related more to file processing than to TimeSheet processing. It can be left aside for the moment.

In the second paragraph, the noun phrases suggest an employee class that contains attributes of status, employee number, personal details, leave history and year-to-date pay.

The verb phrase weekly pay added indicates that a public method, called addWeeklyPay, is required. This method is public, because the parameter, weeklyPay, will be passed to it from the TimeSheet object. The verb phrase update year_to_date pay amount is covered in the next session.

The Employee Object can now be added to the object table.

Object	Attributes	Methods
Employee	empNumber Details Status LeaveHistory ytdPay	+addWeeklyPay (weeklyPay)

1.4 TimeSheet Class revisited

Public methods

To <u>update the year-to-date pay amount</u>, we need to go back to the methods listed in the TimeSheet class:

Object	Attributes	Methods
TimeSheet	empNumber payRate hoursWorked	+ readTimeSheet(validInput) + printTimeSheet( ) − validateInput(validInput) − calculatePay( ) + printPay( )

The printPay( ) method in the TimeSheet class will need to be changed to make the weekly pay available to update the year-to-date pay in the Employee object, and so will now appear as printPay(weeklyPay).

To be able to update the year-to-date pay in the Employee object, a means of matching the empNumber in a TimeSheet object and an Employee object is required. All the attributes in an object are private and therefore invisible to external objects. A public TimeSheet method, called getEmpNumber (EmpNumber), will be required to make the empNumber available to external objects. The 'get' in the method name, getEmpNumber( ), indicates that this method allows external objects to access private attributes. These are sometimes called *accessor methods*.

The object table for the TimeSheet object can now be updated to:

Object	Attributes	Methods
TimeSheet	empNumber payRate hoursWorked	+ readTimeSheet(validInput) + printTimeSheet( ) − validateInput(validInput) − calculatePay( ) + printPay(weeklyPay) + getEmpNumber(EmpNumber)

1.5 EmployeeStore Class

To avoid searching through all the employees whenever a time sheet is to be matched to an employee record, a new data structure (such as an array), called <u>EmployeeStore</u>, accessible by employee number, is required to store the Employee objects in memory.

A data structure can be contained in a single object. EmployeeStore will need methods to transfer Employee objects between secondary storage and memory, called readEmployees( ) and writeEmployees( ). It will also need a method, getEmployee( ), that uses an employee number to locate an employee in the structure.

The object table for EmployeeStore is as follows:

Object	Attributes	Methods
EmployeeStore	Employee	+ readEmployees( ) + writeEmployees( ) + getEmployee(empNumber)

The object table below shows the entire class structure for the program and highlights the advantages of object-oriented design for large programs. In spite of the substantially more complicated problem definition, the only work required is in the unshaded areas. The other parts of the program can be developed later or are already in place and hidden from us except when we need them.

Object	Attributes	Methods
TimeSheet	empNumber payRate hoursWorked	+ readTimeSheet( ) − calculatePay( ) − validateInput( ) + printPay(weeklyPay) + printTimeSheet( )
TimeSheet::ProgrammerTimeSheet TimeSheet::SalesRepTimeSheet	bonus sales	+ getEmpNumber(EmpNumber) + setBonus(projects) + setSales(sales) − calculateCommission(commission)
Projects Sales		+ earlyProjects(empNumber, numBonus) + getSales(empNumber, Sales)
EmployeeStore Employee	Employee empNumber ytdPay	+ readEmployees( ) + writeEmployees( ) + getEmployee(empNumber) + addWeeklyPay(weeklyPay)
	Details Status LeaveHistory	

Step 2: Determine the relationships between objects

In Step 1, ProgrammerTimeSheet and SalesRepTimeSheet classes were identified as types of TimeSheet. However, they are different from the TimeSheet class because they contain additional features or different ways of calculating values. ProgrammerTimeSheet and SalesRepTimeSheet are child classes of TimeSheet.

The ProgrammerTimeSheet and SalesRepTimeSheet classes will inherit their own copies of all attributes and methods in the TimeSheet class and augment them with some that specifically relate to their requirements. Notice in the object table that the child classes are shown next to the parent class, with the relationship indicated by the colon separating them.

An EmployeeStore object contains Employee objects. An Employee object contains Details, Status and LeaveHistory objects. Each of these objects encapsulates the data and methods required to perform their particular function, quite separate from the rest of the program. Because an Employee would be incomplete without each of these objects in its composition, the objects can be shown in UML notation as attributes with a capital letter, or as separate boxes, as follows:

Employee
empNumber ytdPay Details Status LeaveHistory
+ addWeeklyPay( )

Class diagram

It is useful to view a simple graphical representation of the relationships between the program's classes.

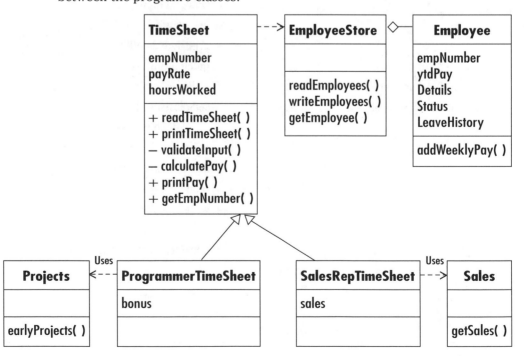

The open-headed arrows connecting TimeSheet to ProgrammerTimeSheet and SalesRepTimeSheet show the child–parent relationship. Notice that the diamond line connecting Employee and EmployeeStore is open rather than shaded. Employee class objects can exist independently of the EmployeeStore, perhaps in other parts of the program, but they are needed to make up EmployeeStore class objects.

Because the program needs to have communication between an EmployeeStore object and a TimeSheet object, regardless of which of the three types of TimeSheet is instantiated, the relationship is shown as a general case, with the parent class. The dashed arrows show that services can be provided by the classes pointed to.

This is a very simple representation of the classes in the program. By using all the features of UML a much more complete picture can be created. Because UML is a sophisticated modelling language it cannot be covered in detail in this book, but it is certainly worth exploring in more depth to further develop your object-oriented design skills.

Step 3: Design the algorithms for the methods using structured design

An algorithm is required for each method in the object table. However, the shaded parts of the object table have methods that already exist. So, the only methods that require algorithms are those unshaded in the object table.

3.1 TimeSheet Class

The method getEmpNumber( ) will return the private TimeSheet attribute empNumber to external objects. It simply returns a value attributed to a variable.

```
getEmpNumber(EmpNumber)
      EmpNumber = empNumber
END
```

The algorithm for printPay( ) will remain the same as in Example11.1, except that the algorithm will return the parameter weeklyPay.

```
printPay(weeklyPay)
      calculatePay(weeklyPay)
      Print weeklyPay
END
```

3.2 ProgrammerTimeSheet Class

Public methods

The ProgrammerTimeSheet object needs a constructor to create a ProgrammerTimeSheet object and to initialise the attribute, bonus.

```
ProgrammerTimeSheet( )
        inherit methods and attributes from TimeSheet
        set bonus to 0
END
```

The method setBonus( ) uses the public method earlyProjects( ) to help calculate the value, bonus. The constant PROJECT_BONUS is set at $50.00.

```
setBonus(projects)
        projects.earlyProjects(empNumber, numBonus)
        bonus = PROJECT_BONUS * numBonus
END
```

Private methods

All the information to calculate the pay for a programmer is available. Each ProgrammerTimeSheet object has the data, constants and methods inherited, because it is a type of TimeSheet object. It also contains bonus information specifically required for programmers.

However, the algorithm that has already been designed to calculate pay in normal TimeSheets does not include the programmer's bonus. A new method is required to calculate the pay for ProgrammerTimeSheets.

Using polymorphism, the calculatePay( ) method can be defined differently in the ProgrammerTimeSheet class, overriding the version inherited from its parent. Inside each ProgrammerTimeSheet object, the TimeSheet calculatePay( ) method will be replaced by the ProgrammerTimeSheet calculatePay( ) method.

```
calculatePay(pay)
        pay = (payRate * NORM_HOURS) + bonus
END
```

3.3   SalesRepTimeSheet Class

Public methods

A constructor is required to create a SalesRepTimeSheet object and to initialise the sales attribute.

```
SalesRepTimeSheet( )
        inherit attributes and methods from TimeSheet
        Set sales to 0
END
```

The method setSales( ) calls the public method, getSales( ), to return a sales value for the sales representative. The sales attribute will store the sales results used to calculate the commission.

```
setSales(sales)
        sales.getSales(empNumber, Sales)
        sales = Sales
END
```

Private methods

A method is required to calculate the commission for the sales representative, based on the sales attribute. MIN_SALES and MAX_SALES are the constants $10 000 and $19 999 respectively.

```
calculateCommission(commission)
    IF (sales < MIN_SALES) THEN
        commission = 0.0
    ELSE
        IF (MIN_SALES<=sales AND sales< MAX_SALES) THEN
            commission = 100.0
        ELSE
            IF (sales >= MAX_SALES) THEN
                commission = 200.0
            ENDIF
        ENDIF
    ENDIF
END
```

The method, calculatePay( ), inherited from the TimeSheet class will need to be changed for the SalesRepTimeSheet, to add the calculated commission to the pay calculation. Again, using polymorphism and method overriding, the calculatePay( ) method for the SalesRepTimeSheet replaces the inherited method.

```
calculatePay(weeklyPay, commission)
    IF hoursWorked <= NORM_HOURS THEN
        weeklyPay = (payRate * hoursWorked) + commission
    ELSE
        overtimeHours = hoursWorked − NORM_HOURS
        overtimePay = overtimeHours * payRate * 1.5
        weeklyPay = (payRate *  NORM_HOURS) + commission + overtimePay
    ENDIF
END
```

3.4   Employee Class

One algorithm is required for the public method, addWeeklyPay( ), where the weekly pay is to be added to year-to-date pay.

```
addWeeklyPay(weeklyPay)
    ytdPay = ytdPay + weeklyPay
END
```

3.5   EmployeeStore Class

There are three methods required to store the Employee details into temporary storage. Assuming that an array data structure is used, the algorithms for the methods of this class are straightforward and can be found in Chapter 7. The methods are:

readEmployees( )	Reads the Employee file into an array
getEmployee(empNumber)	Searches the array for employee details, using empNumber
writeEmployees( )	Writes the contents of the array to the Employee file.

Step 4: Design the mainline algorithm

Now that the new classes have been defined, structured design techniques as introduced in Chapter 8, are used to define the internal methods of the program, processTimeSheets.

A Define the problem

Input	Processing	Output
employee	Read Employee objects from file	timeSheet details
empType	Read empType, timeSheet	WeeklyPay
timeSheet	Validate input	employee
• empNumber	Calculate pay	
• hoursWorked	Print timeSheet details, pay	
• payRate	Add pay to employee ytd pay	
projects	Write Employee objects to file	
• numBonus		
sales		
• sales		

This defining diagram is similar to:

1 the defining diagram for the top-down solution to this problem, found in Chapter 8, Example 8.3, Compute employee's pay; and
2 the mainline algorithm for the previous simpler object-oriented payroll processing example 11.1, computePay, in Chapter 11.

However, there are two main differences. In this example:

1 The first item of payroll data encountered for each employee is the employee type. The processing of the rest of the payroll data in the timeSheet for that employee depends on which of the three types of employee it is: general employee, programmer or sales representative.
2 When the weekly pay has been calculated from the TimeSheet, it will be added to the year-to-date pay in that employee's Employee record. To allow employees to be processed from the file, the Employee objects will be read into an EmployeeStore object which will be responsible for locating each employee using the empNumber, updating the year-to-date pay with the weekly pay, then writing the object back to a file.

B Group the activities in the defining diagram to produce a hierarchy chart

The pre-existing modules are shaded and their descendants are not shown.

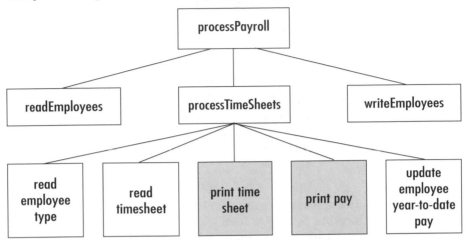

C Establish the logic of the mainline, using pseudocode

Notice that the top modules of the hierarchy chart provide the structure for a mainline. The mainline algorithm is:

```
processPayroll
      Create employeeStore as new EmployeeStore( )
      employeeStore.readEmployees( )
      processTimeSheets(employeeStore)
      employeeStore.writeEmployees( )
END
```

D Develop the pseudocode for each successive module in the hierarchy chart

Having designed the objects from the bottom up, then applied top-down design to the mainline algorithm, you have reached the intermediate level of the design. The following algorithm, processTimeSheets( ), calls all the successive modules in the hierarchy chart.

```
processTimeSheets(employeeStore)
      Set validInput to true
      Create timeSheet as new TimeSheet( )
      Read empType
      DOWHILE more records
            readTimeSheet(empType, validInput, timeSheet)
            IF validInput THEN
                  timeSheet.printTimeSheet( )
                  timeSheet.printPay(weeklyPay)
                  updateEmployee(employeeStore, timeSheet, weeklyPay)
            ENDIF
            Read empType
      ENDDO
END
```

If you look back at the algorithm for readTimeSheet in Chapter 11, you will see that it has one parameter, validInput. The version in the algorithm above has three parameters. This is an overloaded method, and will be the version run when a call is made with three parameters. The single-parameter version is called to validate the inputs to the timeSheet objects. The three-parameter version is called to create the object according to the employee type.

A direct call to the validateInput( ) method of a timeSheet object is not possible because it is a private method of the TimeSheet class. The algorithms for the two public methods developed in Chapter 11 are shown here:

```
readTimeSheet(validInput)
    Set validInput to true
    Read empNumber, payRate, hoursWorked
    validateInput(validInput)
END

validateInput(validInput):
    Set errorMessage to blank
    IF payRate > MAX_PAY THEN
        errorMessage = "Pay rate exceeds $25.00"
        Print errorMessage
        validInput = false
    ENDIF
    IF hoursWorked > MAX_HOURS THEN
        errorMessage = "Hours worked exceeds limit of 60"
        Print errorMessage
        validInput = false
    ENDIF
END
```

To calculate the pay for programmers and sales representatives we need information from the Projects and Sales classes. Therefore the overloaded readTimeSheet method also instantiates Projects and Sales objects from pre-existing classes. It can be assumed that the constructors for these classes make the data accessible to other classes.

```
readTimeSheet(empType, validInput, timeSheet)
    CASE OF empType
        E:  Create timeSheet as new TimeSheet( )
            timeSheet.readTimeSheet(validInput)

        P:  Create timeSheet as new ProgrammerTimeSheet( )
            Create projects as new Projects
            timeSheet.readTimeSheet(validInput)
            timeSheet.setBonus(projects)

        R:  Create timeSheet as new SalesRepTimeSheet( )
            Create sales as new Sales
            timeSheet.readTimeSheet(validInput)
            timeSheet.setSales(sales)
    END CASE
END
```

Each of the three different types of employee time sheets can use its inherited copy of readTimeSheet( ). Notice that polymorphism allows an identical method name to be used in different classes, including the class that contains the mainline algorithm. The method chosen will be determined by:

1   the number of parameters in the parameter list; and
2   the object name which precedes the method call.

Although the readTimeSheet( ) method in the mainline algorithm exists, the programmer and sales representative TimeSheet objects can still use their own individual methods.

Finally, write the algorithm for the method, updateEmployee( ), which updates the employee's year-to-date pay with the calculated weekly pay.

```
updateEmployee(employeeStore, timeSheet, weeklyPay)
    timeSheet.getEmpNumber(EmpNumber)
    employeeStore.getEmployee(empNumber, employee)
    employee.addWeeklyPay(weeklyPay)
END
```

12.3 CHAPTER SUMMARY

Most object-oriented programs need more than one class. Classes can be related to each other through use, by inheritance (being a subtype of a class), or by composition (being part of another class).

When classes are related by inheritance, all subclasses or child classes inherit the attributes and methods of the parent class and supplement them with attributes and methods needed by the subtype.

Through polymorphism, several methods may have the same name.

Using method overriding, a child class may substitute the parent class version of a method with its own specific version. With method overloading, several methods of the same name may have different numbers of parameters and different algorithms.

There are four steps in analysing a multiple class problem: identify the objects and the methods to be performed; determine the relationship between the objects; design the algorithms for the methods using structured design; and develop the mainline algorithm.

12.4 PROGRAMMING PROBLEMS

1   Draw a class diagram to show the relationship between the classes designed in your solution to Programming Problem 7 in Chapter 11. The solution should include at least a book class, a patron class, and a book loan class. Write any method algorithms needed to complete the solution.

2   Prepare the mainline algorithm for Programming Problem 7 in Chapter 11, based on your solution classes.

3   The library loan system in Programming Problem 7, Chapter 11 needs to be able to accommodate non-book loans, such as video, tapes and magazines. Magazines have a title, an ISSN rather than an ISBN, a volume and number, publisher, publication date, call number and a unique accession number. Videotapes have a title, publisher, publication date, call number and a unique accession number. Overdue videotapes are charged at $2 per day. Modify your solution design accordingly, including the class diagram, object tables and algorithms where necessary.

4   Yummy Chocolates requires an object-oriented program for an online catalogue. The catalogue is to display the details of the range of handmade chocolates. Each chocolate product has a product code, a name, a picture and the price per 100 grams. Products can be added to the catalogue, deleted and modified.

Design this program, preparing object tables, a class diagram and algorithms for the methods. Write a mainline algorithm.

Conclusion

OBJECTIVES

* Revision of the steps required to achieve good top-down program design

OUTLINE

13.1   Simple program design
13.2   Chapter summary

13.1 SIMPLE PROGRAM DESIGN

The aim of this textbook has been to encourage programmers to follow a series of simple steps in order to develop solution algorithms to given programming problems. These steps are:

1 Define the problem. To do this, underline the nouns and verbs in the problem description. This helps to divide the problem into its input, output and processing components. These components can be represented in a defining diagram — a table that lists the inputs to the problem, the expected outputs, and the processing steps required to produce these outputs.

At this stage you should be concerned only with *what* needs to be done. When writing down the processing components, simply list the activities to be performed without being concerned about how to perform them.

2 Group the activities into subtasks or functions. To do this, look at the defining diagram and group the activities in the processing component into separate tasks. There are often several activities listed in the processing component, all of which contribute to the performance of a single task. These separate tasks are called functions. By grouping the activities together to form subtasks, you are establishing the major functions of the problem.

Not all the activities to be performed may have been listed in the defining diagram. If the problem is large, only the top-level subtasks may have been identified at this stage. The basic aim of top-down design is to develop the higher-level modules first, and to develop the lower-level modules only when the higher-level modules have been established. You should concentrate on these higher-level functions before attempting to consider further subordinate functions.

3 Construct a hierarchy chart. To do this, study the defining diagram, which now has the major tasks identified in it, and illustrate these tasks or functions on a hierarchy chart. The functions identified on the hierarchy chart will become the future modules of the program.

The hierarchy chart shows not only the modules of the program, but also their relationship to each other, in a similar fashion to the organisational chart of a large company.

Just as a company director can change the organisation of the company to suit its operation, so you can change the organisation of the modules in the hierarchy chart. It is good programming practice to study the way the modules have been organised in the overall structure of the program, and to attempt to make this structure as simple and top-down as possible.

Note that you are still only concerned with the tasks that are to be performed. Once the hierarchical structure of the algorithm has been developed, you can begin to consider the logic of the solution.

4 Establish the logic of the mainline of the algorithm. Use pseudocode and the three basic control structures to establish this logic. Pseudocode is a subset of English that has been formalised and abbreviated to look like a high-level computer language. Keywords and indentation are used to signify particular control structures. The three basic control structures are simple sequence, selection and repetition.

Because you will have already identified the major functions of the problem, you can now use pseudocode and the three control structures to develop the mainline logic. The mainline should show the main processing functions of the problem and the order in which they are to be performed.

We saw that the mainline for most algorithms follows the same basic pattern. This pattern contains some initial processing before the loop, some processing of the record within the loop, and some final processing after exiting the loop.

Chapter 10 developed general algorithms for four common business applications. These algorithms were for the generation of a report with a page break, a single-level control break program, a multiple-level control break program and a sequential file update program. The algorithms that were developed have good program structure and high modular cohesion, and you should use these algorithms as a guide for specific programming problems.

5 Develop the pseudocode for each successive module in the hierarchy chart. The algorithms for these modules should be developed in a top-down fashion. That is, the pseudocode for each module on the first level should be established, before attempting the pseudocode for the modules on the next or lower level. The modularisation process is complete when the pseudocode for each module on the lowest level of the hierarchy chart has been developed.

6 Desk check the solution algorithm. By desk checking the algorithm, you attempt to find any logic errors that may have crept into the solution.

Desk checking involves tracing through the logic of the algorithm with some chosen test data exactly as the computer would operate. The programmer keeps track of all major variables in a table as he or she walks through the algorithm. At the end of the desk check, the programmer checks that the output expected from the test data matches the output developed in the desk check.

This detection of errors, early in the design process, can save many frustrating hours during the testing phase. This is because when the programmer begins coding, he or she assumes that the logic of the algorithms is correct. Then, when errors occur, the programmer usually concentrates on the individual lines of code, rather than the initial logic expressed in the algorithm.

It is essential that the programmer desk checks the solution algorithm, yet this step is so often ignored. Most programmers who bypass this step do so because they either assume the algorithm is correct, or because they believe desk checking is not creative. While it may not be as stimulating as the original design phase, it is really just as satisfying to know that the logic is correct.

13.2 CHAPTER SUMMARY

This chapter has revised the steps required to achieve good top-down program design. Program design is considered good if it is easy to read and understand and easy to alter.

If you follow these six steps in the development of an algorithm, you will rapidly achieve a high level of competence.

Flowcharts

Outline

- Introduction to flowcharts and the three basic control structures
- Simple algorithms that use the sequence control structure
- Flowcharts and the selection control structure
- Simple algorithms that use the selection control structure
- The case structure, expressed as a flowchart
- Flowcharts and the repetition control structure
- Simple algorithms that use the repetition control structure
- Flowcharts and modules

This appendix introduces flowcharts as an alternative method of representing algorithms because many courses require students to be proficient in more than one algorithm design technique. Flowcharts are popular because they graphically represent the program logic through a series of standard geometric symbols and lines connected according to the logic of the algorithm. Flowcharts are relatively easy to learn and are an intuitive method of representing the flow of control in an algorithm. For simplicity, just six standard flowchart symbols will be used to represent algorithms in this text. These are:

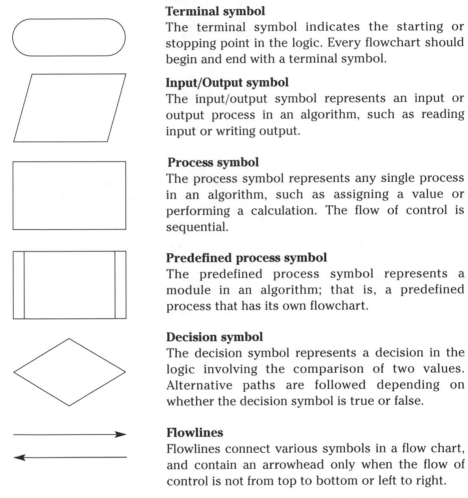

Terminal symbol
The terminal symbol indicates the starting or stopping point in the logic. Every flowchart should begin and end with a terminal symbol.

Input/Output symbol
The input/output symbol represents an input or output process in an algorithm, such as reading input or writing output.

Process symbol
The process symbol represents any single process in an algorithm, such as assigning a value or performing a calculation. The flow of control is sequential.

Predefined process symbol
The predefined process symbol represents a module in an algorithm; that is, a predefined process that has its own flowchart.

Decision symbol
The decision symbol represents a decision in the logic involving the comparison of two values. Alternative paths are followed depending on whether the decision symbol is true or false.

Flowlines
Flowlines connect various symbols in a flow chart, and contain an arrowhead only when the flow of control is not from top to bottom or left to right.

In this appendix the three basic control structures, as set out in the Structure Theorem in pseudocode, will be explained and illustrated using flowcharts.

THE THREE BASIC CONTROL STRUCTURES

1 Sequence

The sequence control structure is defined as the straightforward execution of one processing step after another. A flowchart represents this control structure as a series of process symbols, one beneath the other, with one entrance and one exit.

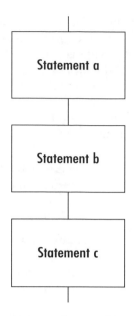

The sequence control structure can be used to represent the first four basic computer operations; namely, to receive information, put out information, perform arithmetic, and assign values. For example, a typical sequence of statements in an flowchart might read:

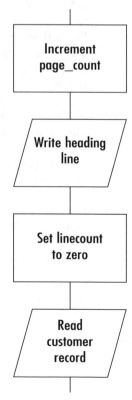

These instructions illustrate the sequence control structure as a straightforward list of steps, written one after the other, in a top-to-bottom fashion. Each instruction will be executed in the order in which it appears.

2 Selection

The selection control structure can be defined as the presentation of a condition, and the choice between two actions depending on whether the condition is true or false. This construct represents the decision-making abilities of the computer, and is used to illustrate the fifth basic computer operation, namely, to compare two variables and select one of two alternate actions. A flowchart represents the selection control structure with a decision symbol, with one line entering at the top, and two lines leaving it, following the true path or false path, depending on the condition. These two lines then join up at the end of the selection structure.

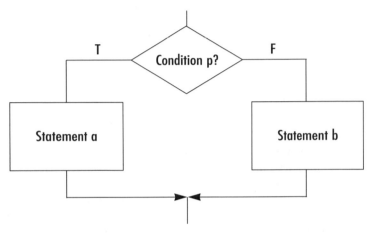

If condition p is true, the statement or statements in the true path will be executed. If condition p is false, the statement or statements in the false path will be executed. Both paths then join up to the flowline following the selection control structure. A typical flowchart might look like this:

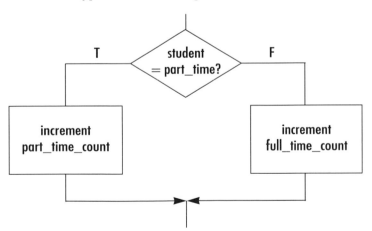

A variation of the selection control structure is the null ELSE structure, which is used when a task is performed only if a particular condition is true. The flowchart that represents the null ELSE construct has no processing in the false path.

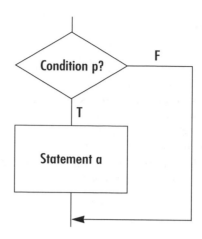

3 Repetition

The repetition control structure can be defined as the presentation of a set of instructions to be performed repeatedly, as long as a condition is true. The basic idea of repetitive code is that a block of statements is executed again and again, until a terminating condition occurs. This construct represents the sixth basic computer operation, namely, to repeat a group of actions. A flowchart represents this structure as a decision symbol and one or more process symbols to be performed while a condition is true. A flowline then takes the flow of control back to the condition in the decision symbol, which is tested before the process is repeated.

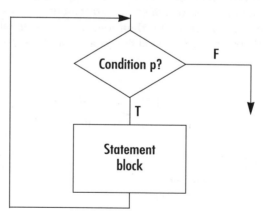

While condition p is true, the statements inside the process symbol will be executed. The flowline then returns control upwards to retest condition p. When condition p is false, control will pass out of the repetition structure down the false path to the next statement. We will now look at a flowchart that represents the repetition control structure:

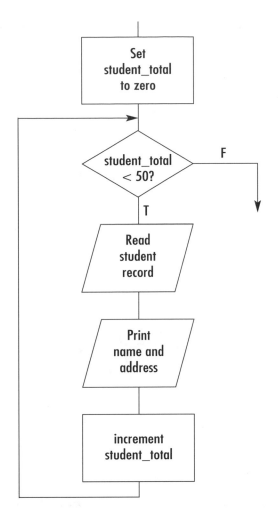

SIMPLE ALGORITHMS THAT USE THE SEQUENCE CONTROL STRUCTURE

The following examples are the same as those represented by pseudocode in Chapter 3. In each example, the problem is defined and a solution algorithm developed using a flowchart. For ease in defining the problem, the processing verbs in each example have been underlined.

Example 3.1 *Add three numbers*

A program is required to <u>read</u> three numbers, <u>add</u> them <u>together</u> and <u>print</u> their total.

A *Defining diagram*

Input	Processing	Output
number_1	Read three numbers	total
number_2	Add numbers together	
number_3	Print total number	

B Solution algorithm

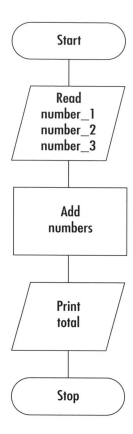

Example 3.2 *Find average temperature*

A program is required to <u>prompt</u> the terminal operator for the maximum and minimum temperature readings on a particular day, <u>accept</u> those readings as integers, and <u>calculate</u> and <u>display</u> to the screen the average temperature.

A Defining diagram

Input	Processing	Output
max_temp min_temp	Prompt for temperatures Get max, min temperatures Calculate average temperature Display average temperature	avg_temp

B Solution algorithm

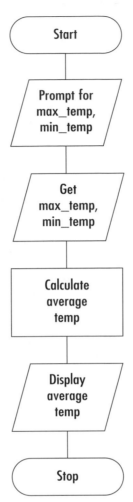

Example 3.3 *Calculate mowing time*

A program is required to <u>read</u> in the length and width of a rectangular house block, and the length and width of the rectangular house that has been built on the block. The algorithm should then <u>compute</u> and <u>display</u> the time required to cut the grass around the house, at the rate of 2 square metres per minute.

A *Defining diagram*

Input	Processing	Output
block_length	Prompt for block measurements	mowing_time
block_width	Get block measurements	
house_length	Prompt for house measurements	
house_width	Get house measurements	
	Calculate mowing area	
	Calculate mowing time	

B Solution algorithm

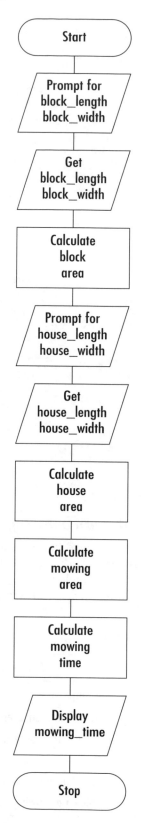

Start

Prompt for
block_length
block_width

Get
block_length
block_width

Calculate
block
area

Prompt for
house_length
house_width

Get
house_length
house_width

Calculate
house
area

Calculate
mowing
area

Calculate
mowing
time

Display
mowing_time

Stop

FLOWCHARTS AND THE SELECTION CONTROL STRUCTURE

Each variation of the selection control structure developed in Chapter 4 in pseudocode can similarly be represented by a flowchart.

Simple IF statement

Simple selection occurs when a choice is made between two alternative paths, depending on the result of a condition being true or false. This structure is represented in a flowchart as follows:

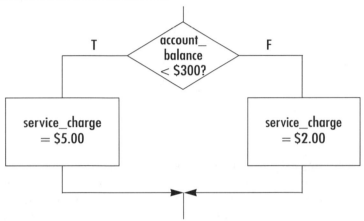

Only one of the true or false paths will be followed, depending on the result of the condition in the decision symbol.

Null ELSE statement

The null ELSE structure is a variation of the simple IF structure. It is used when a task is performed only when a particular condition is true. If the condition is false, no processing will take place, and the IF statement will be bypassed. For example:

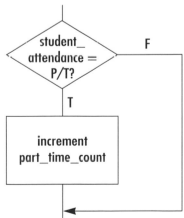

In this case, the part_time_count field will only be altered if the true path is followed; that is, when the student's attendance pattern is part time.

Combined IF statement

A combined IF statement is one that contains multiple conditions in the decision symbol, each connected with the logical operators AND or OR. If the conditions are combined with the connector AND, both conditions must be true for the combined condition to be true. For example:

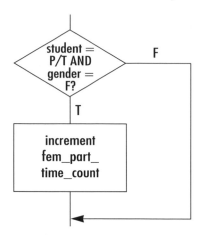

In this case, each student record will undergo two tests. Only those students who are female, and whose attendance pattern is part time, will be selected, and the variable fem_part_time_count will be incremented. If either condition is found to be false, the counter will remain unchanged.

Nested IF statement

The nested IF statement is used when a field is being tested for various values, with a different action to be taken for each value. In a flowchart, this is represented by a series of decision symbols, as follows.

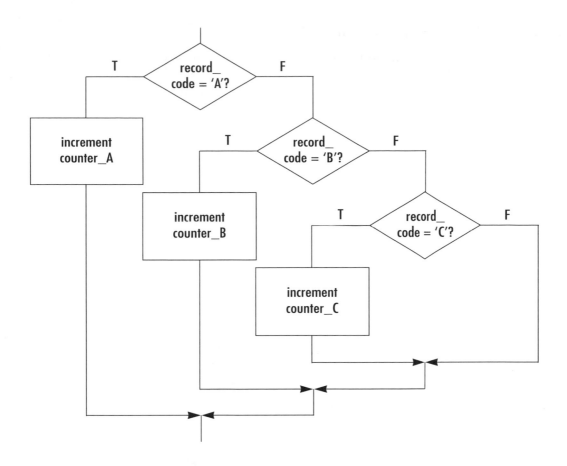

SIMPLE ALGORITHMS THAT USE THE SELECTION CONTROL STRUCTURE

The following examples are the same as those represented by pseudocode in Chapter 4. In each example, the problem is defined and a solution algorithm developed using a flowchart. For ease in defining the problem, the processing verbs in each example have been underlined.

Example 4.1 *Read three characters*

Design an algorithm that will <u>prompt</u> a terminal operator for three characters, <u>accept</u> those characters as input, <u>sort</u> them into ascending sequence and <u>output</u> them to the screen.

A *Defining diagram*

Input	Processing	Output
char_1	Prompt for characters	char_1
char_2	Accept three characters	char_2
char_3	Sort three characters	char_3
	Output three characters	

B Solution algorithm

The solution algorithm requires a series of decision symbols to sort the three characters into ascending sequence.

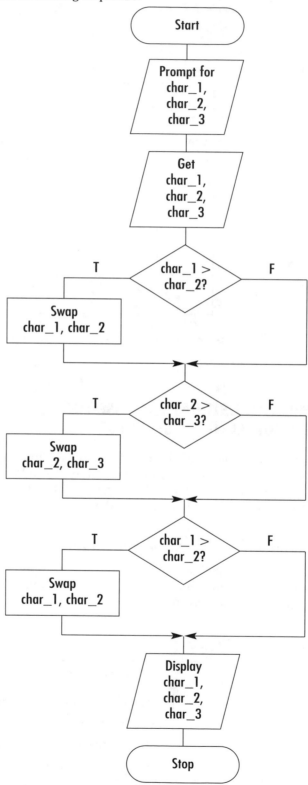

Example 4.2 *Process customer record*

A programmer is required to <u>read</u> a customer's name, a purchase amount and a tax code. The tax code has been validated and will be one of the following:

0 tax exempt (0%)
1 State sales tax only (3%)
2 Federal and state sales tax (5%)
3 Special sales tax (7%)

   The program is required to <u>compute</u> the sales tax and the total amount due, and <u>print</u> the customer's name, purchase amount, sales tax and total amount due.

A Defining diagram

Input	Processing	Output
cust_name	Read customer details	cust_name
purch_amt	Compute sales tax	purch_amt
tax_code	Compute total amount	sales_tax
	Print customer details	total_amt

B Solution algorithm

The solution algorithm requires a nested IF statement to calculate the sales tax.

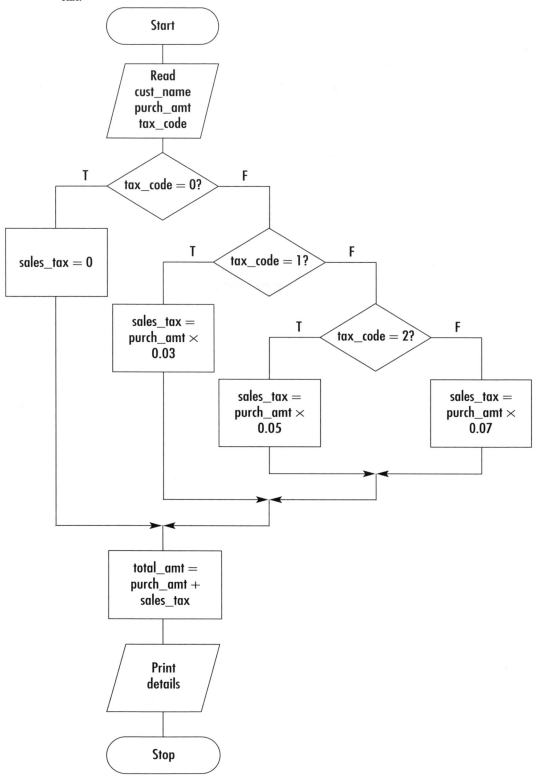

Example 4.3 *Calculate employee's pay*

A program is required by a company to <u>read</u> an employee's number, pay rate and the number of hours worked in a week. The program is then to <u>compute</u> the employee's weekly pay and <u>print</u> it along with the input data.

According to the company's rules, no employee may be paid for more than 60 hours per week, and the maximum hourly rate is $25.00 per hour. If more than 35 hours are worked, payment for the overtime hours worked is calculated at time and a half. If the hours worked field or the hourly rate field is out of range, the input data and an appropriate message are to be <u>printed</u> and the employee's weekly pay is not to be calculated.

A *Defining diagram*

Input	Processing	Output
emp_no	Read employee details	emp_no
pay_rate	Validate input fields	pay_rate
hrs_worked	Calculate employee pay	hrs_worked
	Print employee details	emp_weekly_pay
		error_message

B *Solution algorithm*

The solution to this problem will require a series of simple IF and nested IF statements. First, the variables pay_rate and hrs_worked must be validated, and if either is found to be out of range, an appropriate message should be printed.

The employee's weekly pay is only to be calculated if the variables pay_rate and hrs_worked are valid, so another variable valid_input_fields will be used to indicate to the program whether or not these input fields are valid.

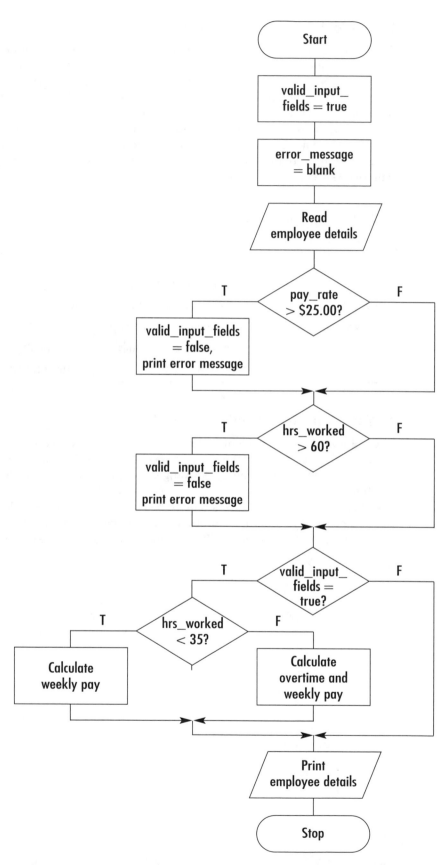

THE CASE STRUCTURE EXPRESSED AS A FLOWCHART

The case control structure is another way of expressing a nested IF statement. It is not really an additional control structure; but one that extends the basic selection control structure to be a choice between multiple values. It is expressed in a flowchart by a decision symbol with a number of paths leading from it, depending on the value of the variable, as follows:

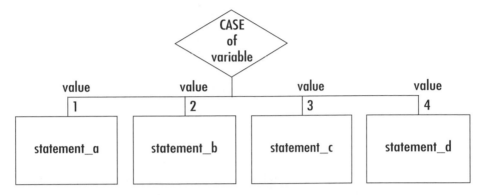

Let us now look again at Example 4.2. The solution algorithm for this example was earlier expressed as a nested IF statement. However, it could equally have been expressed as a CASE statement.

Example 4.4 *Process customer record*

A programmer is required to <u>read</u> a customer's name, a purchase amount and a tax code. The tax code has been validated and will be one of the following:

0 tax exempt (0%)
1 State sales tax only (3%)
2 Federal and state sales tax (5%)
3 Special sales tax (7%)

The program is required to <u>compute</u> the sales tax and the total amount due and <u>print</u> the customer's name, purchase amount, sales tax and total amount due.

A *Defining diagram*

Input	Processing	Output
cust_name	Read customer details	cust_name
purch_amt	Compute sales tax	purch_umt
tax_code	Compute total amount	sales_tax
	Print customer details	total_amt

B Solution algorithm

The solution algorithm will be expressed using a CASE statement.

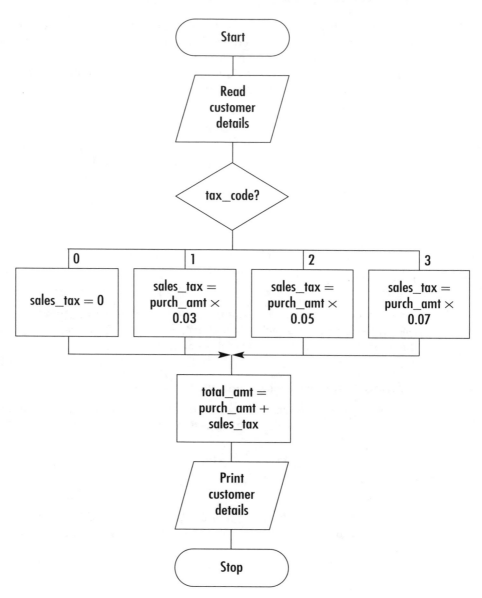

FLOWCHARTS AND THE REPETITION CONTROL STRUCTURE

In Chapter 5 the DOWHILE construct was introduced as the pseudocode representation of a repetition loop. This can be represented in a flowchart as follows:

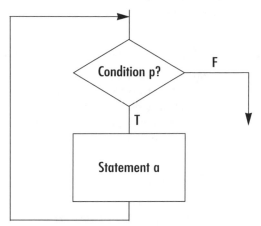

As the DOWHILE loop is a leading decision loop, the following processing takes place:

a The logical condition p is tested.
b If condition p is found to be true, the statements that follow the true path will be executed once. Control will then return upwards to the retesting of condition p (Step a).
c If condition p is found to be false, control will follow the false path.

As a result, the DOWHILE structure will continue to repeat a group of statements WHILE a condition remains true. As soon as the condition becomes false, the construct is exited.

There are two important considerations about which a programmer must be aware before designing a DOWHILE loop.

First, the testing of the condition is at the beginning of the loop. This means that the programmer may need to perform some initial processing to set up the condition adequately before it can be tested.

Second, the only way to terminate the loop is to render the DOWHILE condition false. This means that the programmer must set up some process within the repeated processing symbols that will eventually change the condition so that the condition becomes false. Failure to do this may result in an endless loop.

SIMPLE ALGORITHMS THAT USE THE REPETITION CONTROL STRUCTURE

The following examples are the same as those represented by pseudocode in Chapter 5. In each example, the problem is defined and a solution algorithm developed using a flowchart. For ease in defining the problem, the processing verbs in each example have been underlined.

Example 5.1 *Fahrenheit–Celsius conversion*

Every day, a weather station receives 15 temperatures expressed in degrees Fahrenheit. A program is to be written to <u>accept</u> each Fahrenheit temperature, <u>convert</u> it to Celsius and <u>display</u> the converted temperature to the screen. After 15 temperatures have been processed, the words 'All temperatures processed' are to be <u>displayed</u> to the screen.

A *Defining diagram*

Input	Processing	Output
f_temp (15 temperatures)	Get Fahrenheit temperatures Convert temperatures Display Celsius temperatures Display screen message	c_temp (15 temperatures)

Note that the defining diagram still only lists what needs to be done; the equation to convert the temperature will not need to be known until the algorithm is developed.

Having defined the input, output and processing, the programmer should now be ready to outline a solution to the problem. This can be done by writing down the control structures needed and any extra variables to be used in the solution algorithm. In this example, the programmer will need:

- a DOWHILE structure to repeat the necessary processing, and
- a counter, initialised at zero, that will control the fifteen repetitions. This counter, called temperature_count, will contain the number of temperatures read and processed.

The programmer should now write down the solution algorithm.

B Solution algorithm

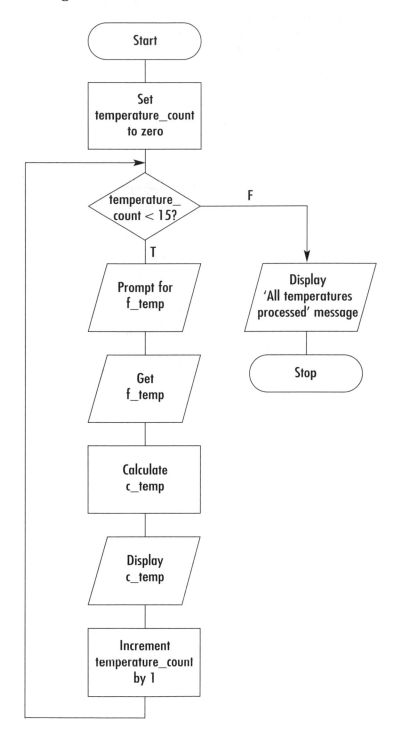

Example 5.2 *Print examination scores*

A program is required to <u>read</u> and <u>print</u> a series of names and exam scores for students enrolled in a mathematics course. The class average is to be <u>computed</u> and <u>printed</u> at the end of the report. Scores can range from 0 to 100. The last record contains a blank name and a score of 999, and is not to be included in the calculations.

A Defining diagram

Input	Processing	Output
name exam_score	Read student details Print student details Compute average score Print average_score	name exam_score average_score

The programmer will need to consider the following requirements when establishing a solution algorithm:

- a DOWHILE structure to control the reading of exam scores, until it reaches a score of 999
- an accumulator for total scores, viz total_score
- an accumulator for the total students, viz total_students.

B Solution algorithm

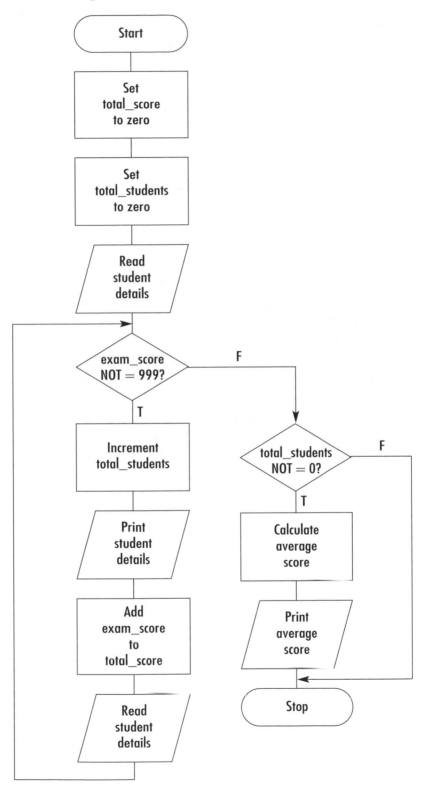

Example 5.3 *Process student enrolments*

A program is required to <u>read</u> a file of student records, and <u>select</u> and <u>print</u> only those students enrolled in a course unit named Programming I. Each student record contains student number, name, address, postcode, gender and course unit number. The course unit number for Programming I is 18500. Three totals are to be <u>printed</u> at the end of the report: total females enrolled in the course; total males enrolled in the course, and total students enrolled in the course.

A *Defining diagram*

Input	Processing	Output
student_record	Read student records	selected student records
• student_no	Select student records	totals
• name	Print selected records	
• address	Compute total females enrolled	
• postcode	Compute total males enrolled	
• gender	Compute total student enrolled	
• course_unit	Print totals	

The programmer will need to consider the following requirements, when establishing a solution algorithm:

- a DOWHILE structure to perform the repetition
- an IF statement to select the required students, and
- accumulators for the three total fields.

It should be noted that there is no trailer record for this student file. In cases like this, the terms more data, more records, records exist, or, not end of file (EOF) can be used in the decision symbol.

B Solution algorithm

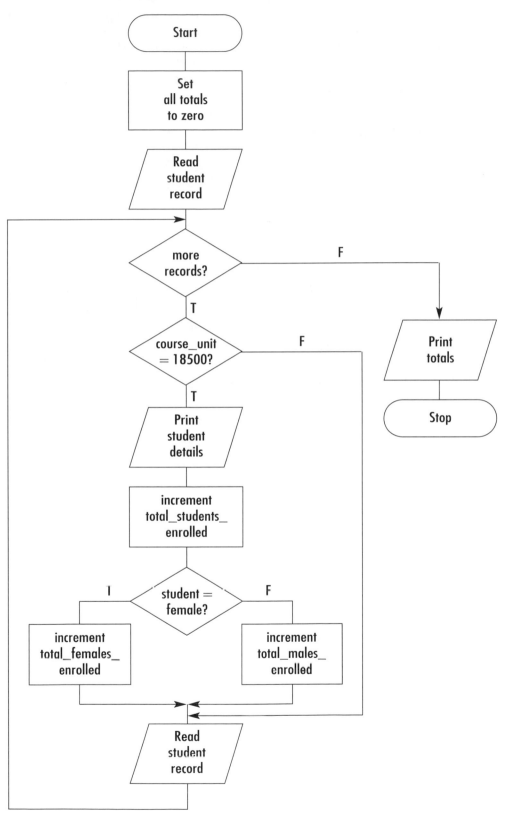

Example 5.4 *Process inventory items*

A program is required to <u>read</u> a series of inventory records that contain item number, item description and stock figure. The last record in the file has an item number of zero. The program is to <u>produce</u> a 'Low Stock Items' report, by <u>printing</u> only those records that have a stock figure of less than 20 items. A heading is to <u>print</u> at the top of the report and a total low stock item count to <u>print</u> at the end.

A Defining diagram

Input	Processing	Output
inventory record • item_number • item_description • stock_figure	Read inventory records Select low stock items Print low stock records Print total low stock items	heading selected records • item_number • item_description • stock_figure total_low_stock_items

The programmer will need to consider the following requirements when establishing a solution algorithm:

- a DOWHILE structure to perform the repetition
- an IF statement to select stock figures of less than 20, and
- an accumulator for total_low_stock_items.

B Solution algorithm

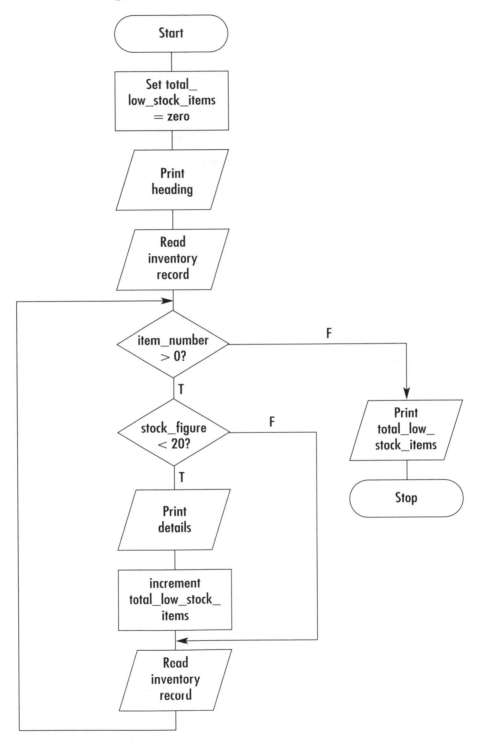

FLOWCHARTS AND MODULES

When designing a modular solution to a problem, using a flowchart, the predefined process symbol is used to designate a process or module. This keeps flowcharts simple, because, as in pseudocode, the main flowchart contains the name of the process, or module, and each process has its own separate flowchart.

Let's look at an example from Chapter 8, to see how a flowchart can represent modules.

Example 8.1 *Read three characters*

Design a solution algorithm that will prompt a terminal operator for three characters, accept those characters as input, sort them into ascending sequence and output them to the screen. The algorithm is to continue to read characters until 'XXX' is entered.

A *Defining diagram*

Input	Processing	Output
char_1	Prompt for characters	char_1
char_2	Accept three characters	char_2
char_3	Sort three characters	char_3
	Output three characters	

B *Hierarchy chart*

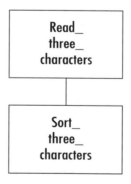

C *Solution algorithm using a predefined process symbol*

The flowchart solution consists of two flowcharts; a main flowchart called Read_three_characters and a process flowchart called Sort_three_characters. When the main flowchart wants to pass control to its process module, it simply names that process in a predefined process symbol. Control then passes to the process flowchart, and when the processing in that flowchart is complete, the module will pass control back to the main flowchart. The solution flowchart is simple and easy to read.

Read_three_characters

Sort_three_characters

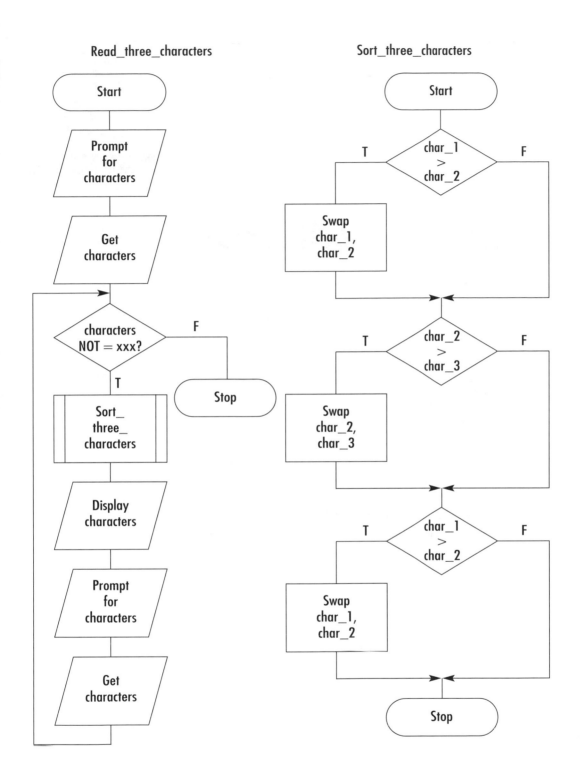

Nassi–Schneiderman diagrams

Outline

- The three basic control structures
- Simple algorithms that use the sequence control structure
- N-S diagrams and the selection control structure
- Simple algorithms that use the selection control structure
- The case structure expressed as an N-S diagram
- N-S diagrams and the repetition control structure
- Simple algorithms that use the repetition control structure

This appendix offers Nassi-Schneiderman diagrams as a third method of representing algorithms because they offer a diagrammatic approach to algorithm design but are not as bulky to draw as flowcharts. Nassi-Schneiderman diagrams use pseudocode-like text in rectangular boxes for those who prefer a more visual method of representing algorithm design than pseudocode.

In this appendix, the three basic control structures, as set out in the Structure Theorem, will be explained and illustrated using Nassi-Schneiderman diagrams.

THE THREE BASIC CONTROL STRUCTURES

1 Sequence

The sequence control structure is the straightforward execution of one processing step after another. An N-S diagram represents this control structure as a series of rectangular boxes, one beneath the other:

statement a
statement b
statement c

The sequence control structure can be used to represent the first four basic computer operations: receive information, put out information, perform arithmetic, and assign values. For example, a typical sequence of statements in an N-S diagram might read:

Add 1 to page_count
Write heading line
Set linecount to zero
Read customer record

These instructions illustrate the sequence control structure as a straightforward list of steps, written one after the other, in a top-to-bottom fashion. Each instruction will be executed in the order in which it appears.

2 Selection

The selection control structure is the presentation of a condition, and the choice between two actions depending on whether the condition is true or false. This construct represents the decision-making abilities of the computer and is used to illustrate the fifth basic computer operation, namely to compare two variables and select one of two alternative actions. An N-S diagram represents the selection control structure pictorially as the testing of a condition which can lead to two separate paths:

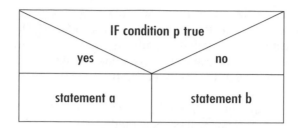

IF condition p is true, the statement or statements in the yes box will be executed. If condition p is false, the statement or statements in the no box will be executed. Both paths then lead to the next box following the selection control structure. A typical N-S diagram might look like this:

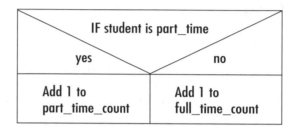

A variation of the selection control structure is the null ELSE structure, which is used when a task is performed only if a particular condition is true. The N-S diagram that represents the null ELSE construct simply leaves the 'no' box blank, or includes the words 'no action' in that box.

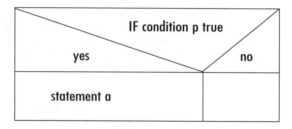

3 Repetition

The repetition control structure can be defined as the presentation of a set of instructions to be performed repeatedly, as long as a condition is true. The basic idea of repetitive code is that a block of statements is executed again and again, until a terminating condition occurs. This construct represents the sixth basic computer operation, namely to repeat a group of actions. An N-S diagram represents this structure as one rectangular box inside an L-shaped frame:

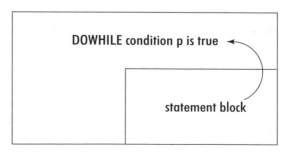

While condition p is true, the statements inside the rectangular box will be executed. The last line of the box acts as the delimiter, and returns control to retest condition p (see up arrow). When condition p is false, control will pass out of the repetition structure down the false path to the next statement (see down arrow).

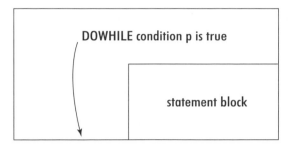

This N-S diagram represents the repetition control structure:

Set student_total to zero
DOWHILE student_total < 50
Read student record Write student name, address to report Add 1 to student_total

SIMPLE ALGORITHMS THAT USE THE SEQUENCE CONTROL STRUCTURE

The following examples are the same as those represented by pseudocode in Chapter 3. In each example, the problem is defined and a solution algorithm developed using a Nassi-Schneiderman diagram. To help define the problem, the processing verbs in each example have been underlined.

Example 3.1 *Add three numbers*

A program is required to <u>read</u> three numbers, <u>add</u> them <u>together</u> and <u>print</u> their total.

A Defining diagram

Input	Processing	Output
number_1 number_2 number_3	Read three numbers Add numbers together Print total number	total

B Solution algorithm

Add_three_numbers

Read number_1, number_2, number_3
total = number_1 + number_2 + number_3
Print total

Example 3.2 *Find average temperature*

A program is required to <u>prompt</u> the terminal operator for the maximum and minimum temperature readings on a particular day, <u>accept</u> those readings as integers, and <u>calculate</u> and <u>display</u> to the screen the simple average temperature [(maximum + minimum/2)].

A Defining diagram

Input	Processing	Output
max_temp min_temp	Prompt for temperatures Get max, min temperatures Calculate average temperature Display average temperature	avg_temp

B Solution algorithm

Find_average_temperature

Prompt operator for max_temp, min_temp
Get max_temp, min_temp
avg_temp = (max_temp + min_temp)/2
Output avg_temp to the screen

Example 3.3 *Calculate mowing time*

A program is required to <u>read</u> in the length and width of a rectangular house block, and the length and width of the rectangular house that has been built on the block. The algorithm should then <u>compute</u> and <u>display</u> the time required to cut the grass around the house, at the rate of two square metres per minute.

A Defining diagram

Input	Processing	Output
block_length block_width house_length house_width	Prompt for block measurements Get block measurements Prompt for house measurements Get house measurements Calculate mowing area Calculate mowing time	mowing_time

B Solution algorithm

Calculate_mowing_time

Prompt operator for block_length, block_width
Get block_length, block_width
block_area = block_length * block_width
Prompt operator for house_length, house_width
Get house_length, house_width
house_area = house_length * house_width
mowing_area = block_area − house_area
mowing_time = mowing_area/2
Output mowing_time to screen

N-S DIAGRAMS AND THE SELECTION CONTROL STRUCTURE

Each variation of the selection control structure developed with pseudocode in Chapter 4 can similarly be represented using a Nassi-Schneiderman diagram.

Simple IF statement

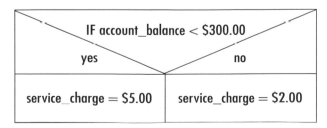

Null ELSE statement

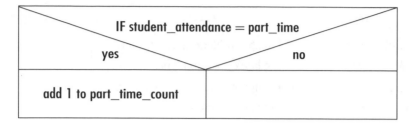

Combined IF statement

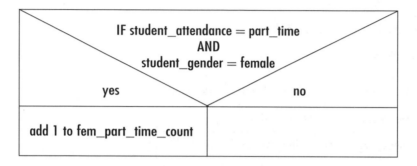

Nested IF statement

A Linear nested IF statement

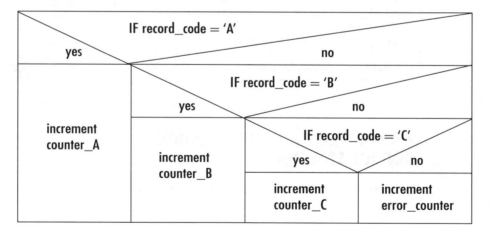

B Non-linear nested IF statement

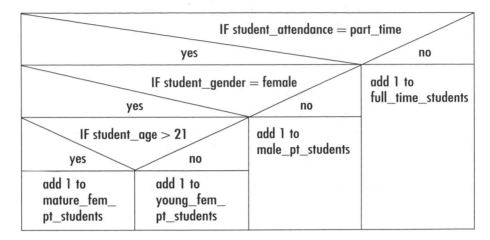

SIMPLE ALGORITHMS THAT USE THE SELECTION CONTROL STRUCTURE

The following examples are the same as those represented by pseudocode in Chapter 4. In each example, the problem is defined and a solution algorithm developed using a Nassi-Schneiderman diagram. The processing verbs in each example have been underlined.

Example 4.1 *Read three characters*

Design an algorithm that will <u>prompt</u> a terminal operator for three characters, <u>accept</u> those characters as input, <u>sort</u> them into ascending sequence and <u>output</u> them to the screen.

A *Defining diagram*

Input	Processing	Output
char_1	Prompt for characters	char_1
char_2	Accept three characters	char_2
char_3	Sort three characters	char_3
	Output three characters	

B Solution algorithm

The solution algorithm requires a series of IF statements to sort the three characters into ascending sequence.

Read_three_characters

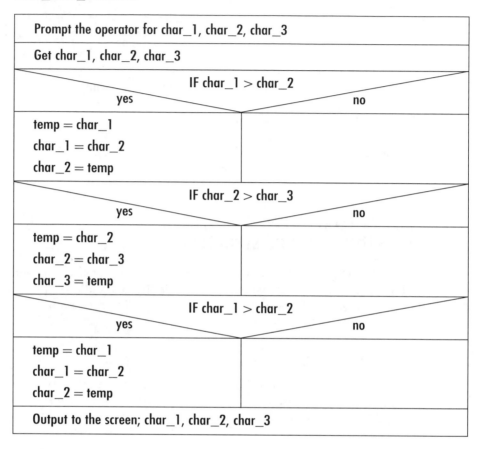

Example 4.2 *Process customer record*

A program is required to <u>read</u> a customer's name, a purchase amount and a tax code. The tax code has been validated and will be one of the following:

0   tax exempt (0%)
1   state sales tax only (3%)
2   federal and state sales tax (5%)
3   special sales tax (7%)

The program must then <u>compute</u> the sales tax and the total amount due and <u>print</u> the customer's name, purchase amount, sales tax, and total amount due.

A Defining diagram

Input	Processing	Output
cust_name	Read customer details	cust_name
purch_amt	Compute sales tax	purch_amt
tax_code	Compute total amount	sales_tax
	Print customer details	total_amt

B Solution algorithm

The solution algorithm requires a linear nested IF statement to calculate the sales tax.

Process_customer_record

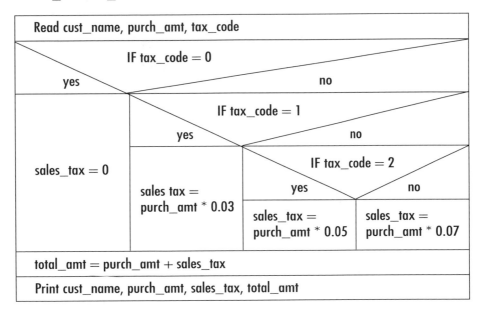

Example 4.3 *Calculate employee's pay*

A program is required by a company to <u>read</u> an employee's number, pay rate and the number of hours worked in a week. The program is then to <u>compute</u> the employee's weekly pay and <u>print</u> it along with the input data.

According to the company's rules, no employee may be paid for more than 60 hours per week, and the maximum hourly rate is $25.00 per hour. If more than 35 hours are worked, payment for the overtime hours worked is calculated at time and a half. If the hours worked field or the hourly rate field is out of range, the input data and an appropriate message are to be <u>printed</u> and the employee's weekly pay is not to be calculated.

A Defining diagram

Input	Processing	Output
emp_no	Read employee details	emp_no
pay_rate	Validate input fields	pay_rate
hrs_worked	Calculate employee pay	hrs_worked
	Print employee details	emp_weekly_pay
		error_message

B Solution algorithm

The solution to this problem will require a series of simple IF and nested IF statements. Firstly, the variables 'pay_rate' and 'hrs_worked' must be validated, and if either is found to be out of range, an appropriate message is to be placed into a variable called 'error_message'.

The employee's weekly pay is only to be calculated if the variables 'pay_rate' and 'hrs_worked' are valid, so another variable 'valid_input_fields' will be used to indicate to the program whether or not these input fields are valid.

The variable 'valid_input_fields' acts as an internal switch or flag to the program. It will initially be set to true, and will be assigned the value false if one of the input fields is found to be invalid. The employee's weekly pay will be calculated only if 'valid_input_fields' is true.

Compute_employee_pay

Set valid_input_fields to true	
Set error_message to blank	
Read emp_no, pay_rate, hrs_worked	

IF pay_rate > $25.00 — yes / no

yes:
error_message = 'Pay rate exceeds $25.00'
valid_input_fields = false
Print emp_no, pay_rate, hrs_worked, error_message

IF hrs_worked > 60 — yes / no

yes:
error_message = 'Hours worked exceeds limit of 60'
valid_input_fields = false
Print emp_no, pay_rate, hrs_worked, error_message

IF valid_input_fields — yes / no

yes:
IF hrs_worked ≤ 35 — yes / no

yes:
emp_weekly_pay = pay_rate * hrs_worked

no:
overtime_hrs = hrs_worked − 35
overtime_pay = overtime_hrs * pay_rate * 1.5
emp_weekly_pay = (pay_rate * 35) + overtime_pay

Print emp_no, pay_rate, hrs_worked, emp_weekly_pay

THE CASE STRUCTURE EXPRESSED AS AN N-S DIAGRAM

The case control structure is another way of expressing a linear nested IF statement. It is not really an additional control structure; but one that extends the basic selection control structure to be a choice between multiple values. It is expressed as a Nassi-Schneiderman diagram, as follows:

CASE OF single variable			
value 1	value 2	value n	value other
statement block_1	statement block_2	statement block_n	statement block_other

Let us now look again at Example 4.2. The solution algorithm for this example was earlier expressed as a linear nested IF statement, but it could equally have been expressed as a CASE statement.

Example 4.4 *Process customer record*

A program is required to <u>read</u> a customer's name, a purchase amount and a tax code. The tax code has been validated and will be one of the following:

0   tax exempt (0%)
1   state sales tax only (3%)
2   federal and state sales tax (5%)
3   special sales tax (7%)

The program is required to <u>compute</u> the sales tax and the total amount due and <u>print</u> the customer's name, purchase amount, sales tax, and total amount due.

A *Defining diagram*

Input	Processing	Output
cust_name	Read customer details	cust_name
purch_amt	Compute sales tax	purch_amt
tax_code	Compute total amount	sales_tax
	Print customer details	total_amt

B *Solution algorithm*

The solution algorithm is expressed using a CASE statement:

Process_customer_record

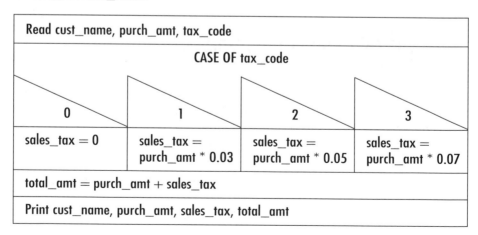

N-S DIAGRAMS AND THE REPETITION CONTROL STRUCTURE

In Chapter 5 the DOWHILE construct was introduced as the pseudocode representation of a repetition loop. This can be represented by an N-S diagram as follows:

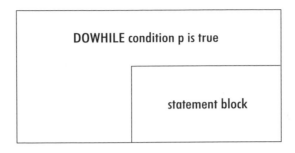

As the DOWHILE loop is a leading decision loop, the following processing takes place:

a   The logical condition p is tested.
b   If condition p is found to be true, the statements within the statement block will be executed once. Control will then return to the retesting of condition p (step a).
c   If condition p is found to be false, control passes to the next statement after the DOWHILE box, and no further processing takes place.

As a result, the DOWHILE structure will continue to repeat a group of statements WHILE a condition remains true. As soon as the condition becomes false, the construct is exited.

There are two important things to consider before designing a DOWHILE loop.

First, the testing of the condition is at the beginning of the loop. This means that you may need to perform some initial processing to set up the condition adequately before it can be tested.

Second, the only way to terminate the loop is to render the DOWHILE condition false. This means that you must set up some process within the statement block that will eventually change the condition so that it becomes false. Failure to do this may result in an endless loop.

SIMPLE ALGORITHMS THAT USE THE REPETITION CONTROL STRUCTURE

The following examples are the same as those represented by pseudocode in Chapter 5. In each example, the problem is defined and a solution algorithm developed using a Nassi-Schneiderman diagram. To help define the problem, the processing verbs in each example have been underlined.

Example 5.1 *Fahrenheit-Celsius conversion*

Every day, a weather station receives 15 temperatures expressed in degrees Fahrenheit. A program is to be written that will <u>accept</u> each Fahrenheit temperature, <u>convert</u> it to Celsius and <u>display</u> the converted temperature to the screen. After 15 temperatures have been processed, the words 'All temperatures processed' are to be <u>displayed</u> to the screen.

A Defining diagram

Input	Processing	Output
f_temp	Get Fahrenheit temperatures	c_temp
(15 temperatures)	Convert temperatures	(15 temperatures)
	Display Celsius temperatures	
	Display screen message	

The defining diagram still only lists what needs to be done; the equation to convert the temperature will not need to be known until the algorithm is developed.

   Having defined the input, output and processing, you should now be ready to outline a solution to the problem. This can be done by writing down the control structures needed and any extra variables that are to be used in the solution algorithm. In this example you will need:

- a DOWHILE structure to repeat the necessary processing, and
- a counter, initialised at zero, that will control the 15 repetitions. This counter, called temperature_count, will contain the number of temperatures read and processed.

B Solution algorithm

Fahrenheit_Celsius_conversion

Set temperature_count to zero
DOWHILE temperature_count < 15
Prompt operator for f_temp
Get f_temp
Compute c_temp = (f_temp − 32) * 5/9
Display c_temp
Add 1 to temperature_count
Display 'All temperatures processed' to the screen

Example 5.2 *Print examination scores*

A program is required to <u>read</u> and <u>print</u> a series of names and exam scores for students enrolled in a mathematics course. The class average is to be <u>computed</u> and <u>printed</u> at the end of the report. Scores can range from 0 to 100. The last record contains a blank name and a score of 999 and is not to be included in the calculations.

A Defining diagram

Input	Processing	Output
name exam_score	Read student details Print student details Compute average score Print average_score	name exam_score average_score

You will need to consider the following requirements when establishing a solution algorithm:

- a DOWHILE structure to control the reading of exam scores, until it reaches a score of 999,
- an accumulator for total scores (total_score), and
- an accumulator for the total students (total_students).

B Solution algorithm

Print_examination_scores

Set total_score to zero
Set total_students to zero
Read name, exam_score
DOWHILE exam_score NOT = 999

> Add 1 to total_students
> Print name, exam_score
> Add exam_score to total_score
> Read name, exam_score

| IF total_students NOT = zero |
| yes   no |
| average_score = total_score/total_students | |
| Print average_score | |

Example 5.3 *Process student enrolments*

A program is required to <u>read</u> a file of student records, and <u>select</u> and <u>print</u> only those students enrolled in a course unit named Programming I. Each student record contains student number, name, address, postcode, gender and course unit number. The course unit number for Programming I is 18500. Three totals are to be <u>printed</u> at the end of the report: total females enrolled in the course; total males enrolled in the course, and total students enrolled in the course.

A *Defining diagram*

Input	Processing	Output
student_record • student_no • name • address • postcode • gender • course_unit	Read student records Select student records Print selected records Compute total females enrolled Compute total males enrolled Compute total students enrolled Print totals	selected student records totals

You will need to consider the following requirements, when establishing a solution algorithm:

* A DOWHILE structure to perform the repetition,
* an IF statement to select the required students, and
* accumulators for the three total fields.

There is no trailer record for this student file. In cases like this, the terms 'more data', 'more records', 'records exist' or 'not EOF' (end of file) can be used in the DOWHILE condition clause.

B Solution algorithm

Process_student_enrolments

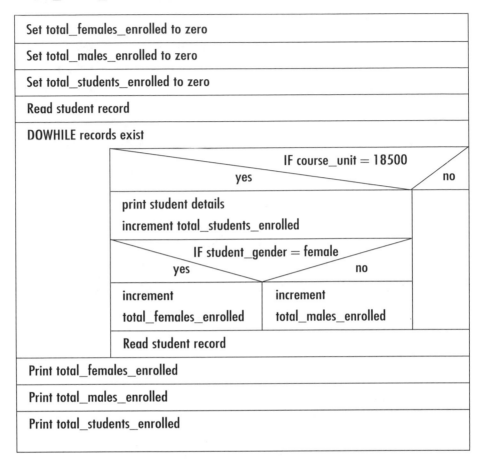

| Set total_females_enrolled to zero |
| Set total_males_enrolled to zero |
| Set total_students_enrolled to zero |
| Read student record |

DOWHILE records exist

IF course_unit = 18500
- yes:
  - print student details
  - increment total_students_enrolled
  - IF student_gender = female
    - yes: increment total_females_enrolled
    - no: increment total_males_enrolled
  - Read student record
- no:

| Print total_females_enrolled |
| Print total_males_enrolled |
| Print total_students_enrolled |

Example 5.4 *Process inventory items*

A program is required to <u>read</u> a series of inventory records that contain item number, item description and stock figure. The last record in the file has an item number of zero. The program is to <u>produce</u> a 'Low Stock Items' report, by <u>printing</u> only those records which have a stock figure of less than 20 items. A heading is to be printed at the top of the report and a total low stock item count is to be printed at the end.

A Defining diagram

Input	Processing	Output
inventory record • item_number • item_description • stock_figure	Read inventory records Select low stock items Print low stock records Print total low stock items	heading selected records • item_number • item_description • stock_figure total_low_stock_items

You will need to consider the following requirements when establishing a solution algorithm:

- A DOWHILE structure to perform the repetition,
- an IF statement to select stock figures of less than 20, and
- an accumulator for total_low_stock_items.

B Solution algorithm

Process_inventory_records

Set total_low_stock_items to zero
Print 'Low Stock Items' heading
Read inventory record
DOWHILE item_number > zero
IF stock_figure < 20 — yes / no
Print item_number, item_description, stock_figure / increment total_low_stock_items
Read inventory record
Print total_low_stock_items

Special algorithms

Outline

- Sorting algorithms
- Dynamic data structures

This appendix contains a number of algorithms that are not included in the body of the book but may be required at some time in your career.

The first section contains three sorting algorithms: bubble sort, insertion sort, and selection sort. The second section introduces three dynamic data structures (queues, stacks, and linked lists) and provides algorithms to manipulate them.

SORTING ALGORITHMS

Bubble sort algorithms

This algorithm sorts an integer array into ascending order using a bubble sort method.

On each pass, the algorithm compares each pair of adjacent items in the array. If the pair is out of order they are switched; otherwise they remain in the original order. So at the end of the first pass, the largest element in the array will have bubbled to the last position in the array.

The next pass will work only with the remaining elements, and will move the next largest element to the second-last position in the array and so on.

In the algorithm:

Array = array to be sorted
number_of_elements = number of elements in the array
elements_switched = flag to record if the elements have been switched in the current pass
temp = temporary area for holding an array element which is being switched
I = index for outer loop
J = index for inner loop

Assume that the contents of Array and number_of_elements have already been established.

```
Bubble_sort_algorithm
    set I to number_of_elements
    set elements_switched to true
    DOWHILE (elements_switched AND I ≥ 2)
        set J to 1
        set elements_switched to false
        DOWHILE J ≤ I − 1
            IF Array (J) > Array (J + 1) THEN
                temp = Array (J)
                Array (J) = Array (J + 1)
                Array (J + 1) = temp
                elements_switched = true
            ENDIF
            J = J + 1
        ENDDO
        I = I − 1
    ENDDO
END
```

Insertion sort algorithm

This algorithm sorts an integer array into ascending order using an insertion sort method.

In the algorithm, the array is scanned until an out-of-order element is found. The scan is then temporarily halted while a backward scan is made to find the correct position to insert the out-of-order element. Elements bypassed during this backward scan are moved up one position to make room for the element being inserted.

This method of sorting is more efficient than the bubble sort.

In the algorithm:

> Array = array to be sorted
> number_of_elements = number of elements in the array
> temp = temporary area for holding an array element while correct
>   position is being searched
> I = current position of the element
> J = index for inner loop

Assume that the contents of Array and number_of_elements have been established.

```
Insertion_sort_algorithm
    set I to 1
    DOWHILE I ≤ (number_of_elements − 1)
        IF Array (I) > Array (I + 1) THEN
            temp = Array (I + 1)
            J = I
            DOWHILE (J ≥ 1 AND Array (J) > temp)
                Array (J + 1) = Array (J)
                J = J − 1
            ENDDO
            Array (J + 1) = temp
        ENDIF
        I = I + 1
    ENDDO
END
```

Selection sort algorithm

This algorithm sorts an integer array into ascending sequence using a selection sort method.

On the first pass the algorithm finds the smallest element in the array and moves it to the first position in the array by switching it with the element originally in that position. Each successive pass moves one more element into position. After the number of passes is one number less than the number of elements in the array, the array will be in order.

In the algorithm:

Array = array being sorted
number_of_elements = number of elements in the array
smallest_element = area for holding the smallest element found in
    that pass
Current_smallest_position = the value of the current position in
    which to place the smallest element
I = index for outer loop
J = index for inner loop

Assume that the contents of Array and number_of_elements have been established.

```
Selection_sort_algorithm
        Set current_smallest_position to 1
        DOWHILE current_smallest_position ≤ (number_of_elements − 1)
            Set I to current_smallest_position
            smallest_element = Array (I)
            Set J = I + 1
            DOWHILE J ≤ number_of_elements
                IF Array (J) < smallest_element THEN
                    I = J
                    smallest_element = Array (J)
                ENDIF
                J = J + 1
            ENDDO
            Array (I) = Array (current_smallest_position)
            Array (current_smallest_position) = smallest_element
            Add 1 to current_smallest_position
        ENDDO
END
```

DYNAMIC DATA STRUCTURES

An array is called a static data structure, because in common programming languages the maximum number of elements must be specified when the array is declared. A dynamic data structure is one in which the number of elements can expand or contract as the problem requires. The elements in these data structures are called nodes.

In building dynamic data structures, pointers are used to create new nodes, and link nodes dispose of those no longer needed. A pointer is a variable whose memory cell contains the address in memory where a data item resides. Therefore, a pointer provides an indirect reference to a data item.

This section covers several examples of dynamic data structures, including queues, stacks and linked lists. Algorithms that manipulate these structures are also provided.

Queues

A queue is a data structure holding data items that are processed on a first-in-first-out basis, like a line of people going through a cafeteria: the first one in the line is the first to reach the cash register and get out of the line.

There are two operations that can be performed on a queue: a node can be added to the end of a queue, and a node can be removed from the head of a queue.

Some programming languages do not support the notion of dynamic data structures, and so do not provide a pointer type. In such cases, the easiest way of representing a queue in an algorithm is by declaring it to be an array. The effect of a pointer is then achieved by using an integer variable to hold the subscript of the array element representing the node that is currently being operated on. Pointers are required to locate the position of the head of the queue and the tail of the queue, as these must be known. Most queues are designed so that the head of the queue wraps around to the tail when required.

Names used in the algorithms are:

Queue = queue to be manipulated
max_size = maximum number of items in the queue
queue_counter = current number of items in the queue
queue_head = position of the head of the queue
queue_tail = position at which the next item will be inserted in the queue.

The pseudocode to add an item and to delete an item from a queue are:

```
Add_item_to_tail_of_queue
     IF (queue_tail = queue_head AND queue_counter > 0) THEN
          Print error message ('queue overflow')
     ELSE
          Queue (queue_tail) = new item
          queue_tail = queue_tail + 1
          IF queue_tail > max_size THEN
               queue_tail = 1
          ENDIF
          queue_counter = queue_counter + 1
     ENDIF
END

Remove_item_from_head_of_queue
     IF queue_counter = 0 THEN
          Print error message ('queue is empty')
     ELSE
          required value = Queue (queue_head)
          queue_head = queue_head + 1
          IF queue_head > max_size THEN
               queue_head = 1
          ENDIF
          queue_counter = queue_counter - 1
     ENDIF
END
```

It is not necessary to alter the data item that is 'removed' from the queue, because it will simply be overwritten if its place is required.

Stacks

A stack is a data structure holding data items that are processed in a last_in_first_out basis, like a stack of trays in a cafeteria: when a tray is required, it is removed from the top of the stack, and when one is added to the stack, it is also placed on the top. These operations on stack data structures are often called 'pop' (for removing the top element) and 'push' (for adding a new element to the stack).

Once again, the easiest way of representing this stack in an algorithm is by declaring it to be an array.

In the algorithms:

Stack = stack to be manipulated;
max_size = the maximum size of the stack;
top_of_stack = the position of the top of the stack.

```
Add_item_to_top_of_stack (Push)
     IF top_of_stack NOT = max_size THEN
          top_of_stack = top_of_stack + 1
          Stack (top_of_stack) = new item
     ELSE
          Print error message ('stack overflow')
     ENDIF
END

Remove_item_from_top_of_stack (Pop)
     IF top_of_stack NOT = zero THEN
          value required = Stack (top_of_stack)
          top_of_stack = top_of_stack − 1
     ELSE
          Print error message ('stack underflow')
     ENDIF
END
```

Once again, it is not necessary to alter the data item that is 'removed' from the stack, as it will be overwritten when the next item is added.

Linked lists

A (linear) linked list is a data structure holding a series of elements or cells that contain both a data item and a pointer to the next element in the list. A linked list can be illustrated as follows:

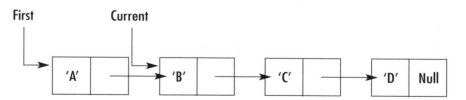

In the above diagram the pointer called 'First' points to the first cell in the list and the pointer called 'Current' points to the current cell in the list. The pointer in the last cell is labelled 'Null', as it indicates the end of the list. Null does not point to a data value.

The advantage of such a data structure is that the elements in the list may be added or deleted by manipulating the pointers rather than by physically moving the data. The data structure thus can be maintained in a logical sequence, without that logical sequence being physically implemented.

Again, where the programming language does not support a pointer type, the easiest way of representing a linked list is by using a technique of 'parallel arrays'. Here, one array holds the items in the list and the other array holds, at corresponding positions, the 'link' to the (logically) next item, i.e. the value of the subscript of the next item. An integer variable is needed to hold the subscript of the 'first' item (in logical order), and some convention must be adopted whereby an impossible subscript value is understood to be a Null pointer.

Names used in the algorithms are:

Items = an array holding the list values;
Links = an array holding subscripts of the next items;
first = the subscript of the first item in the list;
current = the subscript of the list item currently being operated on;
last = the subscript of the 'previous' item to the 'current' item;
continue = a Boolean variable set to true to indicate that the search for a value is to continue.

Pseudocode examples that manipulate a singly linked linear list follow:

1 Traverse a list, printing its value

```
Traverse_and_print
        current = first
        DOWHILE current NOT = Null
                Print items (current)
                current = Links (current)
        ENDDO
END
```

2 Search a list for a particular value ('value')

```
Search_list_for_value
        current = first
        continue = true
        DOWHILE (continue AND current NOT = Null)
                IF items (current) NOT = value THEN
                        last = current
                        current = Links (current)
                ELSE
                        continue = false
                ENDIF
        ENDDO
END
```

Note that continue will still be true if the value was not in the list, in which case current will be Null.

3 Remove a designated value from the list. (This algorithm follows on from the one above, where the value was located.)

```
Remove_value_from_list
    IF NOT continue THEN (i.e. the value was found on the list)
        IF current = first THEN
            first = Links (current)
        ELSE
            Links (last) = Links (current)
        ENDIF
    ENDIF
END
```

In practice, the position of the space just freed would be recorded for later use. This would require the definition of an integer variable 'free' to hold the subscript of the first element of free space. Then after a remove operation the free list would be updated with the statements:

Links (current) = free
free = current

More complex linked structures, such as binary trees and graphs, and the algorithms to manipulate them are beyond the present scope of this book. They may be found in more advanced programming texts and introductory Computer Science texts.

Glossary

algorithm
A set of detailed, unambiguous and ordered instructions developed to describe the processes necessary to produce the desired output from given input.

attribute
A characteristic or property of an object.

array
A data structure made up of a number of variables that all have the same data type and are accessed by the same name.

audit report
A detailed list of all transactions that occurred during the life of the program.

binary search
A search that involves halving the number of elements to search for each time the logic is executed, until an element is found or its absence is detected.

Boolean variable
A variable that can contain only one of two possible values; true or false.

CASE control structure
A structure that extends the basic selection control structure from a choice between two values to a choice from multiple values.

class
A template or pattern that defines the basic attributes and methods available to its objects.

cohesion
A measure of the internal strength of a module; i.e. how closely the elements or statements of a module are associated with each other. The higher the cohesion, the better the module.

constant

A data item with a name and a value that remain the same during the execution of a program.

control structures

The Structure Theorem states that it is possible to write any program using only three basic control structures:

i sequence: the straightforward execution of one processing step after another.

ii selection: the presentation of a condition, and the choice between two actions, depending on whether the condition is true or false.

iii repetition: the presentation of a set of instructions to be performed repeatedly, as long as a condition is true.

constructor

A set of instructions that creates an object and initialises its attributes.

coupling

A measure of the extent of information interchange between modules. The fewer the connections between modules, the more loosely they are coupled. The looser the coupling, the better the module.

data structure

A collection of elementary data items.

data type

A set of values and a set of operations that can be performed on those values.

defining diagram

A diagram that arranges the input, output and processing components of a problem into separate columns. It is constructed when the programmer defines the problem.

dynamic data structure

A structure in which the number of elements can expand or contract as the problem requires.

elementary data item

One containing a single variable that is always treated as a unit.

error report

A detailed list of the errors that occurred during the life of the program.

file

A collection of related records.

flowchart

A graphical representation of program logic, using a series of standard geometric symbols and lines.

functional decomposition
The division of a problem into separate tasks or functions as the first step towards designing the solution algorithm. Each function will be dedicated to the performance of a single specific task.

global data
Data that is known to the whole program.

graphical user interface (GUI)
An interface that enables the programmer to select the program's interface from a pre-existing range of options.

hierarchy chart
A diagram that shows the name of each module in the solution algorithm and its hierarchical relationship to the other modules.

information hiding
A term used in object-oriented design whereby the structure of the data and the performance of its operations are 'hidden' from the user.

interface
A device in a program connecting a user's responses with the program's actions.

intermodule communication
The flow of information or data between modules.

linear search
A search that involves looking at the elements one by one until an element is found or the end of the input is reached.

linked list
A data structure that holds a series of elements containing both a data item and a pointer to the next item in the list.

literal
A constant whose name is the written representation of its value.

local data
Data that is defined within the module in which it will be referenced and is not known outside that module.

mainline
The controlling module of a solution algorithm, which ties all the modules together and coordinates their activity.

master file
A file that contains permanent and semipermanent information about the data entities it contains.

method

A set of operations that an object can perform. Public methods are those producing services requested by other objects. Private methods are those performing internal operations in an object and cannot be accessed directly from outside the object.

method overriding

A term used in object-oriented design to refer to the situation in which a parent class provides a method, but the inheriting child class defines its own version of that method.

modular design

Grouping tasks together because they all perform the same function. Modular design is directly connected to top-down development, as the tasks into which you divide the problem will actually form the future modules of the program.

module

A section of an algorithm that is dedicated to the performance of a single task or function.

multidimensional array

An array constructed in such a way that two or more subscripts are required to locate an element in the array.

Nassi-Schneiderman diagram

A diagram that uses pseudocode-like text in rectangular boxes to represent program logic.

object

A container for a set of data, and the operations that need to be performed on that data.

object-oriented design

A methodology that views the system as a collection of interacting objects, rather than functions, whose internal structure is hidden from the user.

overloading

A term used in object-oriented design to refer to methods in a single class that have the same name.

paired arrays

Two arrays that contain the same number of elements and whose elements correspond in the same position.

parameter

A variable, literal or constant, which is used to communicate between the modules of a program.

- Data parameters contain the actual variables or data items that will be passed between modules.
- Status parameters act as program flags and should contain just one of two values, true or false.

pointer
A variable whose memory cell contains the address in memory where a data item resides.

polymorphism
A term used in object-oriented design to refer to the use of methods of the same name for a variety of purposes.

priming read
A statement that appears immediately before the DOWHILE condition in a solution algorithm.

pseudocode
A subset of English that has been formalised and abbreviated to look like a high-level computer language. Keywords and indentation are used to signify particular control structures.

queue
A data structure holding data items that are processed on a first-in-first-out basis.

record
A collection of data items or fields that all bear some relationship to each other.

scope of a variable
The portion of a program in which a variable has been defined and can be referred to; i.e. a list of all the modules in which that variable can be referenced.

sentinel
A special record placed at the end of valid data to signify the end of that data. It is also known as a trailer record.

sequential file update
An update of a sequential master file, using a sequential file of update transactions.

side effect
An event that occurs when a subordinate module alters the value of a global variable, inside that module.

stack
A data structure holding data items that are processed on a last-in-first-out basis.

string
A collection of characters.

Structure Theorem
The Structure Theorem states that it is possible to write any computer program by using only three basic control structures. These control structures are simple sequence, selection and repetition.

structured programming

A method of writing programs so that each instruction obeys the Structure Theorem. Structured programming also incorporates top-down development and modular design.

top-down design

The division of a problem into separate tasks as the first step towards designing the solution algorithm. The programmer develops an algorithm that incorporates the major tasks first, and only considers the more detailed steps when all the major tasks have been completed.

transaction file

A file that contains transactions designed to update a master file.

variable

A collection of memory cells that store a particular data item.

visibility

A term used in object-oriented design to refer to the public or private nature of a method. A method is visible if it can interact with the rest of the program.

Index